MW01446195

At times I think it will be unbearable to hear one more story of anger, grief, and loss that queer and questioning Christians and their allies have experienced at the hands of churches. Yet reading this book, as a woman who grew up in the BIC and continues to hold the BIC story in high regard, drew me in. I would never have thought that, in my lifetime, so much honesty would be expressed by those who are also part of the BIC story. In this volume's accounts, both from people I know and others I have never met, I was particularly struck with references to the BIC Core Values. I encourage all readers to take time with this book, holding alongside these two Core Value assertions as they read: "We value wholehearted obedience to Christ Jesus through the empowering presence of the Holy Spirit," and "We value integrity in relationships and mutual accountability in an atmosphere of grace, love, and acceptance."

—**Dr. Nancy R. Heisey**, Professor Emerita of Biblical Studies, Eastern Mennonite University

This collection of essays offers poignant storytelling, advocacy, and reflection favoring LGBTQ+ inclusion in the church. Here the context is the Brethren in Christ community, an Anabaptist fellowship whose core values—often cited here—offer ample grounds for, at the very least, a *conversation* about inclusion. But instead, outright rejection, closed doors, fired pastors, exiled Christians, harm after harm! From every corner of the Christian family, in every corner of the world, the same struggle is taking place: will the church change its mind and open its heart to its own wounded children? These essays offer a heartfelt plea for YES.

—**Rev. Dr. David P. Gushee**, Distinguished University Professor of Christian Ethics, Mercer University, and author of *Changing Our Mind*

An Invitation to Conversation: Becoming More Inclusive of LGBTQ+ People in the Brethren in Christ Church is a unique gift to the church, one shared with vulnerability, courage, and grace. The Brethren in Christ have long valued dialogue, in a posture of humility, mutual respect, and a commitment to relationship, to better discern how to follow the way of Jesus as a community. *An Invitation to Conversation* provides us this opportunity. May we be willing to accept this gracious invitation.

—**Darrell Winger**, served as a BIC pastor, missionary, and denominational leader in North America and as Executive Director of the International Brethren in Christ Association

Invitation *to* Conversation

Becoming More Inclusive of LGBTQ+ People in the Brethren in Christ Church

Helena Cicero, Eric A. Seibert, Julie Weatherford, EDITORS

FOREWORD BY John R. Yeatts

SacraSage

Copyright © 2024 by Helena Cicero, Eric A. Seibert, Julie Weatherford

All rights reserved. This book or any portion thereof may not be reproduced or used in any manner whatsoever without the express written permission of the publisher except for the use of brief quotations in a book review or scholarly journal.

NO AI TRAINING: Without in any way limiting the author [and publisher's] exclusive rights under copyright, any use of this publication to "train" generative artificial intelligence (AI) technologies to generate text is expressly prohibited. The author reserves all rights to license uses of this work for generative AI training and development of machine learning language models.

Print: 978-1-958670-40-8
Ebook: 978-1-958670-39-2

Printed in the United States of America

Library of Congress Cataloguing-in-Publication Data
Invitation to Conversation: Becoming More Inclusive of LGBTQ+ People in the Brethren in Christ Church / Helena Cicero, Eric A. Seibert, Julie Weatherford, editors

Acknowledgements

We gratefully acknowledge that inspiration and formatting for this book came from Thomas Jay Oord and Alexa Oord, eds., *Why the Church of the Nazarene Should Be Fully LGBTQ+ Affirming* (Grasmere, ID: SacraSage, 2023).

Partial lyrics from the song "Goodness Of God" by Jenn Johnson, Ben Fielding, Jason Ingram, Ed Cash, and Brian Johnson (CMG Song# 204512) and from the song "People of God" by Wayne Watson (CMG Song# 1906) are used by permission of Capitol CMG, Inc.

All royalties from the sale of this book will be used to support those who identify as LGBTQ+ (along with family members and allies) or to advance efforts to encourage the church to become more inclusive of those who identify as LGBTQ+.

Table of Contents

Acknowledgements vii

Foreword - John R. Yeatts 1

Introduction - Helena Cicero, Eric A. Seibert, Julie Weatherford 5

PART I: LGBTQ+ INDIVIDUALS OFFER THEIR PERSPECTIVE

The Truth Will Set You Free - Tammy Astuto-Goodman 13

My First Kiss - Kirsten Buckwalter 17

The Song in Each of Us - Seth Chamberlain 19

Wanting to Thrive - Spencer Davis 27

I Will Sing of the Goodness of God (Even If I'm Gay) - Tim Dawson 33

I Wish I Had Left Differently - John Doe 37

Everyone Needs Love and Compassion - Liz Johnson 41

Free to Be Reverend Me - Martha J. Lockwood 49

Queer Rights Are a Matter of Life and Death - Jonny Rashid 53

Proved Wrong - Hannah Stolpe 59

An Open Letter to Queer Kids Growing up BIC - Erin Taylor 65

Invitation to Conversation

PART II: PARENTS AND GRANDPARENTS OF LGBTQ+ CHILDREN DESCRIBE THEIR EXPERIENCE

Woman, Mother, Pastor Integrating Roles as a Follower of Jesus - Anne Findlay-Chamberlain............................71

So Much Groaning - Joanna Hadley-Evans 77

Wonderfully Made - Martha Truxton Heller 85

Walking the Tightrope Between Love and Judgment - Jean L. Keller-Thau............................91

PART III: COMMITTED CHRISTIANS EXPLAIN THEIR JOURNEY TO AFFIRMATION

Confessions of a Recovering Homophobe - Jennifer Larratt-Smith 99

A Moment of Clarity - Keith Miller...........................103

Evolution of an Affirming Christian - Meg Purdum 109

PART IV: FORMER BIC PASTORS SHARE THEIR STORIES

Once Upon a Time There Was a Church Called The Bridge - Justin Douglas............................115

I Once Was a Minister in Good Standing - Jay McDermond 123

Full Inclusion - Keith Miller...........................131

I Don't Want to Have a Gay Policy - Rod White 135

PART V: ALLIES CALL FOR FULL INCLUSION

Biblical Considerations

A Biblical Journey Toward Loving, Committed, Same-Sex Unions - Fred Miller............................145

Healing the Bible How the Bible Became a Weapon—and What to Do about It - Jeff Miller............................153

God's Love Wins - George Payne 159

Evolving Faith and Revolutionary Love - Kimberly Tucker 165

PART V (CONTINUED): ALLIES CALL FOR FULL INCLUSION

General Reflections

A Fountainhead of Justice - John Alfred 171

A Last Ditch Letter - Lindsay Barnes 177

Let's Join LGBTQ+ Christians on a Journey toward Holiness - Susan Felix 181

I Wish the BIC Church Offered Unconditional Love to Queer People - Wanda L. Heise 185

The Tent Is Getting Smaller—Let's Enlarge It! - Vernon Hyndman 191

Table for Few? Why the BIC Needs to Reconsider LGBTQ+ Inclusion - Jackie Inouye 197

The BIC Church is Failing the Queer Community (and People Are Leaving) - Dinah Knisely 203

The BIC Church Is in Grave Danger - Andrew Larratt-Smith 209

The Gift of God is Available to Everyone - Christine Martin 217

A Pathway to Inclusion in the Anabaptist Vision - Matthew G. O'Brien 223

"You are My Arm Outstretched" A Vision for God's People - Mama Sarah 227

The Longing to Belong Is from God (So Why Are We Making Our LGBTQ+ Siblings Sit in the Back of the Bus?) - Elisa Joy Seibert 231

Are You 100% Sure? - Lin Taylor 239

Extending Grace and Full Inclusion If Not Now, When? - Daniel Weatherford 243

Who's Missing from These Pictures? - Jami West 249

Dealing with Reality Discovering How God Created Our Neighbors - Sam Wilcock 251

APPENDIX

Suggestions for Using This Book 259

Discussion Questions 261

Glossary of LGBTQ+ Terms and Vocabulary 265

Resources for Further Exploration. 273

Just Because He Breathes - LINDA ROBERTSON 279

About the Editors 287

Foreword

John R. Yeatts

This collection of testimonies and insights compose an informative, inspiring, and convicting book that will make us better followers of Jesus. The stories shared reveal that the Brethren in Christ (BIC) have a variety of views about same-sex relationships and the participation of LGBTQ+ persons in the church. Yet we all want to follow Jesus's greatest commandment to "love God and others." To do so, we listen to people who differ from us in their understanding of this controversial issue.

Reading this book, I was moved and inspired by how writers were transformed as a result of their love for family members who identify as LGBTQ+. But I was also concerned and convicted by sad stories of people who found only rejection from their church family, leading them to move on to a community where they could receive love and inclusion.

As Brethren in Christ, one way we follow Jesus is by loving those who experience rejection in our society. We gain insight into loving others, as Jesus instructed us, from reading this book of stories from our LGBTQ+ brothers and sisters and those who love them.

Throughout my life of three-quarters of a century, I experienced love and acceptance among the Brethren in Christ. Let me begin by witnessing to my own experiences in our church, experiences I see echoed in the stories recorded in this book.

My parents were converts to the BIC, although my mother grew up in a sister denomination. I conformed to the teachings of my church and avoided drinking alcohol and smoking tobacco—the two most preached about "sins" of that time.

In my growing-up years, we had two-week revival meetings in the spring and fall. When I was about five years old, a BIC bishop, who was the evangelist, came to our home for dinner. Before the meal, I was called upon to recite the twenty-third Psalm. After a successful recitation, that bishop rewarded me with a quarter. This was one of my first memories of being seen and loved by the church.

With some pressure from my parents, I attended our denomination's college. During the introduction to academic life, we were taught the concepts of "liberalism" and "conservatism." We learned that "liberals" advocate change and "conservatives" support the *status quo*. Today, those words have become fraught with political agendas, so I'll use the words "progressive" and "traditional" here.

In my college years, I gravitated toward "progressivism," as I understood it. This was in stark contrast to my upbringing. I had long discussions and many arguments with my father about what I was learning, but he never rejected me, and I never doubted his love and faith in me. Again, I was seen and loved.

In one Old Testament course, I became frustrated that we were only reading "traditional" scholars, and I communicated that to the professor. Instead of chiding me, he assigned me to read a few essays supporting a more "progressive" perspective. Not only that, he asked me to report on those readings to the class. Again, I was seen and loved.

While in seminary, the bishop who had given me a quarter for quoting the 23rd Psalm visited my wife and me. In the course of our conversation, he asked me what I was working on. I told him that I had just completed a paper on abortion. He asked if he could read it. I hesitated because I was sure that it was more "progressive" than he would have been comfortable with. After I shared the paper with him, he did not mention it. But within a year or two, he assigned me to a BIC pastorate. I have often thought that my treatment by that bishop is one of the main reasons that I felt accepted among the BIC and consequently stayed for life.

Later, I was asked to write a regular, anonymous article in our denominational periodical. After one entry, I was told that a bishop said: "Well, I guess he's a heretic." I do not know whether that Bishop ever learned that I was the person who wrote the article, but I would have been happy if he did. Why? Because I am confident that even though he disagreed with me, he would have continued to love and accept me. This is exactly what my BIC mentors did throughout my life in the church. Had they not done so, and had they insisted on me adopting their more "conservative" views, I would likely have left the BIC like many writers in this book you are about to read.

The same type of gracious reception I experienced is precisely what we can extend to our brothers and sisters whose beliefs about LGBTQ+ people may be regarded as "progressive." This book helps us understand and support people calling on us to love those who are same-sex attracted and those who are in same-sex relationships.

Following the example of the love and support I received, I have tried to reach out to those among us on both sides of the LGBTQ+ issue. Unfortunately, some who are affirming of same-sex relationships are no longer with the BIC. Credentialed ministers have lost their credentials and left the denomination because they were required to conform *both* in belief and practice to the traditional BIC position. Even ministers who believe and support the BIC position on same-sex relationships are asking for guidance on how to treat people in their congregation who do not hold the traditional BIC position. We need to find ways to talk together and listen to one another as we move forward.

I was told by one bishop, "LGBTQ+ persons want to change our BIC position." My response was: "Of course they do. They want to belong and be accepted." So, an important question is: How do we love and include LGBTQ+ persons like those whose stories are in this volume? What does it mean to fully include these individuals in the life of the church? How do we love them as Jesus loves us?

In the afterward of his book, *People to Be Loved,* Preston Sprinkle challenges the church to "listen to the stories of LGBT people" (p. 179). He writes, "I believe that every single Christian needs to think deeply about this issue.

And since it is not an issue, but *people*, every Christian needs to listen to the stories of LGBT people" (p. 180). As long as we treat those who identify as LGBTQ+ as an issue, we will never see them as Jesus would: people to be loved.

In conclusion, I pray that those who experience same-sex attraction and/or are in LGBTQ+ relationships receive the same kind of loving support that I received from our BIC spiritual family. As we read this book together with all our brothers and sisters, both those who affirm a traditional position and those who affirm a progressive position, let us see it through the lens of Jesus's greatest commandment to love God and others.

John R. Yeatts
Grantham, Pennsylvania

***John R. Yeatts** has been a BIC pastor for nine years, a BIC administrator for three years, a college professor at a BIC related institution for 33 years, and a member of seven BIC churches. John has served in a variety of roles in his home churches and at the denominational level. He currently serves as a mentor, teacher, and evaluator of individuals seeking pastoral credentialing within the BIC.*

Introduction

HELENA CICERO, ERIC A. SEIBERT, JULIE WEATHERFORD

The book you hold in your hands was born out of a desire to follow Jesus faithfully and to fulfill the command to love our neighbor as we love ourselves. It is offered in the spirit of Christian charity and has been published with the hope it will help the church do a better job of celebrating, and caring well for, all who come through its doors.

We Value All People

The Brethren in Christ (BIC) Church has a long and rich tradition of emphasizing God's love for us and, in turn, our responsibility to share that same love with others. As a denomination, the BIC emphasizes service, compassion, the importance of being in community, and the necessity of pursuing peace with all people.

Many of these convictions are nicely summarized in ten core values articulated twenty-five years ago as a result of communal conversation and discernment. They are discussed in a book edited by Terry Brensinger titled *Focusing Our Faith: Brethren in Christ Core Values*.[1] One of these core values, signified by the phrase pursuing peace, states that "we value all human life." The word "all" is wonderfully inclusive. *All* people are to be valued, regardless of whether they are white or black, gay or straight, rich or poor, Republican or Democrat, transgender or cisgender, Catholic or Protestant,

---

[1]. An updated version of this book titled *Compelling Convictions: Finding Our Future in a Modern World*, edited by Terry L. Brensinger, Jennifer Lancaster, and Alan Robinson, will be released this summer.

U.S. citizen or undocumented worker—the list goes on. Each and every person is of infinite worth regardless of their race, ethnicity, (dis)ability, nationality, socio-economic status, sexual orientation, or gender identity.

But the sad reality is that many people from the LGBTQ+ community who attend our churches have not—and currently do not—feel particularly valued there. Rather than experiencing the warm, loving embrace of acceptance, they have felt the cold edge of rejection and condemnation. They have not been well-cared for or welcomed, let alone "valued." The current policy and practices of the church have often made them feel sinful, unimportant, and invisible.

We grieve the harm that has been done to LGBTQ+ people, and those who love them, and are concerned about the way this impedes the mission of the church. We are also distressed by the number of people leaving the BIC Church because of its posture toward the LGBTQ+ community. The way this impacts our youth is especially troubling. Young people today are not inclined to align themselves with a faith tradition at odds with some of their most fundamental beliefs about how people should be treated. If something doesn't change, we are likely to lose this generation from the BIC Church.

With so much at stake, it is imperative that we find a way to address these concerns that is consistent with our commitment to valuing all people and following Jesus faithfully. We need to have an open and honest conversation about how we can do better and where we should go from here. There is no other way forward.

The Conversation We Envision

The conversation we envision is one that is respectful and Spirit-led. It needs to happen in the context of Christian love, peacebuilding, forbearance, and safety in individual congregations and across the wider BIC U.S. family of churches. This is essential for the long-term health and well-being of the church.

Such a conversation must prioritize the voices of LGBTQ+ individuals and allies within the church. It goes without saying that any conversation *about* LGBTQ+ people should *include* LGBTQ+ people. Yet, to our knowledge, this has not been the case. These individuals have not had a seat at the table. LGBTQ+ people (and allies) have not been invited to participate in the planning and facilitation of denominational discussions around issues and concerns that are of special importance to them. This is absolutely essential if the church is to have any hope of addressing the harm that has been done and discovering more appropriate ways of relating to the LGBTQ+ community.

It is also important that this conversation is one in which *real* dialogue happens. A *genuine* conversation is one where the outcome is not predetermined. We realize that some people feel we have already had (and are having) this conversation in various events initiated by the church (e.g., the Full of Grace and Truth Impact Seminar in 2015). But we believe there is a huge difference between *conversation* with no predetermined outcome and *instruction* designed to encourage conformity to an established position. The denomination has sponsored events that fall into the latter category; we are suggesting there is a pressing need for the former.

For a conversation like this to happen in any meaningful way, the denomination needs to stop decredentialing ministers who affirm same-sex relationships. As some of the stories in this book illustrate (see part three), BIC ministers have lost their credentials because they chose to be inclusive of LGBTQ+ people. This is problematic for many reasons, not least of which because it stifles conversation. When sincere followers of Jesus differ on issues that directly impact the health and well-being of congregants, there needs to be space for discussion. If ministers cannot express their views without losing their jobs, they have no chance of engaging in genuine dialogue, and the denomination has no hope of following the Spirit's leading.

One of many things we love about the BIC is that historically it has had a big tent. Time and again, the denomination has found a way to stay together regardless of the issue at hand (e.g., plain dress, divorce, women in ministry) or the intensity of disagreement among members. We believe that is not only desirable but entirely possible in this present moment as well.

It has been suggested that the BIC U.S. won't survive a full-on discussion of LGBTQ+ inclusion and the church. Likewise, it has been said that the BIC won't survive another couple of decades in the United States *without* the discussion. We're aware of both of these possibilities. Yet we strongly believe that God has equipped the BIC U.S. to find a path forward *together*, with courage and mutual forbearance, in ways that have eluded other denominations. Our Core Values spell out how, having experienced God's love and grace, we are committed to believing the Bible, following Jesus, belonging to the community of faith, witnessing to the world, serving compassionately, pursuing peace, and relying on God. These things have united us and steadied our faith community as we've discerned the way of Jesus and journeyed together through difficult times and challenging issues. We are confident they will once again as we engage in this crucial conversation.

Finally, and this is *very* important, the church must be open to changing its policies and practices when sound biblical/theological interpretations, pastoral considerations, and other factors merit it. This is normal and healthy. From its earliest days, the church has had to consider how best to follow Jesus in unique times and particular contexts. As a denomination, we have made numerous modifications to church polity and practice since our humble beginnings. This has served us well and enabled us to remain relevant and faithful to the Spirit's leading over the years.

We believe this book can serve as a catalyst for this kind of conversation, a conversation about how BIC U.S. churches can be more fully inclusive of LGBTQ+ people in their midst. So we offer this book as an invitation, an invitation to come to the table humbly and respectfully, with hope and expectation that the Spirit will lead us forward as we listen to each other and speak graciously to one another.

The Nature and Structure of This Book

Invitation to Conversation contains a collection of brief essays written by people from all walks of life who have a connection, past or present, to the BIC Church. Some of the contributors are current members; others have left the denomination for various reasons. Some are relatively young, while others are in their golden years. Some identify as LGBTQ+, others are allies, family members, and friends. All advocate for fuller inclusion of LGBTQ+ individuals within the church. As a denomination, the BIC has not heard from these individuals in any collective way, making this book an especially valuable and important contribution to the conversation at hand.

It is important to note that we (the editors) did *not* assign particular topics to people. Rather, each contributor was free to shape their essay however they saw fit. As you will discover, some share very personal (and powerful) stories. Others make a biblical/theological case for inclusion. Some emphasize pastoral perspectives while others make a case for why full inclusion is consistent with BIC core values and commitments. Still others combine several of these approaches or do something altogether different with their essay. Each contribution is unique. Each is persuasive and compelling in its own way. We hope you will read them all.

Readers who are familiar with the Moth Radio Hour know that each episode ends with the saying, "Moth stories are true as remembered and affirmed by the storytellers." We make the same claim about the stories contained in this book.

In order to provide some organization to the book, we chose to group the essays into one of five categories. The first group of essays comes from people who identify as LGBTQ+. The second part of the book contains stories written by parents and grandparents of LGBTQ+ children who talk about their experiences as these relate to their children or grandchildren. The third section features essays in which people describe their journey to full inclusion. The contributors in the fourth part of the book are all former BIC pastors, some of whom paid a high price for their convictions. The final section ends with essays from allies who, in various ways, call for full inclusion.

In addition to reading these essays, we strongly encourage you to look through the appendix. It includes a guide for using this book, a glossary of terms, additional resources for further study, and a final, heartbreaking story that highlights why we cannot continue to maintain the status quo.

A Word of Gratitude to the Contributors

It has been an honor and a privilege to work with the contributors of this book. Thank you one and all! We are so grateful for all the hard work you did writing these essays. It has been very humbling to be entrusted with your stories. At various times, as we edited your work, we felt like we were holding something sacred in our hands. Thank you for sharing, even when it brought up difficult memories and emotions. We remain convinced that your stories will make a difference and will help the church become a safer and healthier place for all people, not least of which those who identify as LGBTQ+.

A Brief Note about Terminology

Using the right language to talk about people who are same-sex attracted and/or gender diverse is very important. It is also quite challenging since people have different preferences and not everyone agrees on which terms are most appropriate. We have included a glossary of terms at the end of the book that should help clarify the meaning of some of the terms that are found in this book, as well as others that are commonly used today.

The initialism LGBTQ+ in the title of this book stands for lesbian, gay, bisexual, trans, queer/questioning, and more (hence the plus). Whenever the word "queer" is used to refer to these individuals, it is not meant in any negative or pejorative way. Though it was once used this way, and still is by some, many in the LGBTQ+ community have reclaimed and redeemed this term to say something positive about who they are and how they experience the world.

An Important Disclaimer

Finally, we want to offer an important disclaimer. We (the editors) do not speak in any official capacity for the BIC U.S. Church. Therefore, this book should not be regarded as representing the views of the BIC U.S. Church, any of its individual congregations, or any institutions or organizations associated with it. *Invitation to Conversation* is an independent publication that has not been sanctioned by the denomination.

Part I

LGBTQ+ Individuals Offer Their Perspective

The Truth Will Set You Free

Tammy Astuto-Goodman

A person with a deep sense of God and the truth experiences hypocrisy and rejection by the church when her sexual identity becomes known.

If one part suffers, all the parts suffer with it. (1 Cor 12:26, NLT)

Just as I have loved you, you should love each other. (John 13:34, NLT)

The truth will set you free. (John 8:32, NLT)

These Bible verses have much in common for me. First, I heard them in church many times. Second, I believed them to be true with all my heart. Third, as I grew up in the church, I became aware of a disconnect between what was taught and how people lived—specifically, the way church people treated each other.

Don't get me wrong, people in the church seemed to enjoy each other. Sunday dinners, small groups, and church picnics pointed towards community. Singing during worship made me feel like I was part of the whole. As Wayne Watson sings ("People of God"):

People of God, called by His name
Called from the dark and delivered from shame

Invitation to Conversation

One Holy race, Saints every one
Because of the blood of Christ Jesus the Son

What declarations! What unity! What belonging!

Well, it seemed that way until whispers made me wonder. Why are the people of God whispering about the "wayward kids" of so and so who, after all, *seemed* like such good parents. Why did I see that dad slap his child in the backseat of the car immediately before he walked through the parking lot with his family and then into the church with a cheery "Good morning!" to everyone he passed? Why were the ladies giggling about the Director of Music probably being gay? What straight man is that good at the piano?

My mind was perplexed. If the "wayward kids" were suffering, shouldn't we suffer with them? Shouldn't that dad love his kids as Christ loves him? He looks unphased, but his kid looks wounded. Shouldn't someone go love the kid? And if the Music Director is gay, rather than giggling, wouldn't we want the truth to set him free?

Was church just a performance? Did anyone believe what we read and sang about? I did! I mean, I knew I wasn't perfect, but I was "called by His name," and I was "delivered from shame"! Remember guys? I saw you singing with your hands raised! Hello?

I have had a deep love for God since I was a small child. I also had a strong sense that God loved me. But the divide between knowing God and understanding His people grew wider and wider. My behavior in the church became mischievous rather than directly confrontational, mostly because I knew I would get in trouble for more drastic actions like yelling "This is BS!" in the middle of a service. Still, I knew there were rules to follow. I knew no one at church saw me as one of the *good* Christian kids. But church was still home, even if it was confusing.

There was real life, and there was church life. And the two did not meet very often. If I got married (to a man, of course) and had kids, or if I fell in love with a new worship song, church was a great place to be. If I was confused, lost, angry, or being abused, church was a place from which I knew I should hide.

When my first husband suspected I was gay, he went to the church leaders. He wanted to punish me. And what better place to go to get a few "good" men on your side? I was not asked if I was OK or safe. I was not asked what I was feeling. I was told that if what my husband said was true, I needed to repent and go on a marriage retreat. It was also suggested that I have more sex with my husband. For many reasons, I was trying to get away from my husband. Going on a retreat with him and having more sex with him was an impossible proposition. Still, I knew I had an army against me. Among other things, these "good Christian men" helped my husband in his attempt to take my young children from me, a surefire way to beat a young Mom into submission.

The truth is, I was gay. But that truth certainly did not set me free. And the church did not love me as Christ loved them. I was suffering, and yet "the parts" turned against me (see 1 Cor 12:26). The same recognizable paradox from my childhood reared its head. But this time I was the one suffering. I cried and I begged God to change me, an all too familiar routine for queer Christians. I wanted to be delivered from my shame. I wanted to die. I turned into the biggest homophobe I knew.

A friend gave me a book titled *From Wounded Hearts* (edited by Roberta Showalter Kreider) that contained a foreword written by Peggy Campolo in which she affirmed gay Christians in the church. As I read, it was hard to accept the truths contained in the book. My overriding thought was that my friend was excusing the fact that she had succumbed to a sinful lifestyle. The voice of the church (which said same-sex relationships were inherently sinful) was much louder than God's voice (which celebrated committed relationships regardless of sexual orientation or gender identity). Although the church claimed it wanted people to be more like Christ, I later realized that its *true* mission—at least with regard to human sexuality—was to make people adopt its heteronormative views. It was effective.

It took a process of twenty years, after my ex-husband went to church leaders about my sexuality, for me to understand who I am and who God created me to be. I attribute this transformation to God's relentless pursuit of my heart and to hours upon hours of studying anything with a title close to "Does God love me if I'm gay?" Thankfully, He sure does!

When I met the woman who is now my wife, it took me over a year to imagine a life with her. I could get my head around being gay, but having a partner out of the closet? Being outwardly truthful about it? And people at church would know? Yikes! But the truth will set me free, right? Yes. The truth did set me free, freer than I have ever been. I am married to the most beautifully kind woman, who cherishes me and our family with the most pure and selfless love.

In the process, however, my relationship with the church has been severed. It was clear that we not only disagreed on same-sex marriage, but my heart's desire to love and honor all people did not align with the church. I have many family members and friends who belong to the LGBTQ+ community. I enjoy going to many places with my loved ones. But I cannot imagine bringing them to a worship service at what used to be my home church. People who used to hug me every week and ask about my kids now act like I don't exist. Again, the paradox.

A couple of years ago, when I started being open about my sexuality, I asked the church for simple dialogue. I didn't insist on them being welcoming or, heaven forbid, affirming. I wanted to gain understanding together. But dialogue seemed to be too big an ask, as calls would take months to be returned. I had a couple of roles in the congregation that I loved, and I was never directly told that I was not wanted. But when I asked a few times if I was still welcome, I was never answered. So, eventually, I stepped away.

Despite the rift with the church, my life is more beautiful now than I could have imagined it. Do I wish I could couple it with *how I imagine* the church can be? A church where when one suffers all the parts suffer? A church where we love one another as Christ has loved us? A church where the truth sets everyone free? Yes, I do. But I am part of different communities that exemplify these things wonderfully. Hopefully, someday the church will get there.

Tammy Astuto-Goodman *is a Clinical Consultant who lives in Harrisburg, Pennsylvania. She and her wife, Mindy, enjoy the outdoors, playing pickleball, and any time with their four kids, grandkids, and extended family. Tammy grew up attending Manor BIC and Harrisburg BIC, where her dad, Lou Astuto, was a pastor.*

My First Kiss

Kirsten Buckwalter

A former BIC Bible Quizzer shares her journey to self-acceptance.

Dear Church,
    I don't think you want to reject your own children. I don't think you want to believe gay people are going to hell. I think many of your members really do care about the marginalized. You think you need tough love. You think God must have a good reason for prohibiting same-sex romantic relationships and that even if you don't understand, you need to trust that God knows best. I know this is how I used to feel.

I am the granddaughter of Brethren in Christ (BIC) missionaries. I have memorized over two thousand verses of the New Testament through BIC Bible Quizzing. I have most likely had your children as my campers at Kenbrook Bible Camp. I spent time serving overseas with Youth With A Mission (YWAM), and I graduated top of my class from a Christian College with a Bachelor's Degree in Ministry. I have dedicated the majority of my thirty years of life to God and the church.

If anyone has reason *not* to be gay, it's me.

Having loved God my whole life, one day I decided to take a risk and trust that God's love would take care of me if I was wrong. I was so tired of experiencing the heartbreak of repressing my love for women. So I prayed, "God, I'm in love with this girl, and I'm pretty sure she likes me back, so I'm going to kiss her. And if the Holy Spirit convicts me in the morning,

I'll repent." So at the age of twenty-five, I had my first kiss, and here I am, five years later, still waiting for that conviction.

In place of the conviction and condemnation I thought would come, I hear the voice of Jesus saying instead, "My yoke is easy and my burden is light" (Matt 11:30, NIV). According to Jesus, it's the teachers of the law who "tie up heavy, cumbersome loads and put them on other people's shoulders" (Matt 23:4, NIV). Jesus also says:

> Woe to you, teachers of the law. . . . You shut the door of the kingdom of heaven in people's faces. (Matt 23:13, NIV)

> You have neglected the more important matters of the law—justice, mercy and faithfulness. (Matt 23:23, NIV).

> You strain out a gnat but swallow a camel. (Matt 23:24, NIV)

In the queer community, we talk about the "clobber passages," a handful of verses that have been weaponized against us. I believe these verses are the gnat and that God cares more about the unhoused folks living under city bridges than about me marrying my girlfriend. And maybe the camel in this metaphor is the fact that the Trevor Project reported that 45% of LGBT youth reported seriously considering suicide in 2022.

The theology of homophobia is bearing bad fruit. It's time for us to stop treating the Bible as if it's a legal code and instead focus on the bigger picture of who God is. God is love (1 John 4:8). Don't miss the forest for the trees. It really is as simple as that. God is love; homophobia is fear. "Perfect love casts out fear" (1 John 4:18). The Kingdom of God is inclusive. It's time for the BIC Church to catch up.

Kirsten Buckwalter *is a barista at a small coffee shop in Harrisburg, Pennsylvania. She enjoys listening to audiobooks and going on adventures with her dog, Sophie.*

The Song in Each of Us

Seth Chamberlain

For those who struggle with sexuality and spirituality, remember:
God gives each of us a song. God is right in your
bones, your gut, your soul, singing to you.

There's a song in each of us. That song gives rhythm to our days and direction to our steps. The song adds passion, bounce, and delight. The song colors in the bleak spots and mellows out abrasive tones. (For some of us, that song might not even be music.) It's there. It's in your bones, in your gut, in your very essence.

God gave us each a song. Sometimes more than one.

The more we listen for that song, the more we can follow where it leads. The more we follow where it leads, the more our lives fill with light and love. It doesn't give us answers. In fact, some of the places it leads can make us question, make us confused, make us scared that we've lost our way. But it's still there, whether we choose to follow it or not. And if we're not ready to listen, we need not worry. It will still be there when we're ready to connect with it again.

I loved music from my young childhood. I started taking piano lessons at age five from the pianist at Harrisburg Brethren in Christ (BIC) Church where we attended. I'm sure I irritated my parents as I belted out Cindy

Lauper, Amy Grant, Petra, and the B-52s. I later composed music and once forced my grandmother to listen to a ten-song recital. I always had a tune in the back of my mind.

I loved church music. I mean, I *really* loved church music. I loved hymns. I recorded myself singing campfire songs I learned at Kenbrook Bible Camp and, eventually, led songs as a camp counselor there. I attended Goshen College, a Mennonite undergraduate institution, and discovered the beauty of unaccompanied four-part harmony. The power of the organ bass pedals, the passion of a gospel vamp, the ethereal chants of monks, the quiet-but-fervent guitar of Phil Keaggy—they all enthralled me. They still do. In time, I started to realize that this song was my song.

Although I'm not unaware of the advantages I enjoy, there are many ways my song is similar to the songs of others. I am a white, cisgender male and a citizen of the United States. I am a Christian (though others might disagree, even vociferously). I have enjoyed a middle-class lifestyle, with some lean years and some when I have enjoyed plenty. I have a slight stutter but otherwise have similar abilities to others. I grew up in a loving family with no abuse. I have a master's degree from a prestigious university. I am a professional, a social services program manager with no gap in employment history and strong performance reviews. I am incredibly privileged: I can *choose* (and have chosen) to set aside my privilege to help others in order to increase equity among all people. I have the ability to choose to serve others as a career and still have the means and energy to support my family. I have so much that sometimes I agonize that I have not given enough of my resources and time to others.

But growing up, there was one part of my song that I came to be suspicious of: I realized I might be gay. As a child, I rejected that part of my song. I believed my feelings were wrong. Although my church never discussed homosexuality, the messages I heard and internalized from the broader culture were that homosexuality was repugnant and abhorrent. So, as an adolescent, I tried to sing like others. I dated girls and even kissed a few.

But there was a bigger part of my song that terrified me. By the time I graduated from high school, it opened before me like a giant sinkhole.

I was worried that key tenets of my spirituality might be wrong. Prior to this, I embraced what I thought was the "right" theology, a BIC blend of Anabaptism and American evangelicalism. Unfortunately, my faith eventually grew bleak and dogmatic, more typical of authoritarian evangelicalism than Anabaptism, despite my Anabaptist roots and my mother's encouragement to consider alternative perspectives.

When I was nineteen, I suffered a crushing depression, and the music stopped. Yes, the depression was partly activated because I was finally facing my sexuality. And there was certainly a biochemical component. But if I'm really being honest, the depression was prompted mostly by a loss of faith.

I don't know if you've felt that way before, but it's awful. Shaken to your core, uncertain if the God you thought you knew truly exists. Physically ill, trying to rectify how evil—especially depression—could happen if God were all-knowing, all-powerful, and kind. Feeling abandoned by the God you thought you had served faithfully. Unwelcome in your church's faith—or at least the faith you think your church has—and unsure where to turn next. It consumed me.

My depression lasted through my early 20s. After attending college in Goshen, Indiana, a small, semi-rural town, I began life in Chicago. There, in that huge city, I could hide my loss of faith by avoiding church altogether. And I could hide my sexuality by day and explore it by night. I could conceal all those parts of me that I thought others would disapprove of. I would not need to work through hard issues or defend myself.

But it was music that saved my life. I mean that both metaphorically and literally. As I wandered in my 20s, there was always a quiet song in the back of my mind, gently guiding me. Music gave me ways to express my full range of emotions and thoughts. Sometimes, on the dance floor at midnight, the incredibly deep bass resonated through my bones, reminding me that there was a song in me. Even when I made risky decisions, a song would either guide my feet or help me back onto them. When I was desolate, music sustained me.

As I progressed through my 20s, I began to hear and accept the song that was true for me. It was a song that acknowledged my sexuality and, more than that, embraced my struggling spirituality with authenticity and integrity. The more I listened to the song, the more peace I experienced.

In Chicago, I experimented with a few different churches—Metropolitan Community Church (MCC) and a Unitarian congregation—and never found a good fit. But whenever I attended church, I basked in the music, whether it was an organ solo, a hymn in a Mennonite congregation, or an African American spiritual.

At twenty-eight, I relocated to Washington, D.C., to complete a fellowship. As luck (or providence?) would have it, I moved into an apartment a block away from a thriving MCC church, a denomination founded specifically for LGBTQ+ individuals. At the first service I attended, I was immediately captivated by the choir. And within three Sundays, I joined the gospel and praise-and-worship choirs. I had found my way back to church—this time to one where my sexuality was not just tolerated but affirmed. On top of that, the more I spoke with people at this church, the more I realized that they struggled with faith issues as much as I did.

Over the next two decades, I met and married an amazing man, and eventually, we adopted two daughters. We attend a different church now, an Episcopal church in the suburbs of Washington, D.C., that focuses on service and community (which resonates with my Anabaptist upbringing) and includes high church practices (which resonates with my ex-Catholic husband). There is a rainbow spectrum of families, and our daughters are friends with children of different races, family structures, and origin stories.

At this church, people are real about the struggles they have with hard questions of faith. I continue to hold a faith that does not reflect mainstream evangelicalism. For example, I don't believe in a conversion moment. I believe God is always with us, and we choose every moment whether to follow. I don't believe that God intervenes in this world (save to inspire us), and I don't believe in hell. When we finally stand before the unfiltered love of God, how could anyone reject God's love, and how could God withhold love from any of us? And, of course, I certainly don't believe I am damned for acting on the sexuality God has given me. I still consider myself a Christian. I still hearken to the model and heart of Jesus. I continue to grapple with and marvel at the ever-deepening mysteries of incarnation, crucifixion, and resurrection. My fellow church-members have other (and similar) atypical beliefs. Church is not a place for assimilation, but rather common pursuit of the revelation God has given each of us, the song God has placed in each of our hearts.

At this church, I have sung in the choir for years, and I even spent a year as the part-time music director. I also teach kindergarten-level Sunday school. Rather than instruct these young tykes in evangelicalism or concern them with ongoing questions I may have, I focus on how each of them is special, how God loves them, and how their church family loves them. Period. And I accompany each lesson with a Spotify playlist of soft piano hymns in the background.

I want to be clear. I did not accept my true self—as a gay man embracing nontraditional faith beliefs—based on an epiphany. I didn't discover a hidden Bible verse that resolved my struggles. No theological argument spurred my growth. I have never had a Damascus road experience, nor have scales fallen from my eyes. I can't offer any breakthrough insight. Apologies for that.

While some well-meaning folks base their life decisions on Scripture, church tradition, and/or reason, it seems to me that your faith (and sexuality) needs to resonate with your experience. Otherwise, your faith will be unsatisfying in the short-term and ultimately not long-lived because it won't be authentic to you. Our personal song matters. And I dare say each of us should pursue a life of integrity between our experience, and our faith and sexuality, even when that faith and sexuality don't exactly match certain "established" views on Scripture, tradition, and reason.

To be frank, by now, I've heard all the arguments related to evangelicalism and sexuality. I know all the relevant Bible verses. I have read so many books and essays, and I have sat through endless hours of debate. I don't want to dissuade you from seeking answers or from conversing with those who care for you. But for me, I eventually grew tired of defending my faith struggles and justifying my sexuality. I've grown tired of people limiting me to my sexuality.

Simply put, I am following the song I was given. I am gay, and I am so much more than just "gay." As a later forty-something, I have given up trying to convince people that I'm following the "right" music. If they're marching to a different drummer, I tell them to march on, and I no longer argue. If they tell me my drummer is wrong, oh well, I'll metaphorically shake the dust from my feet and march on to the next town, recognizing the incredible privilege I have by not needing to sacrifice my sexuality or my spirituality for a church community.

This is not an "anything goes" or "if it feels good, do it" approach to theology and sexuality. If anything, the song I have followed has required of me an incredible amount of diligence, honesty, and prayer. And it feels scary not to stick to well-trodden paths. At times, I have not been sure I'm following the right music or, better put, the music God put in my heart. I've found a few ways to help me discern that I am:

- I've found the fruit of the Spirit in Galatians 5:22-23 (NLT) to be incredibly helpful. I'll ask, "Which alternative represents love, joy, peace, patience, kindness, goodness, faithfulness, gentleness, and self-control?"

- I'll bend the ear of a few family members or friends, churched or otherwise.

- I'll ask, "Does this choice bring a feeling of consolation or desolation?" The right music inevitably brings me more peace.

- I'll sit quietly, often with a candle (whether this is meditation, prayer, or something else doesn't really matter), and listen to what my soul is saying.

- I'll have a hard look at myself and ask, "Will I have more or less integrity if I make this choice? Specifically, will I have more integrity to the song God gave me (and not the song others, or my own selfish intentions, want me to hear)?" Honesty with oneself is critical. I've sometimes quipped to my daughters, "The worst person you can lie to is yourself."

For those who wander, and who wonder, I'm not sure where you are in your faith or sexuality journey. I encourage you to read Scripture and books, to ask really hard questions, and to talk with church friends and others. Some may strongly disagree with you. Discern the best for yourself, for example, by considering whether the action you or others may take demonstrates the fruit of the Spirit. When you are tired of defending yourself, acknowledge it, shake the dust from your feet, and move on to more affirming communities. Please know they are out there. You are not alone. Above all, listen to the song God gave you in your soul.

In my house, we have a medium grand piano in an airy, light-filled room. When our daughters were newborns, I would gently place each of them on the piano lid (before they could roll) and oh-so-softly key "Jesus Loves Me" (with major sevenths, of course—the original is so prosaic by now), the "Lord's Prayer," and their specific lullaby (I made one for each of them). I wanted them to hear the music and to *feel* the music. I wanted the bass to resonate in their bones and the treble to echo in their sinuses, with the almost imperceptible taps of the piano hammers accenting each beat. Now, at nine and six years of age, I've been gratified to hear them singing to themselves as they go about daily tasks.

I'm not sure what song my daughters will follow. It's almost certainly going to be different from mine. It might lead them further from church, or closer. They may question their sexuality, or they may not. They will certainly make choices that I wouldn't make, some of which may terrify me. I'll ask them to consider the fruit of the Spirit, to ask hard questions, and to consult family and friends. But mostly, I'll ask them—in ways they can hopefully hear—whether they're following the song God has given them.

There's a song I have written. The chorus goes:

> *You gave me song*
> *And with the song that you gave*
> *You gave me everything*

From where I sit on the metaphorical piano bench, nearing fifty years of age, I don't think God gives us answers. In fact, some of the places God leads us can make us question, make us confused, make us scared we've lost our way. But God is still there. Trust me. God is right there in your bones, your gut, your soul, singing to you.

I wish you much discernment, much integrity, much grace, and much music to carry you to ever brighter life.

This piece is the author's own work and does not represent the views of his employer.

Seth Chamberlain *is a social services program manager. Until the age of eighteen, he was a member of the Harrisburg BIC Church where he was baptized. In his late 20s and 30s, he attended the Metropolitan Community Church in Washington, D.C. He now attends St. George's Episcopal Church in Glenn Dale, Maryland, where he sings in the choir and teaches Sunday School. Seth lives in Maryland with his husband, two daughters, and two guinea pigs. He plays the piano, enjoys fantasy novels, and loves to goof around with his kids.*

Wanting to Thrive

Spencer Davis

We are viewed as rebellious, loud, and harmful when in reality, we are only trying to stay alive in an environment designed to stifle us.

Growing up as a child, I found making friends to be very difficult. Most of my classmates did not want to be friends with me, and those who did ended up not being the kindest people. Church was different. Most people in church were incredibly friendly to me, and I felt welcomed there. The adults would ask what was going on in my life, and I was genuinely valued by them.

When I became old enough to sit quietly through sermons, I began listening to what the pastor had to say. He would bring up various topics and point out ambiguities and differing interpretations of Scripture regarding them. For example, he would talk about whether it was sinful to get a tattoo or get drunk. Often, there were gray areas in what was considered right or wrong, and the pastor would encourage us to become comfortable with the lack of certainty in our world.

I struggle to remember the first time I learned the meaning of the word "gay." I initially heard the word thrown around in middle school when it was a catch-all insult, but I had no idea what it actually meant. The first time I ever talked about it with anyone was around the time the Westboro Baptist Church began to make headlines on the news because of their protests against homosexuality and the gay rights movement. I was initially told that being gay meant you were married to someone of the same gender and that such an act was a sinful choice.

Initially, this confused me. When I reflected on what exactly made a particular act sinful, I would begin by trying to identify what harm was being done and who was being victimized by the act. Stealing from someone, for example, was sinful because there was an act of thievery, and a victim of theft who was being harmed. The same could be said for adultery, murder, and deceit. To my way of thinking, marrying somebody did not involve any victims, as no apparent harm was being done to anybody. But since I was told that marrying someone of the same sex was sinful, I wondered if gay marriage could cause harm by hurting God in some indefinite, uncertain way, similar to how it seemed that tattoos and divorce could hurt God. Since I did not want to press the matter out of fear of losing social connections, I kept these thoughts to myself.

During high school, I began to make more friends and to have a social life outside of the church. I remember making a friend who was gay, and he informed me that he was being bullied for it. Another gay friend had scars across her wrists, clear marks from a point in time when she had tried to take her own life. Regardless of how sinful I had been taught it was to be gay, I knew the social stigmas were unnecessary and caused significant harm to real people.

Until my senior year of high school, I had never dated. I never had much interest in dating anybody, and I found the sexual, romantic desires of my peers to be distracting and silly. Eventually, in March 2014, a close friend of mine confessed his feelings for me. Indifferent, I decided to at least give dating a try for his sake. Surprisingly, I found myself thoroughly enjoying his company every day. Neither of us was harming the other, and we were not harming anyone around us. I could not see how something like this could be even remotely considered sinful. And to this day, I still do not believe same-sex relationships are wrong.

I tried my best to keep my relationship a secret from my parents. I later learned that they had asked for advice from the pastor at our church. He believed I was not doing anything wrong, and he explained his viewpoints to them. Fifteen months later, I decided to tell my parents that I had been dating a man. They were nothing but supportive of me. To have supportive friends and family take an interest in the people who made me feel happy was one of the most joyous experiences of my life. At the same time, I wonder what my life would be like now if the pastor had told my parents to intervene in this situation.

During my college years, our church merged with another church, and the leadership changed. As a result of the merger and changes in church policy, gay people could no longer work with children. A close friend of mine, who had plenty of experience working with children, was soon barred from doing so in church. I had trusted the people in my church for years, but this change in policy caused me to leave the church. It even caused me to question what it meant to be a Christian.

While I was able to live a comfortable life with parents who loved and trusted me, I could not say the same for several people whom I knew personally. In the church I left, one member's daughter came out as lesbian, and she was evicted from her home. A family friend who was similarly evicted contemplated suicide. A trans friend of mine experienced harassment at work when a group of outwardly transphobic people falsified a death threat report in his name. This resulted in him being terminated from his job without a proper investigation into the matter. These kinds of injustices should never happen.

As I write this essay, there is a rapidly growing sentiment in the United States that LGBT+ people are intrinsically sex-driven individuals who corrupt and abuse children. News outlets and politicians explicitly connect trans people with heinous acts and crimes in a deliberate attempt to create a society that is openly hostile toward them. This is evident in a surge of newly proposed laws that define religious freedom as the ability to infringe upon the rights of people groups with whom you morally disagree. Texas is labeling gender-affirming care as a form of child abuse, and popular politicians are attempting to restrict the rights of trans people on the pretense that these individuals are inherently harmful.

There is an old saying that goes something like this: "Those who do not learn history are doomed to repeat it." Historically speaking, stigmas against minority groups do not dissipate when they are ignored. Like a festering wound, they will get worse if not addressed. Sometimes, people cherish their fellow citizens and protect them against forces intent on wiping them out. Other times, things get significantly worse before they get better.

Invitation to Conversation

Some countries incarcerate people for being LGBT+, and the United States could become one of them if its abuse of power continues. Propaganda campaigns that are similar to the current onslaught of slander against LGBT+ people have been carried out across history against minority groups. Some of these campaigns ended in the physically violent removal of those groups. We are seeing the beginning of such violence in the increased frequency of deadly attacks at gay bars and LGBT+ deaths by homicide. Think about moments in history when powerful groups explicitly aimed to eliminate less powerful populations of a certain demographic. Think about the way their peers stayed apathetically silent until the dust settled and it came time to count the bodies. Think about how it must feel to sense the looming threat of removal from society, knowing that your former friends and family want you gone. *That is how we feel just about every single day.*

One of the more egregious misconceptions about LGBT+ people relates to the reason why some commit suicide. I have had LGBT+ friends who have committed suicide. I have contemplated suicide myself. Among members of non-binary minority groups, suicidal ideation often follows long periods of discrimination and abuse, resulting in a desire to escape from suffering. Eventually, they give in to nihilism and finally lose the will to live.

This fact, however, is overshadowed by blatant propaganda used to recontextualize the suicides of LGBT+ individuals around Christian ideology. For example, someone's suicide might be incorrectly explained as the person "realizing that they were wrong all along." This lie is quite convenient for the purpose of demonizing minorities, but it does not align with truth. For example, all the research and statistics gathered by The Trevor Project, an organization that functions as a suicide hotline for LGBT+ people, point toward peer pressure, physical abuse, and discrimination—*not* holy epiphanies—as the main reason for suicide attempts. Research from The Trevor Project and Trans Lifeline also demonstrates that an accepting environment results in measurably lower cases of depression and suicides than a non-affirming one. *Accepting LGBT+ people for who they tell you they are quite literally saves lives*, but stigmatizing these individuals can push them toward suicide.

As it stands, I live in a country in which my friends and I lack basic human rights because of the government's desire to hold LGBT+ people, exclusively, to the standards of a single religious group. This is not religious freedom; this is a form of discrimination. A propaganda campaign is being run against an entire minority group, engineered by people fixated on religious dogma and outdated stereotypes. I cannot imagine anyone with these viewpoints doing any of this in good faith. I am tired of people who continue to hold members of the LGBT+ community to a double standard by scrutinizing their lifestyles under the auspices of a religiously-fueled legal system.

Like a plant whose life sprang from a seed that happened to have fallen randomly in a garden, members of the LGBT+ community have been born into an environment that misidentifies us as undesirable and as rebels. The so-called "weed" grows and remains visible for all to see, and it's almost as if its mere existence is a spectacle. However, the plant is not explicitly trying to be "rebellious," nor has it chosen to grow in the garden on its own volition. It is simply there, like us, trying its hardest to stay alive when others seem intent on rejecting it. The plant needs sunlight, water, and soil to grow, not an herbicide spray designed to kill it in order to preserve the conformity of the garden.

If we are to survive *and* thrive, we need people to nurture and accept us, too.

Spencer Davis *is a custodian who previously attended a BIC church but does not currently attend any place of worship. He enjoys making digital art, playing tabletop games, and reading classic works from across the globe. Graduating from college with a degree in Chinese studies, he also took several classes pertaining to media literacy.*

I Will Sing of the Goodness of God (Even If I'm Gay)

Tim Dawson

A former worship leader in the BIC Church emphasizes that God's goodness is available to all of us by sharing his personal story of coming out.

With every breath that I am able
Oh, I will sing of the goodness of God.

Three years after coming out, I found myself leading worship at a United Church of Christ. Singing the words above from "Goodness of God" by Bethel Music, I was overcome with gratitude to God for His unending faithfulness. In my fifteen-plus years leading worship in the Brethren in Christ (BIC) Church, there were similar moments in worship. Singing "And Can It Be," or "Great is Thy Faithfulness," acapella, in four-part harmony, warms the soul. And introducing "contemporary" music like "Shine, Jesus, Shine" and teaching a congregation to clap on beats two and four are all memories that I will cherish.

But singing *Goodness of God* this time was different. For the first time in my life, I was leading others in worship to our God as a gay man.

I love You, Lord
For Your mercy never fails me
All my days, I've been held in Your hands

Invitation to Conversation

Sure, I have always had a same-sex attraction. Growing up in a Wesleyan minister's home, I knew the part I was supposed to play (or so I was led to believe). The church and society in the 70s and 80s made it clear that boys cannot like other boys "in that way." And if they did, it was a path to hell or, worse yet, for a pre-teen, social purgatory. I watched the caricatures with lisps on TV sitcoms that were always accompanied by fake laugh tracks, and I vowed never to let myself be like them. I attended youth conferences and church camp and pledged the same thing to God.

At the same time that I was receiving the message that those strange feelings I had for Bo and Luke Duke and for Magnum P.I. were wrong, I was also hearing my Sunday school teacher and youth camp speaker telling me that I was made in God's image. He loved me no matter what, and "God don't make no junk." During these conflicting times, God and I had lots of talks. Fortunately for me, He was always there to listen to my confusion and to share His voice.

> I love your voice
> You have led me through the fire

God has always been present for me. In the midst of my struggles, there were many internal battles raging. I made deals with Him and broke almost as many as I made. But no matter how many times I failed to "do right," He was still there. He was never more present than in my darkest days leading up to and during my decision to come out.

> In the darkest night
> You are close like no other

Yet it seemed that coming out was never going to be a reality for me. Early in my life it was because of religious and societal pressures. "What will they think of me, a sinner?" But as I got closer to making the decision, my biggest concerns were not about the church, or co-workers, or friends. It was about the people closest to me, my family. "How could I hurt the people that I cared so much for by upending their lives? How could I be so selfish?"

Through that struggle, God was there, showing me His great love and reassuring me that He would see us through. And when all was said and done, it was my spouse of twenty-seven years, my child, and my understanding in-laws who stood by me. Along with a few Christian friends, God gave me people in my life who truly cared for me, gay or not.

I've known You as a father
I've known You as a friend
And I have lived in the goodness of God

God was with me as a loving Father wrapping His arms around His hurting son. God was with my family as we worked through a divorce and adjusted to this new reality. God brought new Christian friends into my life to support me in my new journey and to replace those friends who didn't know how to do so. I have been blessed.

Your goodness is running after
It's running after me

I have been blessed because I have always felt God's presence with me. Unfortunately, there are many brothers and sisters in Christ who have not felt that same presence. They have only heard the condemnation, and they are running away from the church. But God is running after them. He is chasing them over all the hurdles that the world and the church keep putting in their way.

With my life laid down
I'm surrendered now
I give you everything

If they haven't yet run away, how many queer members are in our congregations, holding on to the heavy mask they have been wearing? Despite the weight, keeping up the façade is safer than laying it down and facing the rejection of family, friends, and (they fear) even God. Despite the promise God has made to us all, the thought of surrendering it all to Him can be debilitating. Our sexual thoughts and feelings are probably the deepest and certainly the most intimate parts of our soul. Certainly, God doesn't want that part of our lives. But He does!

> 'Cause Your goodness is running after,
> It's running after me

God's goodness is running after all of us. His goodness is not to be confused with the church. His goodness is in His love. His goodness is not limited by the acceptance of others. His goodness is in His faithfulness. That is why I sing!

> 'Cause all my life You have been faithful
> And all my life You have been so, so good
> With every breath that I am able
> Oh, I'm gonna sing of the goodness of God

Even if I'm gay. No, not *even* if I'm gay. I'm gonna sing *because* I am gay.

Tim Dawson *is a follower of Christ, a father, and a musician from Harrisburg, Pennsylvania. He is a student success advocate in higher education by day, and a lead in Parkside Harmony, an international acapella male chorus from Hershey, Pennsylvania, by night.*

I Wish I Had Left Differently

John Doe

A former employee of a BIC church, who is gay, writes a letter describing how the behavior of the pastor of this church caused considerable harm to him.

To My Former Pastor,
   I wish I had left differently.
   I wish I had told you my departure had to do with how bad you made me feel about being gay and about how hostile it is for gay people to be in your church. "Your church" is a funny expression for me because once I said "our church" and even "my church." I wish I had told you how stifling it is for everyone at this church—not just me and not just those who identify as LGBT.
   When I first came to your church, I was greeted with words I had never heard from another church. I was told that what was important was the state of your heart rather than mere outward appearances. I knew of many churches where people simply dress themselves up to look the part and then start looking down on those who don't. You told me this church would be different. And at the beginning, it was. I was encouraged when you quoted a book that said the things we measure become the things we care about and that we didn't want to measure anything other than heart change.
   But as the years went by, I saw that we did start measuring behavior; we started measuring the facade. As long as your butt was in the seat and your tithe was in the plate, as long as you'd been dunked in the water and you

Invitation to Conversation

cried in your small group, then you were good. You were saved. You were on the good road. Or whatever you want to call it.

But there's another thing that was measured in your church, something that I'm afraid you still don't realize. Because it wasn't enough just to act Christian; you had to *look* Christian. At your church, that meant looking straight and acting straight. You didn't care how many tattoos I had or how many times I volunteered. What you cared about was me fitting a certain mold, a mold that felt suffocating, like wearing a costume that was too tight and too foreign. I remember sitting in the pews, feeling a gnawing sense of being out of place. The more I tried to conform, the more I lost pieces of myself.

I wish I had had the courage then to tell you that your church, the one I once called "home," started to feel more like a prison. A place where I had to hide and pretend. A place where my true self wasn't welcome. I remember the sermons that subtly, and sometimes not so subtly, condemned who I am. I remember the stares and whispers that followed me whenever I dared to be a bit more myself.

You see, Pastor, I joined your church seeking refuge, a place to belong. I was drawn in by the message of love and acceptance. But over time, I realized that this love was conditional. It was reserved for those who fit within a narrow definition of what was deemed "acceptable." I learned that in your eyes, my identity as a gay man was a sin, an aberration.

I recall the day you spoke to me personally with a tone of what you thought was compassion. You told me that I needed to "overcome" my identity, to seek "healing." That conversation broke something in me. It was the moment I realized that no matter how much I loved the community, I would never truly be a part of it.

Leaving was not easy. It felt like abandoning a family. But it was a family that couldn't accept me for who I am. I wish I had told you how much it hurt to walk away, to leave behind friends and memories. But more than that, I wish I had told you about the damage your words and actions inflicted, not just on me but on many others who left silently, carrying their wounds with them.

I wonder if you realize the weight of your words, the impact of your teachings. Do you see the trail of people who have left, feeling rejected and unloved? Do you ever question if the message of love you preach is truly being embodied in your actions and the culture of the church?

I wish I had expressed the deep conflict I felt within the walls of a church that preached love but practiced exclusion. Each sermon, each gathering, felt like an echo of judgment, not just on my identity but on anyone who dared to differ from the norm. The emphasis on appearances and on fitting within a certain mold created an environment where authenticity was lost. It wasn't just about being gay. It was about the suppression of any true expression of self that didn't align with the church's narrow view. The irony of it all was the stark contrast to the initial messages I heard of genuine heart change over outward appearances. The church, which should have been a safe haven, became a place where I felt more judged and less understood.

I wish that when I left I had told you how it felt to be backed into a corner. I wish I had told you this fact: I left because when I came to you as a leader, and I told you my heart was to reach more people for Christ, you told me the real problem was my identity.

I wish I had left angry for my people, people from the LGBT community who would walk through your doors seeking God, only to be pushed out those same doors by you.

I wish I had left loud. Instead, I left sad. Instead, I left quiet. I wish I had left loud because I believe the mission of the Church is important. I love the community I once called family. I want the church to do better. I want you to do better. I want you to reach people in the community for Christ, to accept them as family and not sideline them, have special meetings with them, or add extra burdens they must bear to be Christian. I want you to treat them better than you treated me.

Sincerely,
John Doe

John Doe *has been a Christian since childhood. He attended a BIC church for fifteen years, was on staff in a BIC church for ten years, and is gay. (A pseudonym has been used, and some details have been changed to protect the identity of the writer and the pastor.)*

Everyone Needs Love and Compassion

Liz Johnson

A longtime Christian shares her fraught relationship with the church she loves, a church she believes should be a welcoming community to all people regardless of how they identify since we all are loved unconditionally by God.

Growing up in a conservative, fundamentalist pastor's family, I was introduced early to the concept that I am evil and that the only way to forgiveness is through the blood of Jesus. I got "saved" at the age of four. Told that I "needed to be a good example" to my peers, I was terrified of thinking or acting less than perfectly. I felt shame and guilt almost constantly, even with small mistakes and even though I was a "good" kid.

When I was six, classmates chased kids of the opposite gender at recess. Noticing that no one else chased anyone of the same gender, neither did I. But, in my view, males were unsafe and untrustworthy, and females were attractive, desirable, and relational. I thought I was the only female to feel this way because I had had no exposure to lesbians or even the word "lesbian." I'd been told that "gay" was an evil male thing, so I felt like the most dirty, evil person for being "gay for females," as I thought I was the only person depraved enough to have those thoughts and urges. Having been told that there was no such thing as a gay Christian, I was sure that if I couldn't change, I would go to hell.

I prayed that God would change me and leave me without sexual urges of any kind. God answered: "No, I knew what I was doing when I made you. I made you just how I wanted you." This didn't relieve my guilt and shame, and it didn't deter my pleading prayers, my efforts to "be perfect," or my wish to be anyone else.

At age seven, I developed a serious eating disorder related to my efforts at extreme self-control and punishment. By sixth grade, I was actively suicidal. I knew it needed to look like an accident, or it would cost my dad his job. By ninth grade, I became more passively suicidal. Without taking unnecessary risks, I was nonetheless eating very little—and I was not avoiding things that could kill me. I "knew" everyone would be better off without me. If I died, I reasoned that I would at least stop adding "sins" to the list for which I would be accountable.

In junior high school, a church leader heard a rumor that I had played "doctor" with a couple of girls my age. When she informed my mom, they angrily lectured me about how evil I was, how I "knew better" and "should be a better example, not leading other kids astray." They said it didn't matter that it wasn't my idea. The leader told me, "You can never get married now because before marriage you should tell your fiancé about your past, and no man would agree to marry such a soiled woman." I took this to heart but found it confusing because it was well known from her testimony that she was on her second marriage, that she had had multiple partners, and that before coming to Christ, she and her husband had lived together before marrying. Evidently, same-sex contact of any sort was worse than any heterosexual "sins."

I started avoiding the appearance of any type of attraction or intimate relationships. This made my friendships stiff and lifeless, or extremely one-sided, with my friends sharing everything and with me sharing nothing. I knew I could not show even a hint of what I was struggling with, or it would affect my dad's job and my relationships with church people, including those who said they loved me unconditionally. Even my "best" friends from childhood and high school didn't have the faintest idea. I couldn't tell them and risk them saying something to their parents. This fall, I finally informed one friend from that time that I am queer.

From junior high school through college, purity culture messages focused on perfection and "cleanliness." The fact that I had been sexually assaulted as a child was described as an unerasable stain. I had to dress as unnoticeably as possible, and I had to speak as correctly as possible. My Christian college had rules around appearing "pure" which made being "authentic" nearly impossible. My academic study was negatively affected, my eating disorder worsened, and I came to believe that I didn't deserve to live at all.

In college I did a lot of soul searching, talking to God, and studying the Bible about gender and sexuality. I concluded that the sole purpose of dating was to lead to marriage, and since a lesbian marriage was not possible, I could either stay single for life or date and marry a man. But I had always perceived men as threatening, and I found the male form repulsive. Since I had internalized the message that I was "too dirty" for a man to want to marry me, I prepared myself for a life of singleness and celibacy.

But then I met Nick, a male acquaintance who was so calm and gentle that he slipped by the gender warning flag and became a friend. Nick and my female friend Brooke became my closest friends. At one point, I realized I could comfortably allow either one to pursue me romantically. But gay marriage was still illegal, so I only allowed Nick to be romantic in any way. Before we got too close, I revealed my deepest, darkest secret to both Nick and Brooke so they could leave me if it was too terrible to be associated with me. Their response was reassuring: "I thought it was going to be something awful and a big deal."

In the last semester of college, I joined a Brethren in Christ (BIC) church in Kansas that advertised itself as a new healthy place where "we do church differently," recognizing that "God accepts everyone" and that "God cares more about what's inside than what's outside" (these are paraphrased to avoid identifying a specific church). I was assured that while "shunning" was a part of Anabaptist history, the church no longer encouraged or practiced it.

After dating for three and half years and having received marriage counseling from our pastor, Nick and I married the day after college graduation. We had been very open and honest with each other and were very committed to one another. So, on that day, we began our mixed-orientation, heterosexual-appearing, strongly committed, monogamous marriage. Five years after our wedding, Brooke, then homeless and pregnant by acquaintance rape, was in the middle of a divorce and a mental breakdown. We moved her into our house and eventually adopted her baby. We gave birth to our youngest child five years later.

I was still very private about being a lesbian. I was "out" to my pastor, and since "I wasn't living the lifestyle," it wasn't a concern for him. A few years later, I reevaluated some things. The church's emphasis on authenticity, accountability, and God's acceptance prompted me to be more open with my accountability partners. I realized that my "sin" was no less forgivable than those of other people our church served: porn addicts, angry people, drug addicts, alcoholics, recent prison parolees, and homeless people. All these individuals were welcomed and encouraged to be authentic and open with their struggles. I worked up the courage to broach the topic with my accountability partners. Though shocked, they reassured me that they would love me unconditionally, support me no matter what, and hold me accountable in the same ways they did for other struggles. However, they never brought up the topic when checking in, which seemed like they thought I must not be dealing with it if I didn't mention it.

I was "out" to several people at church, and one was eventually comfortable putting words to their sexuality as well. We were (and are) strong Christians, and we were passionate about this church and its mission. We worked to encourage loving attitudes and to create spaces that would be welcoming and safe for LGBTQ+ people. We weren't trying to change church theology but were simply hoping that LGBTQ+ people could be treated like everyone else: people with sin who are saved through the blood and forgiveness of Christ. Since thieves, embezzlers, murderers, and even convicted sex offenders were told God had unconditional love and forgiveness for them, we desired the church to offer similar love, care, and acceptance to LGBTQ+ people. But we faced pushback and disappointment. We were told any intentional change would be seen as glorifying sin. While the church welcomed these individuals, it would not do the same for LGBTQ+ people.

Over the years, the culture of the church and the reaction of leadership shifted from relative neutrality about LGBTQ+ issues to non-responsiveness (as long as you weren't obviously queer), to occasional sermons denouncing homosexuality and transness, to more frequent sermons on the topic. If you became a regular attender and appeared less than straight or cisgender, you could quickly expect an invitation to meet with leadership for your general vetting. If you stayed around, a sermon about your particular brand of LGBTQ+ identity would surely follow. As time went on, any regular attendee who was contemplating becoming a member came to know that they could not consider membership classes unless they were "not living the lifestyle" and "not identifiably queer." Since I was a longstanding member by this time, a "mature Christian," a leader, had been a staff person for a brief time, and was married to a man, I was spared this treatment.

In the last five or so years, almost every time the word "sin" appeared in the Scripture reading, the pastor's sermon focused on sexual "sins"—divorce, adultery, living together/premarital sex, gender issues (mostly transness), and homosexuality. These "top five sins" were preached on regularly. Yet the pastor would make little or no mention of other sins that affect our congregation regularly. When I brought this up to the pastor, he said it couldn't be accurate: "It must just be 'how it feels to you.'" But when I went back over the last three years of sermon recordings, I realized it was even more true than I originally thought.

In the last year and a half, two trans-appearing adults and two confirmed lesbian couples were among the church's new regular attendees. Pointed sermons were followed by a sermon series on 1 Corinthians that lasted over a year. Although "sin" is a frequent topic in Paul's first letter to the Corinthians, Paul mentions gender and "homosexuality" only briefly. However, in the church's weekly series, sermon after sermon highlighted the "top five sins." Even though the series was billed as "Jesus Above All Things," it felt as though it was about homosexuality, transness, and divorce. In the church hallway and sanctuary, people openly shared off-color and queer-phobic jokes, eliciting agreement and chuckles from others in the vicinity. When we brought up our concern about this with the pastor, he said that he hadn't noticed anything and that he didn't believe his people would talk that way. He suggested that maybe we had misheard or were too sensitive.

———

Last spring, my eldest child, at age eleven, announced to us that they were trans, had a new name, and wanted a haircut and change of wardrobe. They wanted to use their new name primarily at school, not at church or with extended family. For two weeks, everything was one hundred percent masculine for them. I told them that I wouldn't dictate their labels, but there were other labels I felt probably fit a bit better. Following our family norms, I gave them information and resources. After two weeks, my child came back to me asking, "Is it okay if I am just gender fluid instead?" I said, "I love you no matter what labels you use. Use the ones that make sense to you and hold loosely to them as life is full of changes." Since then, they have presented eclectically traditional, gender-wise.

At the beginning of summer, I spoke with our church youth leaders to provide a heads-up about what my child was dealing with and to give them the opportunity to say they were uncomfortable with my child being in the youth group. I was assured that my child would be fine and was told that while they can't condone "those choices," they would not penalize a child for having struggles and being who they are. But in the fall, youth group friends started rumors that my child was sleeping with girls and then that they were trans (even though they had not mentioned their new name in church, and they dressed as gender neutral, or feminine, as they could handle). Along with the rumors came bullying. I had to bring this to the attention of their parents and our youth leaders and explain why this wasn't okay.

Mid-fall, a church leader put a rather inflammatory post on social media about God and gender. The post got lots of "likes" and "hearts" from other church leaders. I made the first comment by asking a discussion question. I shared relatable analogies, used Scripture in context, and wrote in a calm, reasonable, polite tone. None of the people from my church responded to my comment or other comments on "my side." Instead, people from my church "hearted" their approval of the church leader's position, as did the pastor who chastised me and others with responses like mine. I left the post feeling abandoned and shunned by many friends with whom I had shared vulnerably about my sexuality, friends who told me they would love unconditionally and would support me and hold me accountable. The pastor "requested" to have a meeting with Nick and me to talk about how this affects my husband Nick's position on the board, to discuss how it affects our membership status, and to have a conversation as friends. The actual conversation took hours and didn't resolve anything.

While acknowledging that it was admirable to have stayed in the church to advocate for the LGBTQ+ community and to encourage change, my spiritual advisor and therapist said I needed to take into consideration my deteriorating mental health and the lack of safety for my child. Although I started visiting more local, affirming, biblical churches, I hoped I would not have to leave my BIC church. I wanted to keep trying to help create the welcoming space the church claimed to be. Yet the church's current treatment of the LGBTQ+ issue and LGBTQ+ people has created and/or added to the church-related trauma that many people experience. It has communicated that Christ's love and forgiveness are only for certain kinds of people, and it has insisted that people "blend in" and look and act like a certain type of Christian if they want to be included in this church community. This is not the message of Christ. And it is not the message that the BIC Church should be sending.

Several people I know have stopped going to any church, and more have become atheists or have adopted a different religion altogether. I myself have stopped attending on Sundays, limiting my involvement to a small group. Recently, I entered residential treatment for my eating disorder. Although the treatment center generally encourages residents to maintain connections with their spiritual communities for support in the healing process, this has not been possible for me. I lost most of my church friends the day they said the "quiet parts" out loud and stood together in solidarity against me. At this time in my life when I really need their support, I have instead been grieving the loss of my faith community, my pastor, and all but a small number of friends.

Finding myself without many friends and in between spiritual/faith communities, I am grateful to have found pastoral support from a local Christian minister/bishop from another denomination. While I appreciate this, it is a shame that my own BIC faith community has not stood by me and supported me during this time. Everyone needs love and compassion.

Liz Johnson *has been a member of her local BIC church for seventeen and a half years. She has served on staff and in leadership, and she has done a lot of volunteer work. Her husband, Nick, is on the church board. She has a bachelor's degree in Psychology, Ministry, Communication, and English Education. For over a decade, Liz has taught at a small, private Christian school for children with needs that aren't easily met in the traditional classroom. She has been a committed Christian for the last thirty-six years (most of her life). She is a mom and a supportive friend. She also happens to be a lesbian with a child who is bisexual and genderfluid.*

Free to Be Reverend Me

Martha J. Lockwood

―――――――

*The journey of a minister who went from serving the
BIC as a closeted clergy to serving the United Church
of Canada freely as God created her to be.*

On May 9, 1980, at a Brethren in Christ (BIC) church in Canada, I made the decision to become a follower of Christ. For the next twenty-seven years, the BIC Church nurtured me in the faith and gave me opportunities to grow and serve. In 1992, I was ordained at Lancaster BIC Church. At the time, I was only the third woman to be ordained in the BIC Church. I served four churches in Ontario (Heise Hill, Sherkston, North East Calgary, and Fallsview) and two in Pennsylvania (Palmyra and Lancaster).

Even though I was not an "ethnic BIC," I became very involved in the broader church and was encouraged and mentored by many outstanding people. An ongoing joke among my colleagues was that I would be the first woman bishop—an indication of my level of dedication to this small denomination.

During my twelve years in Pennsylvania, the thought that I might be a lesbian never entered my mind. I dated but never found the right man. I believed I was one of those people who functioned better as a single person. When you live in the evangelical world, there really are no other good explanations. I had an incredibly fulfilling life with a wonderful family and friends, and I was content as a single person with considerable freedom.

And since I am not the most introspective person, I continued on, content in my singleness.

After moving back to my hometown in 2000, I began to question my sexual orientation. Perhaps it was due to the "safety" of living back in Canada, or the friendships I had with the queer community, or my season of middle age reflection. I also began to think about the consequences of coming out. It was a seven-year process, so my decision was not made in haste.

I knew if I took this step there would no longer be a place for me in the BIC Church. This was a painful realization but one I had to come to terms with. I wrestled with Scripture, prayed, and sought the wisdom of some of my dearest and trusted friends.

Jesus said in the Gospel of John, "So if the Son sets you free, you will be free indeed" (John 8:36, NIV). And Paul wrote in his letter to the Galatians, "It is for freedom that Christ has set us free" (Gal 5:1, NIV). There is great freedom in being a follower of Christ, freedom to be who God created you to be. The church was forcing me to live a life of slavery, not freedom.

I often thought of those I knew with similar dilemmas. For example, there was a song leader in my church who was old enough to be my dad. One of my closeted friends at the time had run into him at a park in a nearby city where men went to have anonymous sex with other men. (Sunday mornings felt a little awkward after that.) There was also another friend of mine who served on the board of his church, but dated women to hide the fact that he went to gay bars. He knew he would be removed from membership if word ever got out. Both men lived double lives in fear of being outed. And there were others.

I had three choices: (1) stay closeted and live my life as less than I was created to be, (2) live a double life in fear of being caught, or (3) come out in the gentlest way possible and live my authentic life. Each had a cost, and each had its comfort. I chose the third option and have never regretted it. Through the emotional turmoil of it all, I never doubted God's love for me or Jesus' redeeming and transformational love for his church.

For the last sixteen years, I have lived my authentic life as a follower of Christ, a follower who happens to be a lesbian. Some would say it is impossible to be both. I would encourage those who think that way to read

Unclobber: Rethinking Our Misuse of the Bible on Homosexuality by Colby Martin.

I have found a home in the United Church of Canada and now serve as an ordained minister of a great city church. I recently celebrated six years of marriage to my wonderful wife, Michelle Heisey. Her last name tells me that God, indeed, has a sense of humor. Most of my BIC friends have not turned their back on me, and I continue to enjoy great fellowship with them. Many of them have shared their gifts of preaching or worship on a Sunday when they were visiting.

I was thankful to be asked to contribute to this project. I hold no bitterness toward the BIC denomination, only thankfulness for the years of nurturing and ministry and for the wonderful seekers of Christ I worked alongside and served. I am heartened by those who are having this conversation and are showing great courage in standing up for others who have been forced to live in denial, duplicity, or exile.

God created us all with unique gifts, abilities, and personalities. I believe our Creator wants us to be authentic—to be our true selves. How many of God's children will be lost to the church because of fear, a misinterpretation of Scripture, or cultural ignorance? Jesus did not lose me, but the BIC Church did.

Martha J. Lockwood *is a former BIC minister who now serves as pastor of Central United Church in Welland, Ontario, Canada. She serves on numerous Regional Committees, including the Affirm Network for churches in Southern Ontario. Martha is an avid football fan—both CFL and NFL. She lives in Crystal Beach, Ontario, with her wife, Michelle, and two dogs and four cats (all rescues). She is also the proud bonus mom of Lindsay, Spencer, and Zach, and she is Granny to Beau.*

Queer Rights Are a Matter of Life and Death

Jonny Rashid

A pastor issues a plea to respect, value, and protect trans lives—and all queer lives—and to stop behaving as though "trans issues" are simply a matter for debate.

Almost no Christian would disagree that a simple reading of the Gospels makes it clear that we are to love and side with the most vulnerable among us. Jesus reserves his harshest words for people who cause the little ones to stumble, likening their judgment to being worse than a millstone being hung around their neck as they are tossed into the Sea of Galilee (Matt 18:6). As Christians, it is our duty to protect vulnerable people around us. In fact, the Apostle Paul says that church unity is dependent upon giving honor to the most disrespected persons among us. Paul writes, "The members of the body that seem to be weaker are indispensable, and those members of the body that we think less honorable we clothe with greater honor, and our less respectable members are treated with greater respect, whereas our more respectable members do not need this" (1 Cor 12:22-24, NRSVue).

As an explicit application of this teaching, I believe that the clearest way to follow Jesus and to express the Gospel is to love, affirm, and cherish trans folks, and especially trans youth. But unfortunately, Christians seem to be doing the very opposite.

According to one study, "Data indicate that 82% of transgender individuals have considered killing themselves and 40% have attempted suicide, with suicidality highest among transgender youth."[1] This isn't surprising, and it is likely to get worse. The assault on trans rights is happening across the United States, and trans youth are the most victimized. Another study links queer suicidality with religiosity: "Lesbians and gays who reported that religion was important to them were 38 percent more likely to have had recent suicidal thoughts. For lesbians only, religion was associated with a 52 percent increased likelihood of suicidal thinking."[2]

Queer people are at higher risk of suicidal ideation when they name religion as important to them. The risk of suicidality decreases when they name religion as less important to them. So, to stay alive, statistics show that queer people should become *less* religious. *Christians must reckon with the fact that their anti-queer theology is deadly.* Our theology is costing the lives of queer people. If a queer person leaves your church, it is sad to say, they're statistically better off. Our job, then, is to turn the tide and make it so that churches actually reduce, rather than increase, the risk of suicidality among queer people. While suicidality is lower for most people who attend church, this is not so if they are queer. Therefore, it is imperative that we pour resources into changing these toxic outcomes related to our religious communities and our deadly theology.

It is increasingly harder, it seems, to stay queer and out, especially if you are a teen. After passage of the landmark U.S. Supreme Court case that legalized gay marriage, *Obergefell v. Hodges*, we have experienced a radical and wicked backlash against LGBTQIA rights. All over the U.S., LBGTQIA rights are being slashed, and the Republican presidential candidates all seem to be campaigning to end the rights of trans teens. Nikki Haley, a so-called moderate candidate, suggested trans teens are causing an

---

[1]. From the abstract of Austin Ashley, et al, "Suicidality Among Transgender Youth: Elucidating the Role of Interpersonal Risk Factors," *Journal of Interpersonal Violence* 37:5-6 (2022).

[2]. Anne Harding, "Religious Faith Linked to Suicidal Behavior in LGBQ Adults," *Reuters*, April 13, 2018, https://www.reuters.com/article/us-health-lgbq-religion-suicide/religious-faith-linked-to-suicidal-behavior-in-lgbq-adults-idUSKBN1HK2MA.

increase in suicidal ideation in teen girls.[3] Haley's rhetoric is particularly heinous because she ignores the fact that trans teens have higher suicidality rates while suggesting their plight is one they inflict on others. Meanwhile, Ron DeSantis is codifying his hatred of trans teens in Florida law.[4]

Not only have bans on aspects of trans life been codified into law—"sports bills, birth certificate and pronoun bills, drag bills, bathroom bills, 'Don't Say Gay' bills"—trans health care is being legislated against too.[5] The largest threat to trans youth and their families are "aggressive efforts to outlaw what's known as gender-affirming care for minors—a range of interventions from talk therapy and social transition, such as adopting a name, clothing style or pronoun without any medical treatment, to puberty blockers and, for older kids, hormones."[6]

Too often, we treat the issues surrounding trans individuals as abstract. In hopes of achieving unity in our polarized time, Christians reduce the issue to a matter of public debate rather than seeing it for what it is: a matter of life or death. To be clear, the issues at hand are not whether we can watch or read Harry Potter, or whether we are being too harsh to transphobic people or those "just asking questions." The important issues involve the health and well-being of queer youth and their ability to survive. Queer youth depend on our support for their very lives. Yet Christians often lead the way in assaulting their rights and denying them the ability to be who they truly are.

Most of us are not brazenly hateful when it comes to queer folks. But in my experience, even well-intentioned Christians harm trans people by not taking a side. Sadly, this is a choice that many well-intentioned Anabaptist pastors routinely make.

---

3. Rebecca Shabad, "Nikki Haley Suggests Transgender Kids Are Causing Suicidal Ideation in Teenage Girls," *NBC News*, June 5, 2023, https://www.nbcnews.com/politics/2024-election/nikki-haley-suggests-transgender-kids-cause-suicidal-ideation-teenage-rcna87708.

4. Brendan Farrington, "DeSantis Signs Bills Targeting Drag Shows, Transgender Kids and the Use of Bathrooms and Pronouns," *AP News*, May 22, 2023, https://apnews.com/article/desantis-florida-lgbtq-education-health-c68a7e5fe5cf22ab8cca324b00644119.

5. Megan K. Stack, "When Parents Hear That 'Their Child is Not Normal and Should Not Exist'," *The New York Times* (Feb. 18, 2023), https://www.nytimes.com/2023/02/18/opinion/trans-gender-missouri.html?smtyp=cur&smid=tw-nytimes.

6. Stack, "When Parents Hear That 'Their Child is Not Normal and Should Not Exist'."

Much debate circles around a lack of research on things like puberty blockers and hormones. I want to emphasize that while research on trans health is very important, even more pressing needs are (1) to respond caringly to the reality of the increased risk of suicidality among trans children and (2) to oppose attempts to criminalize them and/or their parents. There's nothing wrong with doing more research (which, by the way, the aforementioned legislation makes impossible), but the claim that we need to do more research before we take care of our trans youth has lethal ramifications.

Trans people and their rights are often disregarded in our society because they make up such a small percentage of the population. I've even heard pastors say that they wonder why we are devoting this much time to a group that is so small. The implication is that they aren't worth the sweat or the effort.

Like other minorities whose numbers are small in comparison to more dominant societal groups, trans people's needs are often minimized and dismissed. But trans people are our neighbors, our co-workers, our family members, our children. We must care for them as we do for anyone else. In fact, we must especially prioritize their needs because they are so often dismissed. Once again, this isn't a theoretical or abstract matter; it is a matter of life and death.

However, many Christians miss this point. Raised with homophobic and patriarchal teachings and understandings of the Bible, they focus on—and speculate about—harm done to traditional understandings of gender identity. It is a shame that those leading the death march against trans folks are Christians because Jesus has such a different approach to the most persecuted among us.

I want to encourage all of us who are queer to have pride in who we are and to stand firm in our own identities, despite resistance from those who oppress us. "Pride" can be a confusing word to Christians who understandably see pride as sinful. But LGBTQIA+ pride is not the kind of arrogant pride that the Bible warns against. Instead, our pride is better understood as honor. Queer pride is the opposite of shame, not the opposite of humility. We don't stand in arrogance, but we stand without shame, and we demand that society honor and dignify us. It is the lack of dignity and honor that leads to us being closeted, and that causes some of us to even entertain the idea of taking our own life. So queer folks, stand proud, without shame.

On the other hand, people who exploit our marginalization and oppression for their own gain are the ones who exhibit that sinful, arrogant kind of pride. They are so sure of their moral righteousness that they are willing to hold onto their ideology even when it kills people.

In Romans 12:16, Paul says, "Consider everyone as equal, and don't think that you're better than anyone else. Instead, associate with people who have no status" (CEB). Paul is speaking directly to those who oppressed and opposed marginalized people of his day. Today, the call to Christians is to see marginalized people—like queer people—as equals. It is a call for straight and cisgender Christians to refrain from thinking that they are better than queer folks and instead to humbly come alongside them in their status-poor state with accompaniment and support. Christians who are opposed to the lives and dignity of queer people would be better off "taking a log out of their eye" than attempting to remove "the splinter" from their queer sibling's eye (see Matt 7:3-5). Humility would be their best response.

LGBTQIA+ pride is about a society elevating people who have been oppressed, not so they reign over others, but so they stand on equal footing with others. It is about equality, unity, and an end to division in our society. If it offends people, it is because some people want to put us back in the closet and want us to be hidden and covered up. That sort of closeting is deadly. Queer inclusion is about giving the most honor and dignity to the ones who have been most oppressed.

Christians who oppress us should stand in shame because their theology leads to death. Christians who support and love queer people, who stand in humility and who humbly accept our experience, are the ones who exemplify the meekness and humility of which biblical authors write. Those who are proud of themselves for how they oppress us should take heed of God's warning against the proud. Queer people who stand proud are doing so because of who God made us to be. We are proud of ourselves as members of God's creation. Being proud of who God made us is an act of worship to our Creator. When a queer person embraces their identity, they are thanking and honoring their Creator. When they are forced into closets, they are being forced to be ashamed of who they are. And those who shame them are denying the beauty in God's creation and desecrating people whom God loves. Honoring queer people and allowing them to take pride in themselves honors and gives glory to God.

It is time for Christians to listen to queer folks and their allies and allow them to lead us. If we care about supporting life and defeating death, then queer rights must matter to us. Jesus saw people beyond the gender binary and called us to love the most vulnerable persons among us. It's time to stop engaging in the culture war and instead to start prioritizing the life and health of queer folks among us.

Jonny Rashid *is the pastor of West Philadelphia Mennonite Fellowship, former pastor of BIC church Circle of Hope, and author of* Jesus Takes a Side. *He blogs at jonnyrashid.com.*

Proved Wrong

Hannah Stolpe

When I realized I'm bisexual, I worried my BIC church would no longer be the same welcoming home I've come to cherish. I was delighted to have my fears proved wrong even as I continue to pray for the full embrace and affirmation of queer people in the BIC.

I sat in my room soaking in the last few minutes of an episode of "A League of Their Own," a show that follows the fictional lives of several queer women baseball players in the 1940s. It was the night after a big win. After having to hide their romantic partnerships for so long, the players are celebrating together in an underground bar. The air is laced with joy and welcome in this space of chosen community and freedom.

All of a sudden, their respite is shattered as loud banging pierces the bar. The owners of the bar throw themselves against the door in an attempt to barricade it, but it isn't long before the police break in. Chaos erupts as the police rip through the bar. Like predators narrowly focused on their prey, they brutally attack and detain anyone in their path. The next day, the names of the victims would be published in the newspaper and labeled as sex offenders. Being queer in the 1940s wasn't seen as an act of love; it was regarded as a crime.

I sat there, frozen in that moment, until the credits finally rolled. Tears streamed down my face, and my hands shook as I took in the horror of the violent cruelty. Although the scene was fictional, I knew that it all too

Invitation to Conversation

well represents reality for many queer people, past and present. My heart in pieces, I uttered to God the only word I could muster, "Why?"

A whisper reverberated through my heart and body: "My heart breaks too." Tears spilled down my cheeks, a strange mix of relief and gratitude, pain and heartbreak. I don't know any better word to describe the treatment of LGBTQ people by the church than "heartbreak," but I have found great comfort in believing God's heart breaks over it, too.

The first time I walked through the doors of Harrisburg Brethren in Christ (HBIC) I was struggling with a lot of doubt and disappointment toward faith and the church. The past two years of searching for a church home had opened my eyes to the church's own contribution to injustice. It was hard to see the church as a bearer of "good news," especially to those whose voices have been systematically silenced.

The reason I attended HBIC with a few friends that morning in January 2022 was because we had heard of a Harrisburg church that had recently appointed a queer woman as their worship pastor. As it turned out, HBIC was not that church. Regardless, I did not leave disappointed. That Sunday was a participatory service of congregational prayer in conjunction with the BIC's annual Week of Prayer and Fasting. The space exuded welcome. Before long, I found myself mustering up the courage to add my voice to the choir of prayers and to invite another woman to join my friends in the closing small group prayer. By the time I walked out the door, the spirit of community at HBIC had already left an impression.

I soon made HBIC my home church. That first year was marked by getting to know an incredible community. And, bit by bit, my belief in the church was revitalized. I watched how these people supported and encouraged each other with homemade meals, text messages to check in on each other, and extra hands for yard work. I marveled at how each person contributed something different to the community: their talents, their time, their prayers, and their leadership. I watched my own relationships in the church grow from simple introductions to conversations at young adult lunches and finally to coffee meet-ups, game nights, and deeper talks about the hard things in our lives. I am so profoundly grateful for this *home*.

At the same time, I was navigating my own evolution of beliefs about queerness. For a long time, I had felt a deep unease with the church's view against homosexuality and its damaging impact on queer people. I finally researched the issue for myself and found solid ground to stand on as an affirming ally of LGBTQ+ people. I am so thankful my faith evolved in this way since it enabled me to walk into the next season of my life with hopeful curiosity rather than fear.

It was in the winter of 2023, a year after coming to HBIC, that I first realized I am bisexual. This new insight brought its own joys and challenges. Yet, because of the work I had already done to see queer people as whole, beloved creations, it was not accompanied by a crisis of faith. Instead, I got to see new sides of God's heart.

It was in that season that I heard God's voice of heartbreak and learned to cling to my own relationship with God rather than relying on others' beliefs. I also felt a deep sense of calling. I had the privilege of embracing my own queerness at a time when I had already learned how damaging it had been to try to change the sexual orientation of other queer Christians or to shut down their sexuality entirely. I had read too many stories of self-hatred in search of illusive change. And I had too many queer friends who had been deeply hurt by the belief that homosexuality was sinful. I knew I needed to be a voice for positive LGBTQ+ representation in my family and church, and I began to pray that my own queerness could help create a spirit of curiosity, understanding, empathy, and eventually full embrace of LGBTQ+ people among the people in my own life.

Determined not to hide something that I believed to be part of God's good design and plan for my life, I started coming out to friends and family. Although I was apprehensive because of the BIC's official stance on homosexuality, I also came out to several friends and members of HBIC. Despite the nervousness that often accompanies these conversations, I have been blessed over and over again by the responses from this community. They have shown great care and understanding.

After hearing how I was struggling with internalized homophobia one weekend, a friend texted me the next day to remind me that her home would always love and welcome me. She sent a quote from Bridget Eileen Rivera from a podcast she had done with Jonathan Puddle (April 8, 2022):

> I don't know a single gay Christian who hasn't spent years searching Scripture for how to live out their life and their sexuality. Most LGBTQ Christians obtain the equivalent of a seminary degree just to live in some of the ways straight Christians take for granted.

I teared up when I saw her message. She saw right into the depths of my heart and showed up with so much love and understanding.

That same weekend I spoke with another friend as I was navigating the question of whether HBIC was still a safe place for me in light of my new discovery. She asked in response, "Has it felt like a safe place?" It was a simple question, but it meant so much to know she cared about my experience of safety and belonging in this community enough to ask and to hear my genuine response.

Alongside the kindness of these friends, my experiences with individuals at HBIC have demonstrated that these are people committed to listening and advocating for justice. Despite the official doctrine of the BIC Church on marriage and homosexuality, the people of HBIC have a variety of beliefs on this topic, and many of them support and affirm LGBTQ+ people. I am grateful that HBIC has allowed and welcomed this diversity of perspective. I am thankful I never had to sit through a sermon that condemned queer individuals or that was overly exclusive in the language of partnership and marriage. I have deep gratitude for church friends who have been let go from jobs because they have provided a safe space for queer students. Once again, this church has restored my belief that followers of Jesus can bring good news to *all* people.

Accepting and rejoicing in my queerness has been a beautiful gift. It has given me roads into a new community, one that embraces uniqueness and is unafraid to walk in freedom. It has helped me speak more honestly about hard feelings. It has allowed friends to come alongside me, as vulnerability has created new pathways of trust and support.

However, alongside all that beauty, being queer has opened my eyes to the long history of injustice and unwelcomeness in our churches. It saddens me that a faith based in love, welcome, and justice has not been able to extend that same love to LGBTQ+ people. It frustrates me that many cannot see that queerness only adds more love and freedom to our lives and to our faith tradition.

Although I have deep gratitude for my experiences with people at HBIC, there are still areas in which I regularly pray and hope for change in my congregation and in the BIC denomination at large. I still wonder what it will be like if I date and marry a woman. Will this community I so dearly love be part of our wedding and our lives as a couple? I worry about queer youth in our community and the messages they are hearing. Do they know that they are already loved just as they are, or are they hearing messages that will cause them to reject their created beauty or their church and faith? Do they know that there are many Christians who fully embrace queer people?

I struggle with the fact that despite my deep love for this community, I don't recommend it to other queer people because I want them to be able to attend a faith community where their sexuality is never up for debate. I wrestle with deciding if I will become a member of my church. I am fully committed to this community, but it is hard to officially sign my name to an organization that is still a contributor to exclusion and pain for queer people and youth. Even silent condemnation is damaging. Even unspoken lack of affirmation hurts.

But I continue to stay. Why? Because I love this community and these people. Because they have been a shoulder to cry on, a listening ear, and a source of wise council. Because they continue to fight for justice and work for a more welcoming and diverse church. Because many have sacrificed to be allies and safe places. And because I believe in being part of the change. I was encouraged by the 2022 General Assembly vote to change the official doctrine of the BIC to officially describe women as equal in church leadership. True inclusion requires specificity. I pray consistently that I will get to see the day when a similar change is made to our doctrine to fully embrace queer people.

Our faith is always evolving. It evolved when Jesus was resurrected. It has adapted over time to include new beliefs about science and creation,

Invitation to Conversation

about whom we welcome and about how we interpret Scripture. Change is a necessary and good part of a relationship with a living God. The storyline of God that we see in the person of Jesus and throughout the Bible is one of fuller inclusion and broader welcome. Just as my home church has been a place of deep belonging, I pray that the BIC Church at large will extend this same belonging and welcome to queer individuals as we seek to model God's kingdom on earth.

Hannah Stolpe *teaches Spanish at a high school in Harrisburg, Pennsylvania. She attends Harrisburg BIC Church where she assists with English Language Learner (ELL) classes and can often be found chatting with other young adults in the church. She is an enthusiastic extrovert who enjoys hiking, reading, and dancing salsa when not exploring Harrisburg or planning her next travel adventure. Hannah lives in Mechanicsburg with two friends and their furry companions.*

An Open Letter to Queer Kids Growing up BIC

Erin Taylor

The author shares helpful advice, words of wisdom, and lots of encouragement in a letter to young people who attend Brethren in Christ churches.

Dear queer kid growing up in the Brethren in Christ (BIC) Church,

Hi! You don't know me, but I used to be a queer kid in the BIC Church, just like you. I know there are a lot of different places you could be right now in terms of your own self-understanding. You could know you're queer, disagree vehemently with the church's position on LGBTQ folks, and be counting down the days until you can leave. You could know you're queer, love Jesus, and want to stay but feel strongly that the church should affirm queer people. You could know you're queer, stand by the church's position, and feel sad or scared. You might not be sure if you're queer and may be confused about how to move forward. You may feel like there is something wrong with you. For a long time, that's how I felt. These are just a few of the millions of different ways you might be feeling, and I know people who have gone through all these scenarios and more. Regardless of how you're feeling, you are definitely not alone.

There are so many things I want to say to you and so many things I wish I had known when I was in your shoes. The first is that I strongly oppose the Brethren in Christ Church's stance on LGBTQ+ people. I believe that queer folks are made in the image of God and should be loved, celebrated, and affirmed as members of any religious community. If you feel this way, too, there are many, many churches (and many Christians) that agree with you. In fact, there are churches that have gay, bisexual, lesbian, trans, or queer pastors and leaders. If being a Christian is important to you, you don't have to stay in a community that does not affirm you. You deserve to be in a church where the love of God and membership in the community is offered to everyone with complete and total equity.

The second thing I want to say is that being LGBTQ+ is the most powerful thing I've ever experienced. There is so much beauty and community waiting for you in the future. Being involved in queer community has brought me many wonderful lifelong friends, my lovely girlfriend, and more unconditional love and care than I could have ever imagined. It's made me a sharper and more empathetic person, and it has helped me become more aware of the importance of fighting for equity and justice. I want you to know that there is an unbelievable amount of love and light waiting in your future. You will build relationships with people who love you unconditionally and who love you as your whole self.

That said, you may still find a lot of things challenging even if you decide to leave the BIC and build a life for yourself that is full of people who love you unconditionally and believe in the full personhood and equality of LGBTQ+ people. You may struggle to let go of homophobic mentalities that you learned, and you may feel very deeply hurt about the homophobia you experienced in the church. It can be hard to carry that pain.

When I first left the church, I felt like everyone around me—particularly the folks who had grown up in affirming communities—had years more of experience than I did. They already knew how to affirm their own feelings and how to accept themselves as they are. They had queer friends from middle school and high school and same-gender exes. Seeing this made me feel an immense sense of loss since I did not have those kinds of connections.

A number of years ago, there was a piece in *Rookie Magazine* by Jude Doyle titled "We're Called Survivors Because We're Still Here" (www.rookiemag.com/2012/01/survivors). The piece is specifically about going through sexual assault, but it has a lot of overarching messages about living through trauma and other really, really difficult things. Doyle says:

> You are going to have to walk through more than most to get to "OK," and you may have to keep walking back to it, over and over. But you are not alone, and help exists, and "the rest of your life" is hopefully going to be a very long time.

This is what I want to tell you, too. Getting yourself to "OK" after leaving a homophobic environment will feel really intense at times, but it is possible. You will meet lots of other people who have grown up in similar environments who are doing the same thing. These people will be lifelines for you as you navigate what your life looks like on the other side. You will have your whole life to make connections, build community, and be OK. And life is so long.

Another thing Doyle writes that I want to share with you is that "pain is a message, from the part of you that wants to live, telling you that something is wrong." I share this line because if you feel pain about what happened to you, it's tempting to invalidate those feelings. In fact, if you bring it up to folks who are not affirming, they may also try to invalidate your feelings about what happened to you. That is something that really, really hurts. I want you to know that you feel that pain for a reason. It's because it's a message from your body that what happened to you is *not* OK. It's a message that you deserve better and that you deserve to be OK. Listen to it.

I realize that this piece is a little heavy. The reason it's heavy is that living through intense homophobia is a heavy thing to go through. It stays with you in ways you don't expect. But as Doyle says, the rest of your life is a very, very long time. In that long life, you deserve equity, dignity, and love. You deserve real, loving friendships. You deserve to fall in love, to have relationships, to build a life with someone else. As a baseline, you deserve the dignity afforded to straight and cisgender people. You can and will have that dignity and more. There is so much beauty waiting for you in the future.

Invitation to Conversation

Erin Taylor (she/her) *is a lesbian artist, writer, and occupational therapy student living in Boston, Massachusetts. You can find her newsletter,* Hot or Not With EVT, *on Substack. She also runs a lesbian art and history project at @lesbianbookstoreproject on Instagram. In her free time, you can find her spending time with her friends and girlfriend, going to museums, surfing, and starting four new creative projects every week.*

Part II

Parents And Grandparents of LGBTQ+ Children Describe Their Experience

Woman, Mother, Pastor
Integrating Roles as a Follower of Jesus

Anne Findlay-Chamberlain

Søren Kierkegaard wrote, "Life can only be understood backwards; but it must be lived forwards." This essay reflects what I've come to understand by looking backwards to live as an open and affirming person of the LGBTQ+ community. I do so as a woman, a mother, and a pastor.

Growing Up as a Woman

My name was supposed to be Frederick Carl Findlay in memory of my maternal grandfather, who died six months before my birth. My parents were hoping that I would be the long-awaited son following two daughters. When baby girl Findlay arrived, they scrambled to find a girl's name. Mom thought Fredericka Anne would be a good girl's name. I am grateful that Dad suggested Anne Albrecht (my mom's maiden name). Relatives on my mom's side called me Freddie Anne for years.

As a girl growing up in the 1950s and 1960s, there were times when the grass looked greener on the boys' side. Boys and men had opportunities to do things that girls and women didn't have. My male peers were members of Little League Baseball teams, for which I was ineligible, even though I could run, hit, and catch with the best of them. The same was true with church. Though I felt a call to ministry early in life—preaching to my "congregation" of stuffed animals—there were no female role models to lead the way. I did my best to suppress God's nudge towards ministry and the angst that my gender was an obstruction.

I sensed that call again in my late twenties. By then, I was married, had two young boys, and was an active part of the Brethren in Christ (BIC) Church. I remember the exact time of day and place where I was sitting when God's call to ministry interrupted an otherwise ordinary day. I talked with our bishop. He was kind but firm in saying there would be no assistance for such an endeavor, nor opportunities as a pastor in the denomination. Being a woman seemed to be in conflict with the deep call to serve God as a pastor. So instead, I became a mental health counselor. In that role, I found myself beginning to extend the same sort of grace I offered others to myself as well. And grace began to do its softening work within.

When I was in my late forties, I visited my childhood home. I introduced myself to the current owner who had purchased the house from my parents in 1965. She said, "You were the one who was supposed to be a boy." I felt the lingering sting that I was a mistake. No matter how hard I tried, it wasn't enough because *I* wasn't enough. With the help of spiritual direction, prayer, and grace, that painful but holy moment was a threshold through which I came to know, experience, and believe—in head and heart—that I am deeply loved by God, redeemed by Jesus, and sustained by the Spirit.

Nurturing as a Mother

My spouse and I celebrated our fiftieth wedding anniversary in December 2023. We have two sons—one of whom is gay—and four grandchildren. When our younger son, Dan, was four, I discovered him wearing my old knee-high pantyhose on his arms at bedtime. He said, "I like how it feels." I told him it was "OK for bed, but not a good idea for school attire." He is our straight son.

When our older son, Seth, was in fifth grade, he invited one of his female friends to go on a bike ride and treated her to an ice cream cone, calling it a date. Seth dated girls earlier than Dan, attending proms and homecomings throughout his high school years. When he was in ninth grade, he asked how to kiss a girl. I am still not sure exactly how to teach that lesson! He had girlfriends throughout high school and college. I remember conversations in the car when he wondered about sexuality. I listened without judgment and, like another mother, "pondered these things in my heart." I offered him the grace I experienced through God rather than the judgment I'd put on myself for years. He is our gay son.

I think I knew he was gay before he knew it himself. I wasn't surprised when he came out to me a few years after college graduation. I was not concerned about his soul. I know him to be sincere and open to Jesus. I trust that God was, and is, faithful to this child and loves him more than I can comprehend. God's work is not yet done with my son, nor with any of us. The thing that shocked me was the realization that my son, who was so good with children, might never have children himself. I had no idea I wanted grandchildren until that moment.

Shepherding as a Pastor

I received my third distinct call to ministry in 1997. This time, the same BIC bishop who had previously told me there was no place for women pastors in the denomination welcomed me in the pursuit of that call. I entered seminary in the Midwest, where my husband and I were living. In 2001, we moved to Maui, Hawaii. There were no Anabaptist congregations on Maui, so we looked for a church from a different tradition.

This led us to the United Church of Christ (UCC), which aligned with our sense of community and social justice. I met with the Associate Conference Minister, who welcomed me with open arms and noted that the UCC was welcoming to all. This acceptance included women in leadership and LGBTQ+ persons. I felt a quickening in my heart that this denomination would welcome and affirm my calling graciously, encourage me in solo and senior pastoral positions, and also welcome my gay son. It was an acceptance I knew was not possible at that time with the Brethren in Christ.

I remember walking with Seth on a beach in Maui. He talked about going out to clubs in Boys' Town (a gay neighborhood in Chicago). My protective alarms went off. I imagined all the dangers he was in. My first impulse was to say, "Stop!" My second impulse was to pray for wisdom.

With fifteen years of experience as a counselor, some spiritual formation training, and the Spirit's wisdom, I simply asked, "Where do you sense light and joy in your life?" He replied, "When the music is playing and I'm dancing." I replied, "Follow the light and joy." In 2004, he joined a Christian church in Washington, D.C., and was part of their music ministry. As he was following the light and joy, so was I, as an ordained pastor and teacher in the UCC.

In 2005, the UCC passed a resolution at General Synod requesting that congregations consider marriage equality for all people, regardless of gender. According to UCC polity, these approved resolutions speak *to* congregations, not *for* congregations. Individual congregations make the final decisions. Other aspects of UCC polity state that the pastor is not the chair of the church board or president of the consistory. Therefore, one of my tasks as a pastor has been to empower congregations to wrestle with issues in order to discern what is right in all matters of faith. It is not the role of the pastor to dictate to a congregation what to do or think.

The issue of same-sex marriage was on the minds and hearts of the four congregations I have served. My position has been to be honest about our family. I explained that although my spouse and I don't agree on all theological points, we love our sons and will do everything in our power to love and support them. I reminded each church leadership team of the UCC polity. None of those churches have moved forward as "Open and Affirming Congregations." Some of these congregations may split on this issue in the future. All four of these congregations continue to find common ground on the essentials. I do not take sides.

I mentioned earlier that when Seth came out, I grieved that he would not have children. In 2013 Seth and his partner were married in a civil service. In 2014, they adopted a baby girl. And in 2017 they adopted a second baby girl. In spite of all the obstacles that could have kept them from having children, they are parents, and I get to be the girls' Nana. They attend a church-related private school and have weekly sacred studies. They know the Lord's Prayer, the Beatitudes, and talk regularly about their faith. Our son and his spouse are amazing parents. Their girls are a precious part of our family, along with Dan's daughter and son.

In June 2021, I reconnected with a high school friend whose same-sex partner had died. She'd not darkened a church door since elementary school. I was invited to speak at her partner's memorial luncheon. As a result of that connection, my friend started watching my sermons online and reading my blog. We would occasionally meet for lunch or hike. One day, out of the blue, she asked me if I'd baptize her. After several months, and many conversations about faith and baptism, she and twenty family members and friends traveled over two hours to witness her baptism during our worship service on Pentecost Sunday. Her conversion is one of the most amazing, God-led experiences in my ministry.

Integrating My Roles as a Follower of Jesus

After my son, Seth, and his partner had a civil marriage service in Washington, D.C., they planned to have a Christian blessing in France later that year so that his spouse's family could be present. Seth asked me if I would be willing to perform the service in France. Without hesitation, I said, "Yes." He then proceeded to contact different churches near Montpelier, France, to see if they could accommodate the service. Multiple churches said no. It was against their policy to host same-sex weddings.

Seth finally located an Anglican church that would host the ceremony. In the spirit of full disclosure, he explained that his mother, an ordained UCC pastor, was going to officiate. He was then informed that this congregation had an agreement with the church they rented space from stating that "no women could serve as pastors in any circumstances." Seth thanked the church official and said, "That's a deal breaker for us. Thanks anyway."

Jesus welcomed the little ones, the least, and the last. My own challenges—as a woman, mother, and pastor—have led me to embrace members of the LGBTQ+ community with the grace and love of God. That is how I am called to act as I follow Jesus, who, for the love of the world, became one of us.

Invitation to Conversation

Anne Findlay-Chamberlain *is an ordained United Church of Christ pastor as well as a seasoned spiritual director and retreat leader. She and her spouse, Rod Chamberlain, have two sons and four grandchildren. She has served three UCC congregations in Hawaii and is pastor of St. Paul's UCC in Woodstock, Virginia, where she is an active member of PFLAG, an American organization representing the interests of the LGBTQ Community. She loves accompanying people as they discover God's presence in their lives.*

So Much Groaning

Joanna Hadley-Evans

A longstanding member of the BIC Church withdraws her membership as a result of the church's prolonged failure to come alongside her (and her queer daughter) and its resistance to fostering increased understanding of LGBTQ people.

Adequate words do not emerge as easily as tears when I consider the grief and loss surrounding our departure from the Brethren in Christ (BIC) Church in 2017. It is still raw for me. And my heart still aches at what could have been. When my wounded spirit can only offer groans, I know the Spirit intercedes on my behalf. So I pray the following utterance can be transformed into a reflection that is honoring, primarily to our faithful Lord, but also to the richness of the BIC heritage our family experienced during our twenty-three years within the denomination.

My husband and I were members of three BIC congregations in Dillsburg, Pennsylvania, in which our children were also raised: Dillsburg, NewCreation, and Cumberland Valley, which became The Meeting House (Dillsburg) as it merged with Carlisle. We also briefly attended Engage Community Church in Carlisle, Pennsylvania. We have deep appreciation for the gentle pastors who guided us through our baptisms, the renewal of our wedding vows, and the dedications of our children. Their faithful encouragement led to our service in youth leadership, Bible Quiz coaching, musical worship, administrative support, women's ministry, men's ministry, married couples' ministry, and elder board. At this time, we no longer attend a church, although we still identify with the core values of Anabaptism, thanks, in large part, to our experience in the BIC Church.

Just before her twenty-first birthday, our daughter trusted us with the truth of her queerness and the difficult tension she experienced at Wheaton College as an LGBTQ student. Since I worked in Christian higher education, I was keenly aware of the strain that campus heteronormativity places on queer students. My husband and I (and our son) were fully affirming of her and immediately assured her of our love and support, as well as of her divine design as a child of God. Her queerness and her identity as a Christian were not mutually exclusive. Yet, admittedly, we didn't know of many others who were in our family's situation. So we set out to find "our people." We knew the Lord created our daughter this way. She had not changed nor "chosen" anything—other than to be honest and authentic. Our daughter did not necessarily come out to us. Rather, she let us in.

Prior to these family conversations, and even predating any of the BIC's Full of Grace and Truth conversations that occurred within the denomination in 2015, our church board had drafted a specific response to LGBTQ members wanting to serve in our congregation. This document was even shared by denominational leadership at the Full of Grace and Truth Impact Seminar as an example of how one church was navigating the topic. Our board's document basically said that we would be a welcoming congregation in which LGBTQ individuals could serve in any capacity other than on the elder board. And, in order to remain in compliance with the *Manual of Doctrine and Government* (Ministerial Credentialing, Article 1.3.3), they could not be married by one of our pastors or within our church building. But it did allow our queer attendees to serve on the worship team as well as with children and youth. While not fully affirming, we were certainly more inclusive than other congregations in the area. Sadly, when our church merged, this recommendation from the board was no longer considered valid.

We sought counsel from our pastor when our daughter shared her queerness with us. He was incredibly kind but, unfortunately, ill-equipped to support parents with little more than a few outdated resources. We trusted a small number of individuals among friend and church circles, but primarily, we kept this truth under wraps for the better part of a year—until we discovered an organization that springboarded us from being allies to becoming advocates and equipped us with an array of books to read, podcasts to listen to, and local and online support groups in which to engage.

We finally found our people. The Gay Christian Network (GCN), now Q Christian Fellowship, provided our first experience with a large gathering of LGBTQ Christians. My husband and I flew with our daughter to Portland, Oregon, for the 2015 conference. We did not know a soul there, and yet, within our first few steps into the large conference room of 1,300 people, it was evident we were walking on holy ground. So many believers were joining their voices in prayer, testimony, and song!

Unfortunately, this sacred space was disturbed by Westboro Baptist protesters shouting and displaying hateful signs one rainy morning outside the convention center. Parents and loved ones were invited to create a wall of love for conference attendees to pass through to avoid direct contact with their aggressive protest. Our family even made the front page of the *Oregon Live* newspaper that weekend. You can google it to see us. In the lead photo, our daughter is holding the white sign, and my husband and I stand on either side of her—with a full rainbow in the sky behind us! (See "Portland Christians Protect Members of LGBT Community from Anti-Gay Westboro Baptist Church.") From that weekend on, we were officially out as a family.

Yet, we sensed upon our return back to Pennsylvania that the church was going to be a challenge. Our daughter had served in youth leadership and on their worship team during high school and throughout college when she was home. Despite her relationship with the church, we found homophobic posts and comments on our own social media by members who had led worship or worked on service trips with our daughter. They continued to openly post or privately send Scripture verses with admonishment on how we had strayed from the Bible's literal interpretation. (Newsflash—many of us are not biblical literalists!) It was humbling and wearying to attempt to respond in love.

Attending church on Sunday mornings became anxiety-ridden for both our daughter and for me. It was not long before our daughter discerned that she could no longer identify with the congregation. And we could not blame her. Our son, seeing his sister walk this painful path, eventually left the church as well.

Not every encounter was wrought with conflict. There were a few gentle souls who tried to come alongside us, but for the most part, all we heard were crickets—utter silence. Here we had returned home from the GCN conference full of hope and ready to engage in loving dialogue about what we had seen and learned about the diversity of God's kingdom, but there were no conversations to be had, save for those with an encouraging and affirming associate pastor. Most friends, and even some family, did not want to inquire about the conference lest they appear to be approving of our daughter's "lifestyle choice." The silence was deafening and created greater distance. People would ask about our son and how he was doing, but they did not know how to engage meaningfully in our daughter's journey. They were also not interested in reading books, hearing personal stories, or attending meetings we suggested.

From this, we learned how difficult it was for others to "enter in" at a time when we needed them the most. Having some semblance of church support would have encouraged us as we navigated difficult conversations with family and work colleagues and tried to keep our daughter's mental health in balance—rather than at odds—with the faith foundation on which we had raised her. We sensed a cognitive dissonance between the reconciling BIC we knew from our historical experience and the BIC we were now seeing in practice. It just did not seem reflective of the radically inclusive Jesus we knew and had learned about from the church.

My husband and I prayed for wisdom and direction as the Lord was clearly preparing us for something. As difficult as it was for me personally, we committed to remain in the church for the purpose of bridge-building and educating others about the inherent worth of LGBTQ individuals and the gifts they could bring to our congregation. It wasn't long before seven other families in our congregation of three hundred confessed to us that they were either parents or siblings of queer persons or queer themselves. They did not realize there were others like them. Clearly, there was a need, but none of our requests for education or deeper dialogue were approved by senior leadership in the church or the denomination.

Next, we asked the elder board, of which my husband was a member, to consider sending several pastors to the 2016 GCN conference in Houston, Texas, with us. Our associate pastor was eager to attend, but the church would not pay for his travel expenses. So my husband and I paid for him to come. Even so, his participation was on the down-low as far as the broader congregation was concerned.

The following year, two other elders (a fellow mother of a queer child and a gentleman who was a father figure to our daughter) attended the 2017 conference when it was hosted in Pittsburgh, Pennsylvania. I will not forget the look on my daughter's face (or her tears) when this man showed up and "entered in" to our new community on her behalf.

I was cautiously optimistic following these events, but little fruit came of them after returning to our local congregation. We tried to coordinate several book studies, guest speakers, evening testimony events, and parent support groups. All were denied. We felt marginalized after two decades of loving, supportive fellowship.

Sunday mornings became severely anxiety-inducing for me. From the church parking lot to crossing the threshold of the narthex door, I would have a physiological response that triggered tears that would endure the length of the service, particularly during the musical worship portion when I would grieve the exclusion of my daughter's gifts from the platform. I spent a lot of mornings in the restroom trying to pull myself together. I withdrew from cantata participation and women's ministry leadership because I simply felt phony. This season involved significant groaning and weeping.

After three years of trying to paste on a smile, I realized I needed to step away for my own spiritual health. This felt selfish at the time, but I knew I was no longer contributing to the richness of that fellowship. Nor was I remotely open to receiving fellowship in return. We opted to remain at the church one Sunday a month and then began attending another local congregation that was actively discussing full affirmation of LGBTQ individuals.

Finally, in 2017, we withdrew our membership from the Brethren in Christ Church altogether. My husband Brian and I penned the following letter to our four pastors:

> *With heavy hearts, we would like to request that our membership from The Meeting House be withdrawn. Brian intends to complete his term through December assisting with counting at the Dillsburg campus, but following that, we will continue in fellowship at Engage Community Church. At this time, we are not requesting a transfer of membership, but rather a withdrawal.*
>
> *We have appreciated your gentleness and humility through the process as we discern our path, but it is evident the TMH congregations, and more broadly, the denomination, are not making LGBTQ inclusive support or discussions a priority as we have been seeking reconciling dialogue, education, and support for four years now. It has been wearying and dejecting in the silence of the church. Please know we are not angry, but deeply hurt.*
>
> *With 23 years in the Brethren in Christ, and 12 of those at Cumberland Valley/The Meeting House, including Brian's leadership during the transition with Carlisle, our deepest desire would be to remain in fellowship, but we need to be a part of a community where we can be fully transparent and worship with those who will allow us and those we love to be so. We pray for The Meeting House to someday be a safe space for those like [name removed], [name removed], and our beloved daughter, [name removed], who find themselves on the margins. And we pray for your leadership as you shepherd our brothers and sisters who remain.*

We did not receive a response from our campus pastor. And our senior pastor of the merged congregation could not meet with us to discuss the withdrawal until three weeks later—unfortunate fallout from a large congregation with so many needs to attend to. This was discouraging but also an affirmation of our decision. Since that time, we know of several loving pastors who were "defrocked." Their credentials were not renewed, or they were asked to withdraw them because these ministers believed queer individuals in loving relationships could be celebrated and not just tolerated.

My daughter does not want to be an example or a token queer person representing all LGBTQ individuals. She does not have a "gay agenda," although she will rightly call you out on your heteronormativity. I can testify that the good fruit she bears living out of the closet and in her fullness as a queer woman is bountiful and beautiful. It is nothing like the bad fruit that results from living in the dark closet of captivity.

At one point during the GCN conference, a new friend asked me what keeps us coming back to the conference. I paused as I felt a lump form in my throat, and then softly answered, "Because I get to see my daughter be herself. No code-switching to tone down her queerness in order to make others feel comfortable, which happens frequently at family holidays, wedding celebrations, or even just going out to a restaurant. It is the one place outside our family home where we get to experience her being fully herself, which is such a gift for a parent." Our daughter is the one who invites the outsider in, the one who cracks a joke to lighten the mood, the one who can read a room and take action. These gifts serve her well as an ER nurse, a road long traveled and much celebrated. We see more and more of Jesus Christ in the actions of our adult children outside of the church. They are kind, patient, forbearing, and loving.

An abolitionist minister, Theodore Parker, preached in 1852, "I do not pretend to understand the moral universe; the arc is a long one, my eye reaches but little ways; I cannot calculate the curve and complete the figure by the experience of sight; I can divine it by conscience. But from what I see I am sure it bends toward justice." Most of us are more familiar with Dr. Martin Luther King, Jr.'s clever paraphrase, "the arc of the moral universe is long, but it bends toward justice." This particular arc seems *so* long, but I wholeheartedly believe it bends toward the justice of full inclusion of LGBTQ individuals in our faith communities.

Four long evenings and a box of tissues were spent penning this reflection. And that is after three other attempts in previous months in which I could not pull myself together. I confess that most days now, on the surface,

I am apathetic towards the church. But simmering just below is an ache that is palpable in my body, a lament that extends beyond normal grief. So much groaning.

The Lord is faithful as we find community in other settings now. But I miss our brothers and sisters and the joy of the journey together. I miss the glorious harmonies of voices and instruments in song. I miss the accountability of relationships. I miss the hope of reconciliation. I miss the body of Christ as the BIC taught me it could be.

***Joanna Hadley-Evans** is a part-time administrative assistant, but her true passion is her work as a travel coordinator specializing in bespoke itineraries for friends and family. When not traveling, she enjoys cooking for guests, reading for book club, playing the piano, cross-stitching gifts, and attending concerts and comedy shows. Joanna lives in Carlisle, Pennsylvania, with her husband and one cat. They love to spend time with their adult children—daughter, son, and daughter-in-law—who have blessed them with fourteen grand-pets.*

Wonderfully Made

Martha Truxton Heller

Martha shares her journey as the mother of a queer child navigating her communities of faith: the joy, the uncertainty, and the heartache.

My third child is the only one of my four that I delivered at home. From the moment he was born, I worried about him. His face was purple, and his heartbeat was irregular. I still remember the heaviness in my stomach as I watched my mom (a missionary doctor for forty years) sit on the side of my bed, stethoscope carefully placed on his little chest, listening intently for what felt like hours. But his color did eventually even out, his heartbeat became more regular, and my husband, Jon, and I both melted every time he looked at us with his big, beautiful eyes. His sisters absolutely adored him. They would read to him, snuggle with him, and pat his head and belly with such care.

As he grew, his eyes became bigger and browner, and he was the absolute light of our household. He loved dancing, singing, and playing imaginary games with his sisters. He would dress up in too-large boots, wield plastic swords, and run around with blankets draped over his head, pretending to have long, golden hair. He often imagined he was a princess with magical powers. He was completely delightful.

At the time, our family was attending a Brethren in Christ (BIC) church, and I was well acquainted with people of faith who looked down on a boy having any interest in traditionally feminine things. So, as his infatuation with long hair and flowy dresses grew, my uneasiness with it all began to surface.

While I thought everything about my boy was charming, I found myself trying to talk him out of the dolls he wanted for Christmas and the nail polish he was so proud to wear when we ran errands. I remember a clerk giving him an enthusiastic compliment about the particular shade of yellow he wore on his nails once, and although I felt a burst of pride in that moment, I immediately started questioning whether I should have been happy about it.

I fought endlessly between excitement over my child's individuality and the external voices directing me to make my kid more manly somehow. I stayed awake at night wondering what I might have done to steer my child in this direction, and how I might be able to make it "right" in the eyes of our church. I even began hiding some of his favorite toys because I lived in such fear that I was enabling behavior that might somehow end up being harmful to him. I thought maybe if I could change his behavior, then he might not ever have to hide anything about himself. Life would be easier, and the voices swirling in my head and embedded in my heart—steering me towards feelings of shame and guilt—would all fall silent.

But I was robbing him of his joy, and I knew it.

During one of our family beach vacations, my delightful child curled up in my lap as we sat by the water, his hair bleached from the sun and his beautiful brown eyes looking out at the sea of people around us.

"How come God didn't make me a girl?" he asked.

My heart dropped, and I fought back tears as I tried to wrap my head around a response. Oh, how I adored this lighthearted, colorful child of mine, and he was already questioning his existence at the age of four.

"You are beautifully and wonderfully made," I managed to whisper into his lightly sweaty locks pressed against my cheek, "exactly as you are." I hugged him tighter.

God, why this? Why now?

A few years later, I had a dream that my sweet child died in a car accident. I was so desperately heartbroken in the dream that I had thrown myself to the ground, and the tears came hard and fast, my unspeakable loss mixing with confusion and anger and guilt so deep it held me there for a long, long time. *Why couldn't I let my child just be who I knew they had been created to be?* I woke up weeping uncontrollably and instantly felt God's healing breath on my heart—heard His soft whisper in my spirit—that He made my precious child exactly the way he is. That he is *seen* exactly the way he is. And that he is loved *because* of the way he is.

I struggled long and hard with God after that. I knew in the deepest parts of my being that my kid was not a mistake. I knew God made him and loved him. But what did it look like for me to love and care for my child exactly as he was created to be while also trying to reconcile the voices of God's own people telling me that I was wrong? That my child was not part of God's good design?

The years rolled by as my husband, Jon, and I wrestled with our Creator: waiting for answers, wondering if we were making the right choices in our parenting, and hoping our path through all of this would somehow be made clear. And then, one Sunday morning, as we sat at the back of a large evangelical congregation, the pastor began talking about biblical manhood. He spoke about how certain cultural "lies" were obscuring gender lines, and how sinful that was in God's eyes. And he talked, and he talked. And my sweet, then-solemn teenager reached over to me and grabbed my arm—eyes never leaving the pastor—fingers shaking as they grasped for familiar skin, any shred of warmth and comfort. I looked over at his wide, desperate eyes, and I knew at that moment that my sweet, seeking teen didn't feel safe to be himself in that space. He was wrestling in his spirit, just like I had been, and he didn't feel accepted or loved there amongst God's people. In fact, he felt condemned.

Instantly, I was back on the beach so many years ago when he had curled up in my lap, questioning and wondering. He was still questioning and wondering, but here—in God's house—he didn't feel safe to do so. I felt as if somehow he was a newborn again, struggling to breathe, and I was sitting beside him, desperately needing him to be okay. At that moment, I knew we couldn't ever go back through those sanctuary doors.

After that Sunday morning, my husband and I tried to make it very clear in our demeanor and in our conversations that we loved and accepted all kinds of God's children. *All* kinds. A short few months later, I found a note on my bed one night, carefully written on a piece of lined notebook paper in my teen's bubbly handwriting. He said he felt safe enough to tell Jon and me that he thought he was gay, that he had been hiding it, and that he had been prepared to hide it forever because of what he had heard at church. But he finally felt safe enough to tell us the truth. A short time later, our teenager revealed to us that he had never felt like a boy, and that trying all of these years to act like one—and being referred to as one—had, in fact, been very painful.

Not he. *She.*

I pulled my teenager close as she spoke, never wanting to let go, praying desperately as my tears fell hard that my child would know beyond any shadow of doubt that she was loved just as she is. I prayed that all of my doubt about God's care for *even us* would simply evaporate. That we would be the hands and feet of Jesus and simply *love*.

We returned to our previous BIC church a short time later, hoping to find a welcoming church home for our family. And although the faces were friendly, the smiles genuine, and the sermons free of condemning content, there was a quiet lack of welcome for the queer children of God. And that subtle silence felt heavier than any of the anti-queer sermons our family had sat through to that date. It pushed an unmistakable distance between the people of God and His queer children who are so desperately in need of love and acceptance.

So we walked away.

We walked away from the church family we had worshipped with, cared for, and raised our children with for almost twenty years. And since then, I've gradually seen the light return to my teenager's eyes. Her delightful demeanor. The singing, the nail polish, the zest for life . . . it's all seeping back into every pore and dancing out of her gorgeously deep, brown eyes. Relief that she can finally be herself, the person God created her to be. That she can truly breathe and truly be—and it fills my heart with such joy.

But some of our closest friends and family don't see my child that way. Our church family—"God's people"—didn't see my child that way. They don't see my child as free and freely loved. They see my child as wayward, walking away from God, not living a life of God's design. And how can I even begin to describe the loneliness in that?

My child won't step into a church because of how she was made to feel. Unwanted. Unloved. Unseen. My child now equates her Heavenly Father with the people who refuse to love and accept her for who she is. And as hard as I might try to undo all the years of pain and hurt that the "family" of God has caused, it's going to take much more than my own effort to fix. It's going to take an army of God's people to rise up, hug my kid, and tell her she is fearfully and *wonderfully* made.

This past Christmas Eve (2022), I felt such a deep sadness in my spirit—a yearning for the sweetness of fellowship and communal worship—so I planned to attend a service with my eldest daughter. But I couldn't bring myself to walk through those doors. I ended up sitting in my car, alone, listening to the sermon on the radio. I was yearning for God's word that night, but I couldn't bring myself to worship beside people who did not believe my transgender child could be welcomed as she is. I closed my eyes, put my head back on the driver's seat, and just listened.

The pastor's voice was clear and earnest. He spoke about how Jesus spilling His blood for us was like a safe space . . . a safe space for all. And at that moment, I broke. I wept into my hands in that parking lot full of empty cars. *God, why doesn't it feel safe?* Your people speak of Christ's love, dying for all, but do they really mean *my* child? My precious, queer teenager who wears dresses and sings an unforgettable baritone? Because she hasn't felt loved or welcomed into Your house. And now, because of that, she doesn't feel loved or welcomed in Your presence. So where is the cross in all of this? Where's the acceptance I've heard about on countless Sunday mornings and in devotional books and hymnals? Where's the sacrificial love we have been called to impart for *the least of these*?

Jesus never once left anyone to feel unwanted. Never once told anyone they were on the outskirts of God's kingdom and unworthy of love. *So why do we?*

In my thoughts these days, I return often to that morning on the beach, with my child curled up in my lap, looking for answers. And then I imagine my child curling up in her Creator's lap one day, snuggling in against His loving arms. And my child will hear Him say with a tender smile pressed against those sweaty locks of sun-bleached hair, "You, My child, are *wonderfully* made."

Invitation to Conversation

Martha Truxton Heller *worked for many years as a caregiver in various forms and is currently a Lifeskills Paraprofessional for Cumberland Valley School District. She grew up in Nigeria and now resides in Churchtown with her husband and four kids. She was a member of Cumberland Valley BIC Church for eighteen years, where she was married, raised her children, and served as a deacon. When she's not working or busy being a mom, Martha enjoys gardening, photography, creative repurposing, and writing.*

Walking the Tightrope Between Love and Judgment

Jean L. Keller-Thau

A mother/grandmother's journey of love, not only for her own son and granddaughter, but for all the families who desire a place of acceptance for their children and grandchildren.

Throughout my life, I have honed the ability to read a room. In some ways, I consider it a gift. In other ways, I consider it a curse. The gift is having the ability to avoid landmines, to enter into difficult conversations with a degree of authenticity without putting others on the defensive. I am a "confrontational avoider." I work very hard to be honest, but I'm not sure that translates into complete transparency. That's where the curse comes in. I want to be authentic, but if that means creating a hostile environment, I will step away very quickly. There have been numerous times when I've wanted to express an opinion but, after weighing the consequences, have opted to remain silent. In some cases, that was probably the right choice. In other cases, not so much.

I say all that simply to give some background to help you understand how daunting it is for me to be transparent in an area that has caused me a degree of discomfort over the years. I am the mom of a gay man. I am also the grandmother of a transgender woman.

I was serving as an associate pastor when my son asked to speak with me privately. He was in his early forties. As I sat on the couch, I watched my grown son collapse into my arms in heart-wrenching sobs as he shared

Invitation to Conversation

with me that he was gay. He said he had been aware that he was different since the age of twelve. He had never shared that with anyone and had tried to live what is generally considered a "normal" life. He dated girls, fell in love, married, and eventually divorced. It wasn't until after his divorce that he made a decision to live what he considered his authentic life.

My grandson did not share his journey with members of our family until after I retired. He now pursues what he believes is his authentic self. He now asks to be seen as female and to be known as my granddaughter instead of my grandson.

I share all this not to persuade or to put forward an argument for the rightness or wrongness of these decisions. Instead, I write to help you understand that there are people in Brethren in Christ (BIC) churches who are struggling with this firsthand. What may seem very black and white for many people is very gray for others. It is a reality of our world, and it has a significant impact on our communities and our churches. We need to be able to have authentic, non-confrontational conversations about how we will respond with love and support, not only to those who have come forward as being part of the LGBTQ+ community but also to the families who are walking this journey every day.

I have no desire to proof text verses of Scripture to make a case for the LGBTQ+ community. Nor do I want to enter into a dialogue that is couched in arguments to persuade and change minds. I don't even feel qualified to begin that process. But in the dark of night, I struggle to embrace the notion that even though my son and granddaughter profess a faith in God, some people in the church say that they are condemned to hell. They are kept at arm's length from the church and often are not embraced at all. *Can you begin to imagine the pain a mother and grandmother feel when her children and grandchildren are not welcomed by the BIC community she loves and serves?*

One of the most important passages that guide my thoughts and actions toward the LGBTQ+ community is 1 John 4:7-21 (NIV):

> Dear friends, let us love one another, for love comes from God. Everyone who loves has been born of God and knows God. Whoever does not love does not know God, because God is love. This is how

God showed his love among us: He sent his one and only Son into the world that we might live through him. This is love: not that we loved God, but that he loved us and sent his Son as an atoning sacrifice for our sins. Dear friends, since God so loved us, we also ought to love one another. No one has ever seen God; but if we love one another, God lives in us and his love is made complete in us.

This is how we know that we live in him and he in us: He has given us of his Spirit. And we have seen and testify that the Father has sent his Son to be the Savior of the world. If anyone acknowledges that Jesus is the Son of God, God lives in them and they in God. And so we know and rely on the love God has for us.

God is love. Whoever lives in love lives in God, and God in them. This is how love is made complete among us so that we will have confidence on the day of judgment: In this world we are like Jesus. There is no fear in love. But perfect love drives out fear, because fear has to do with punishment. The one who fears is not made perfect in love.

We love because he first loved us. Whoever claims to love God yet hates a brother or sister is a liar. For whoever does not love their brother and sister, whom they have seen, cannot love God, whom they have not seen. And he has given us this command: Anyone who loves God must also love their brother and sister.

I believe and totally embrace a God who loves. I believe and totally embrace a God who looks at each individual as His own creation. I embrace a God who sent his Son, Jesus, to come and live among us in order to model for us what it means to radically love all people. I embrace a man who was willing to step outside the accepted boundaries of culture and to walk, talk, eat, and be with individuals whom others shunned and ignored. I embrace the Holy Spirit and His work in my life that continues to call me to reach out and love outside of judgment. I don't struggle with embracing that understanding of my faith and my Christian walk.

My struggle comes in honoring what I have been taught all my life regarding sin and balancing that with a mother's love for her son, her granddaughter, her son's husband, and her granddaughter's wife. Unless you have

Invitation to Conversation

walked this journey, I don't believe you can fully understand the pain I experienced when people who claimed to follow the commands of Jesus and the church counseled me to walk away from my son when he came out. Unless you have experienced something similar and received this kind of "counsel," I don't believe you can fully understand the pain I felt when the same people told me I should not allow myself to be part of my son's journey when he decided to marry a man and that the most loving thing I could do for my son was essentially to "shun" him.

I prayed and searched the depths of my soul, seeking to understand what I needed to do as a mom, a grandmother, and as a pastor. How could I explain to those who hold very conservative views about the LGBTQ+ community that I believed I was being asked to unconditionally love my son and his husband, as well as my granddaughter and her wife? I was being called to build a relationship with them rather than to step away. How could I balance what Scripture (as the BIC Church has interpreted it) says regarding the perceived sin of "homosexuality" with the call placed on Christ's followers to love unconditionally, without judgment? If we turn LGBTQ+ folks away, where can they go to be part of a community that will allow them to walk a journey that leads them to a personal relationship with Jesus? If we cannot fully embrace them into the church, where will they go to find Jesus' love?

These questions, and others like them, should spur the conversations that I believe we need to have as a church. We need to engage in conversations that allow us to find a way to love, as commanded by Jesus, while also allowing us to honor our convictions and accountability to God. What a daunting task! But I believe it is one we absolutely need to pursue. If we stand in judgment and do not allow ourselves to engage in thoughtful, prayerful conversations, we stand to lose—and are losing—numbers of young men and women who are truly seeking a relationship with Christ. Can we set aside the need to stand in judgment of what is perceived to be sin and simply reach out to the human being standing in front of us? Can we find a way to embrace and to love? Can we recognize our need to be open and begin to explore the gray areas without fear?

I don't pretend to know what the next steps should be. What I do know is that we are extremely fortunate to have people in BIC leadership who are willing to listen and to have hard conversations, leaders who are strongly grounded in Scripture but who also feel the pain of the people God has called them to serve.

Can I be authentic and express my love for my son and granddaughter without being made to feel that I need to find another place to worship? Can we, as a faith community, begin to grapple with this issue and not allow it to divide and conquer us? I certainly hope we can.

Jean L. Keller-Thau is an ordained pastor who served the Dillsburg BIC Church as an Associate Pastor for ten years. She received her MDiv in 2013 and retired from full-time pastoral service in 2015. Jean continues to attend Dillsburg BIC Church. In retirement, she has focused on family and volunteering, and she serves on the board for Family Promise Harrisburg Capital Region, a non-profit organization working with families with children and with individuals who are facing the very difficult journey of homelessness.

Part III

Committed Christians Explain Their Journey To Affirmation

Confessions of a Recovering Homophobe

Jennifer Larratt-Smith

A mother reflects on her own changed perspective on LGBTQIA+ while trying to raise a daughter with budding faith.

The shadows from the canopy of trees speckled the dirt road ahead of us, and although the sun hung low in the sky, the muggy breeze still carried the day's heat. A glisten of sweat coated our faces and arms as we walked. I savored this rare, unhurried moment with my teen daughter, a luxury of our month-long vacation in Canada.

She sipped the lemonade we'd bought at the market up the road as our conversation meandered at a slow pace, not unlike our tired legs. The lazy flow of topics came to a screeching halt, however, when we wandered onto the subject of same-sex attraction and I said, "Your dad and I used to be homophobic."

Her shoes scraped the dirt as she turned to face me. "What! When?"

"In college. And after."

"Why?"

"Well, because we are Christian. And back in college, we thought it was a sin," I said. "We believed what religious authorities told us, and we did a lot of damage and hurt a lot of people."

Instantly, the faces of old friends blurred my view of the road: my transgender housemate who didn't feel he could come out, gay members of our fellowship who suppressed their desire to be loved, and the student

Invitation to Conversation

to whom I had suggested conversion therapy. The memories tugged at my shoulders, caving them in toward my heart.

"To be fair, the people I am talking about thought it was a sin, too, at the time, but that doesn't minimize the damage we did. There are a lot of Christians who still believe it's wrong."

She shook her head and resumed walking. "I didn't know that. I always thought . . ." She never finished the sentence.

Over the past three years, my daughter has seen her dad and me as allies and advocates. We had guided the church in discussions around LGBTQIA+ concerns. We read books like *God and the Gay Christian: The Biblical Case in Support of Same-Sex Relationships* by Matthew Vines, and *Unclobber: Rethinking Our Misuse of the Bible on Homosexuality* by Colby Martin. We led Bible studies and discussions on ways to respond to what we saw as a problematic doctrinal statement held by the Brethren in Christ Church. We did this even as we knew the denomination might sever ties with us and refuse us access to our church building. The earlier version of her parents, who thought being queer was a "sin," did not compute with her current vision of us.

For her, this has never been a question or a struggle. She has loved and accepted all her friends, whatever their gender identity or sexual orientation. And she is fiercely loyal. My daughter trusts her friends to tell her who they are. And I trust her to make wise, loving decisions.

We never got to finish our conversation that day. A van packed full of family members and camping gear met us at the side of the road to take us to dinner. But I am glad I had the chance to share this bit of my past with her. It illustrates an important truth. We don't have to be stuck in our perspectives. We don't have to follow what we've always been taught. People can change.

Jesus has always been a guide for me, a person of extreme love and a fierce advocate for the vulnerable. He had little patience for religious authorities who used their power to declare themselves holy while harming others. He turned tables, healed on the Sabbath, and called venerable religious leaders "whitewashed tombs" (Matt 23:27). His radically new interpretations of traditional Scriptures and the threat these presented to religious authorities got him killed.

Throughout history, churches have used Bible verses to justify some horrific perspectives. Scripture was used to imprison Galileo for believing the earth to be round. Scripture was the ostensible reason for the Crusades and the Spanish Inquisition. It was used to justify slavery and the genocide of Native Americans in the United States. In fact, there is arguably more scriptural justification for each of these perspectives than for the oppression of the LGBTQIA+ community today. (Consider how many Scriptures buttress the flat-earth theory by referring to the "ends of the earth": Deut 13:7, Job 28:24, Psa 48:10, and Prov 30:4, to name a few.) My point: it pays to be skeptical of religious authorities who claim to know what Scripture is saying and how it should be understood. History suggests they can be very wrong and can do great harm in the process.

According to the Trevor Project's 2023 U.S. National Survey, a shocking 41% of LGBTQ young people seriously considered suicide in the past year. Some 53% of youth reported being verbally harassed at school, and 9% reported being physically harassed. According to the Williams Institute at UCLA School of Law, trans people are four times more likely than cis-gender people to experience violent victimization, including rape, sexual assault, and aggravated or simple assault. These are upsettingly high numbers.

No doubt, Christians who believe they can "hate the sin and love the sinner" will want to wash their hands of this and say that Jesus would not condone violence or persecution of people. But the belief that it is a sin to be queer, and the accompanying legislation that has stigmatized the LGBTQIA+ community, are directly related to the mental health, safety, and well-being of these people. One leads to the other. If we can tell a tree by its fruit (Matt 7:17), then what fruit has our intolerance of the LGBTQIA+ community produced? Does it sound like the kind of fruit that Jesus, the radical ally of vulnerable people, would want for his church?

Back to my daughter. A few weeks after our conversation on the road, she attended a Christian camp. Upon return, while her cousins and her brother talked about axe throwing, swimming, and diving being highlights, she shared that the highlight for her was meeting other young people who nurtured her spiritual life.

"I think I want to be a counselor there in a couple of years," she said.

Her dad was delighted at the mention of this and started talking about his own experience as a teen counselor, memories cast with a warm glow. I listened in silence for a minute before I butted in with what I knew would kill the mood.

"Um, there is a potential issue here."

She paused. "Huh?"

"Well, this particular camp is run by a Christian organization which is not affirming of LGBTQIA+ people. If you were to be a leader there, you might have to sign a statement."

"Oh," she said, her voice shifting from chirpy excitement to soberness.

I want my daughter to have fellowship and community. I want her to know God. She is a straight, cis-gender teen girl, but she cannot participate fully if she has to agree with a set of beliefs that harms people she loves. A policy like this creates barriers to her walk with God and negatively impacts her even though she herself does not identify as LGBTQIA+. Yet, like Jesus, she knows loving people is at the center of following God. And like Jesus, she will not compromise that.

"I'm definitely not going to sign," she said.

"I know," I said. And I couldn't be prouder.

Jennifer Larratt-Smith is a Licensed Clinical Social Worker, a community activist, and a member of Madison Street Church in Riverside, California, where she lives with her husband and two children. She became a Christian as a young teen and has sought to learn what it means to live like Jesus since that time.

A Moment of Clarity

Keith Miller

Close relationships are crucial if we desire to encounter the Spirit of Jesus and take fresh steps toward an inclusive Beloved Community.

Sometimes in life, real transformation can only happen when the theoretical becomes material. This happened for me just a few years ago. I had been a pastor and church planter within the Brethren in Christ (BIC) Church for more than 17 years.

I deeply value the emphasis that our Anabaptist heritage has placed on community, caring for the poor, nonviolent conflict resolution, and the teachings of Jesus. I've celebrated dozens of lives surrendered to Jesus in baptism. As a denomination, our Jesus-centered convictions led to courageous conversations about gender and racial equality, led by dynamic women and by disciples of color. It happened slowly, but there was a lot of movement to celebrate!

But as the years passed, there was one area where courageous conversations didn't seem to be taking place. That was around varying viewpoints regarding same-sex relationships and LGBTQ+ inclusion. And when conversations did happen, they happened without the voices of any queer Christians.

I had become increasingly uncomfortable with the lack of wrestling our family of churches had done over the years with regard to these matters. As I looked into the Scriptures, I began realizing more and more that "clear" biblical restrictions regarding homosexuality were actually quite complicated and culturally nuanced. Scholars did not agree nearly as much as our church tradition suggested, and it was clear that assumptions had been projected onto the text in many places. I began to notice that even when these prohibitions were read at face value, they didn't address same-sex couples who wanted to follow Jesus in faithful relationships.

I also began to ask myself questions from a missional perspective. I was a church planter who longed to see God's kingdom take root in people's lives. What happens when two loving women and their 5-year-old child show up and want to follow Jesus with us? *Does God's kingdom for them really look like divorce and shared custody?* Is that God's ultimate wholeness?

I would have conversations with other people who, like me, were asking the same questions. Even among ministry friends, I would speak passionately about the damage the church had done by rejecting a group of people who had already been deeply marginalized by the culture around them. Even if Christians held a traditional understanding, one that viewed all same-sex behavior as sinful, we still treated the queer community differently than everyone else. No other "sinners" were rejected so publicly and viewed with such suspicion. I was feeling it deeply, and something seemed off. But it was still theoretical. So, I carried on with my sisters and brothers in the BIC, cognizant of the good work being done and genuinely loving this denomination in which I pastored. I lived with tension in my gut, but no situation had arisen at LifePath that forced me to move one way or another.

And then I met Katherine.

It's amazing how something complicated can become clear so quickly. Kat had just moved into the area for her job as a university professor. She had found our church's website, and our ethos as Jesus people resonated with her. But there was a looming unknown. There was something Kat wanted to find out.

> My wife and I are looking for a place where we can worship Jesus, serve in community, and where we would be welcomed as a same sex couple. A Bible-focused but inclusive church can be difficult to find so we have found it helpful to just ask upfront when it isn't clear. I appreciate any clarification you can give!

What courage it must have taken to ask that question! And what beautiful words! This wasn't simply a "What's your stance?" question. It was a desire to walk together: to "serve in community," to "worship Jesus." These phrases communicate a posture that excites any pastor.

In an increasingly disconnected world, I was delighted to encounter a new friend who understood the church through a lens of both community and compassionate service. There was also a sense of humility in those few words. Or maybe it was more mystical than all that, I don't know. But either way, there was an undeniable presence of the Spirit of Jesus in this disciple in front of me. The theoretical became material.

It was an eight-year process marked by a moment of clarity. While I had done plenty of scholarship and study and wrestling, apparently God knew I needed a friend right in front of me to help me finally see clearly. I realized that I could not tell this fellow disciple of Jesus that she could only use her gifts partially in our faith family. I called my bishop, trembling, and shared that I was no longer in process in this area of my theology. God had given me peace in a fresh way.

He was both gracious and saddened, and he walked me through the coming weeks and months with love and care. It would lead to the end of my licensure as a BIC minister and to our church peacefully disassociating from the BIC. It was painful for both of us, but I'm forever thankful for the spirit of family that we both were able to maintain throughout. *[Editors note: The letter Keith wrote to his bishop and conference board is included in a later section of this book.]*

I'm horribly embarrassed that over the years I'd had so few deep conversations with queer Christians. Kat and I began a wonderful friendship defined by a shared love for Jesus and a desire to see the church be a beautiful place of redemption. As I shared with her more about what was going on in my own pastoral journey, she said, "Kind of sounds like the experience of coming out. I'm sure that must be painful." I sat back, tears in my eyes, knowing full well that the comparison was completely unmerited. How could this friend offer such Christlike compassion and understanding when she had been through an exponentially more painful journey of religious rejection and exclusion? I could only conclude that I was experiencing the fruit of the Spirit of Christ in her. It was clear as day. I could see it in her words, her manner, and her marriage. This was my sister in Christ in every way.

So, like Peter, who was also horribly slow to learn even though he should have known better, I have decided, "I will not call anything impure that God has made clean" (see Acts 10:15). These days, it seems absurd to ever have thought otherwise. We missed out on so much beauty in the church for too many years.

I'm deeply aware that other pastors and Christ followers have not come to this conclusion. This entire journey is complicated, and most honest pastors will admit that. But we need space for courageous conversations. Those conversations may not always lead to shared perspectives or an agreed upon theological interpretation. But if embodied in relationships, they *will* lead to understanding. And since Jesus' priority was for us to love God and one another above all, I must believe that there is room within the BIC for understanding to lead us toward genuine inclusion.

I'm still very BIC in the way that I look at things. Luke Keefer famously talked about our theological streams as having "a difference" (see Luke L. Keefer, Jr., "The Three Streams in Our Heritage: Separate or Parts of a Whole," *Brethren in Christ History and Life* 35 [August 2012]: 331-367). We're anabaptists, *with a difference*. We're pietists, *with a difference*. We don't just adopt things. We make sure that they are shaped by Jesus. I think these days my pastoral perspective could probably be understood as affirming, *with a difference*. I don't want to simply affirm that any choices or expressions of sexuality are honoring to Jesus. Jesus changes and transforms each of us as we respond to the Spirit's guidance. He turns us into people of self-control and selflessness, who put the needs of others first and who live gently with nuance, justice, and bold love.

To me, pastoring my amazing queer congregants means affirming their humanity in the same way I affirm the humanity of those who don't identify as queer. It means walking together with them in an effort to follow Jesus faithfully in all areas of life, including our sexuality. I take great joy in seeing loving same-sex marriages as beautiful, redemptive expressions of the selfless character of God we see in Jesus.

Since LifePath Church became more clear about being an inclusive community in 2023, the opportunities to love and share with LGBTQ+

disciples and truth-seekers have been absolutely beautiful. It has strengthened our ability to love and learn together, with Jesus at our center, and we have witnessed a fresh openness for conversations in all sorts of other areas as well. People feel like they can trust that our church takes Jesus' posture of breaking down barriers seriously.

Interestingly, all this has happened without our LGBTQ+ conversation becoming the single defining issue in our church. We're not a large, impressive, or powerful church. But by God's grace, we are one of the many examples of churches that retain Anabaptist distinctives while fully welcoming and sharing life with our queer folks.

Katherine emailed me one day about how valuable it was to her that we remain focused on Jesus and not on this single issue. "For me, attending a church that is clear about their affirmation but does not highlight it allows me to attend as a whole person with no more focus on my identity or family than on anyone else's. Thank you for making space for that."

This is the heart of the issue. We have disciples among us who are eager to move toward Jesus, follow him, and join him in his redemptive work in our world with their whole person. I believe it's time for the church to embrace the high calling of the body of Christ and walk together, showing the world just how beautiful God's unfolding kingdom truly is.

Keith Miller *has been the Lead Pastor of an incredible collection of disciples at LifePath Church Delaware in Newark, Delaware, for thirteen years. His extra time is spent running ultramarathons and coaching his cross-country team. When he's not moving, it's probably because he's watching a migrant at his backyard bird feeder because he believes that God's wonder is everywhere.*

Evolution of an Affirming Christian

Meg Purdum

One millennial Christian's experience growing up (and staying!) in the church while exploring one of the most important personal and theological issues of the twenty-first century.

Over the course of the last fifteen years, I went from being an unaware Christian—when it came to the LGBTQ+ community and the church—to being an affirming one. Here's the story of that evolution.

While I experienced some challenges in my early years, overall, I had a privileged, comfortable, sheltered life in the "Christian bubble." I grew up in a loving Christian home with parents who were Sunday school teachers. I went to a small private Christian school. Weeks at Christian summer camp or Vacation Bible Schools filled my summer schedules. We went to church multiple times a week, mostly with people who looked and lived like us.

Not having internet or cable service at home kept the larger world and its events out of sight and out of mind for me, unless we talked about it at church or school. This created an environment that kept me from thinking about issues that didn't personally affect me, or people like me, until my teen years. Because I didn't have any LGBTQ+ people in my life at that time—at least, none that I knew of—it was one of those things I was never really forced to think about. I don't blame anybody for this. Talking about tough issues is hard, even for adults. But it's made me more intentional about educating myself now.

Invitation to Conversation

I first encountered homosexuality in the Bible and in books. I memorized passages related to this as a Bible quiz team member, including many of the infamous "clobber" verses. I also read John Green and David Levithan's novel *Will Grayson, Will Grayson*, which is about two teenage boys—one gay and one straight—who have the exact same name and end up becoming friends. When it came out, I remember being pretty scandalized by it as a young teen. The language and sexual references in the book were not part of my everyday life. But I hadn't developed opinions about LGBTQ+ issues yet. It took leaving my Christian private school bubble for that to happen.

When I say that public high school radicalized me, I'm only half-joking. It definitely challenged me. I went from a class of forty kids, who all knew each other, to a class of about two hundred. While I only knew about a quarter of them, they all knew each other from middle school. It was hard to make friends. But I tried to be nice to everyone and, for better or worse, I latched onto whoever was nice back to me. In hindsight, I was very lucky that this worked out and nothing bad happened.

A lot of my new friends were the edgy, alternative kids. Many of them were gay, lesbian, or bisexual. I don't remember being shocked or bothered by this, despite everything I had read and learned in church that might have created that response. But I do remember excitedly texting one of my friends when gay marriage was legalized in Pennsylvania, and I recall having heated conversations with relatives who held different views than I did and were more interested in debate than discussion. I also had my first trans friend in high school, and this friendship prepared me to support college friends on their gender identity journeys. Overall, the diversity of thought in my public high school was good for me. I became more politically aware and grew in my faith, developing viewpoints that were my own. I took those viewpoints and experiences with me when I went to college.

Some people say the Christian college I attended is "liberal," which some regard as a liability and others as an asset. Regardless of the label and what it means to you, this institution does things differently than other Christian colleges. I found it was a safe, albeit imperfect, place to explore and expand my beliefs regarding the LGBTQ+ community and the church. Educational opportunities happened both in and outside the classroom. Through friends, I got involved with different student groups related to gender and sexuality. I also had many excellent mentors who modeled affirming Christianity.

I church-hopped all through college. My favorite was an Episcopal church in the closest city to my school. I felt very "plugged in" spiritually there, and I enjoyed the liturgy. The diverse, affirming environment also contributed to my comfort there. I've been in good church environments since I left college, but I haven't found anything quite like it. I still miss it a little bit.

One important caveat: my college experience as a straight, cis person differed from those of many of my LGBTQ+ friends and peers. Certain campus policies, particularly our community covenant of behavioral standards, affected their behavior more than mine. For example, I was in a serious relationship in college. I could be openly physically affectionate with that person on campus without worrying about breaking any rules. My friends couldn't enjoy that same privilege.

I've seen a lot of changes surrounding LGBTQ+ people since then, both in my circle and in society at large. More friends and family members have come out to me. I've seen many people who went to church, school, or camp with me leave the church. Although that saddens me, I can't blame them. They have been hurt by churches, individual Christians, and other groups because of their sexuality and/or gender identity and how they wanted to express it. Leaving an environment where you feel unwelcome or unsafe is an understandable course of action. I hope we will make space for them to come back to church if they choose that.

Something I've noticed lately is that more people are talking about trans issues than they were before the pandemic. I certainly know a lot more trans people than I used to. I've witnessed faith-based ministries loving trans kids and creating safe environments for them. I hope those conversations are happening with youth leaders and youth groups. Young people are the future of the church. We either love them or we lose them, and we've already lost enough people from my generation.

As much work as the church has to do—and I think we can all agree the church has work to do no matter what you think about some of these issues—I also have work to do on myself. As a lifelong people pleaser, I'm not good at asserting controversial opinions. (This may surprise people who know me and know how much I like to talk.) But sharing how you feel is the key to good dialogue, and good dialogue is the key to sustainable and productive change. It's also part of being a supportive ally to LGBTQ+ people within and outside of the church. Writing this essay is part of that journey for me.

***Meg Purdum** is a lifelong BICer with ties to the Elizabethtown, Harrisburg, Grantham, and Conoy BIC churches. A 2018 graduate of Messiah College (now University), she currently works in nonprofit communications as a social media specialist. She lives in Elizabethtown with her beloved husband, an elderly bunny, and one very spoiled cat.*

Part IV

Former BIC Pastors Share Their Stories

Once Upon a Time There Was a Church Called The Bridge

Justin Douglas

A former BIC pastor recounts the harrowing story of losing his ministerial credentials—and the church he pastored—while offering words of warning and blessing to those who continue to work for full inclusion of LGBTQ+ people in the church.

In 2015, I embarked on a new journey when I became a Brethren in Christ (BIC) pastor and began serving at The Bridge Church in Hummelstown, Pennsylvania. This marked a significant shift from my previous role in a rural Wisconsin church. Throughout most of my career, I had been affiliated with traditional evangelical congregations. However, in 2011, I experienced a pivotal moment of introspection, where I began to question the core tenets of my faith, including my beliefs about God, Jesus, the church, the Bible, and more. It was during this period that I started asking previously unexplored questions.

What anchored me to my faith during this transformative time was my exposure to the teachings of numerous Anabaptist thinkers. This led me to radically reorient my theology by placing Jesus Christ at the very center of my beliefs, a departure from the theological approach I had been taught in my youth and during my studies at Liberty University.

Upon joining the BIC, the denomination's Core Values immediately stood out to me. They set it apart from evangelical congregations I had been involved with. There was a strong emphasis on embodying the teachings of

Invitation to Conversation

Jesus, including, and perhaps most notably, some of his more radical statements. For instance, Jesus' call to lay down the sword (Matt 26:52) and to love one's enemies (Matt 5:43-45) was taken seriously as a profound charge. It was central to the BIC's Core Values rather than just being seen as some unattainable ideal.

Not long after joining the BIC, I encountered other pastors who, unlike me, had not been drawn to the denomination because of its stance on peace. Instead, they had joined in spite of it and sometimes had a difficult time appreciating it. For example, in 2018, when I was arrested alongside Shane Claiborne and Doug Pagitt during a nonviolent protest advocating for a ban on assault weapons, I felt compelled to defend my actions to both to my denomination and my fellow pastors. It made me ponder, "Weren't we the ones who rejected the idea of being drafted into war? Where has our prophetic voice for peace gone if we can't even agree that weapons of war do not sow the peace Jesus championed?"

That same year, I was grappling with an anonymous blog post that had gained significant traction within our denomination. This post openly criticized our church's public media which expressed *all are welcome here*, and it even went so far as to criticize other churches and pastors by name. Remarkably, once the anonymous author was unmasked, it turned out to be a lead pastor within the BIC. Surprisingly, this pastor's ministerial credentials remained intact, even though they made no effort to seek reconciliation with me or any of the other pastors who had unjustly suffered the repercussions of that hurtful post. This incident ultimately marked the beginning of the process that led to the revocation of my own ministerial license.

After this harmful, anonymous post had been widely circulated and had sparked numerous inquiries at the BIC U.S. office about our church, I received an invitation to meet with the National Director. Several staff members of The Bridge and I participated in the meeting, which evolved into a rigorous discussion of my theological beliefs regarding sexuality. This included inquiries about various practices at The Bridge, such as whether we permitted LGBTQIA+ individuals to volunteer within our children's ministry. At the time, we did have members from the LGBTQIA+ community serving in various capacities, and we did not perceive any conflicts with the *Manual of Doctrine and Government* (*MDG*).

I'll spare you the intricate details, but the ensuing months proved to be exceptionally demanding for us at The Bridge. We found ourselves engaged in the arduous task of defending our beliefs against a barrage of inquiries and criticisms. While we had previously navigated a certain level of ambiguity regarding matters of sexuality, this ongoing challenge compelled us to delve deeper into our positions as numerous questions were being raised about our beliefs and practices.

In early 2019, after profound introspection, study, and conversation with LGBTQIA+ individuals, I said, "I believe that God can, and does, bless same-sex monogamous marriages." This statement resulted in the removal of my ministerial credentials. It's worth noting that I had not officiated any same-sex marriages. It was the statement of belief alone that led to the revocation of my credentials and my removal as the pastor of a thriving church that had recently established a new campus in Harrisburg.

On May 15, 2019, The Bridge appealed to the denomination to become a non-affiliated partner of the BIC. The following day, I appealed to have my ministerial credentials reinstated. As disturbing as it was to have my ministerial credentials revoked, what was even more disconcerting for me was the appeals process itself. There was no independent entity to which I could turn for an impartial review. Instead, I had to appeal to the very same group—predominantly consisting of older, white, heterosexual men—who had initially rendered the decision. In addition, the actual appeals meeting was constrained by a remarkably tight schedule, as if this was a simple matter that wasn't profoundly impactful on someone's life, not to mention an entire church community! What's more, for half the session, I found myself needing to answer questions about issues related to transgender individuals despite having made no previous statements in this regard.

As part of my appeals process, I highlighted the fact that numerous BIC pastors were allowed to retain their credentials and continue to minister even though they did not fully align with certain aspects of the *MDG*. To demonstrate this, I referenced specific statements from the *MDG* (indicated in italics below) and then offered my observations as follows (in slightly edited form):

*Since the body of Christ is international, love of nation is secondary to fellowship in the body of Christ and mission to people everywhere. (*MDG, Statements of Christian Life and Practice, 4.2*)*

I am aware of multiple BIC churches that display American flags on Sunday mornings during their worship. This would seem to affirm a loyalty to the state. Furthermore, I have watched videos of multiple Fourth of July worship service celebrations. In one of these services, they sang "America the Beautiful" and "God Bless America" during the time of worship. This is a BIC church, and they have videos of these celebrations on their website.

*Christians should build a positive peace witness that permeates their daily lives, and should testify against violence and war, consistently showing love and concern for all. (*MDG, Statements of Christian Life and Practice, 4.2*)*

I entered into the BIC with a strong peace position. I still maintain this conviction. But as I began to create relationships in the BIC, I was shocked that many BIC pastors did not share my peace convictions. What I thought was a core BIC conviction advocating non-violence was revealed to be secondary at best. I have had credentialed BIC pastors argue for war and explain to me how my non-violent approach is unhelpful and unrealistic. Again, for me this is shocking, as I thought the one place I wouldn't experience resistance toward the radical nature of the peace position was in an Anabaptist denomination.

Believers should promote Christian community and fellowship in openness and concern for one another and in sharing one another's burdens. Consideration should be given for those having differing opinions. Schismatic activities should be avoided, but when conflicts do arise, Christians should seek reconciliation as outlined in Matthew 18:15-22. It is inappropriate for Christians to involve a fellow believer in litigation (1 Corinthians 6:1). (MDG, Statements of Christian Life and Practice, 3.1)

> Last year a senior pastor in the BIC Church authored a nine-page essay slandering many within the BIC family. In this essay the author says, "I feel our leaders rather than confronting wolves, we defend them and we ask them to come and teach us. That deeply concerns me." Describing myself, our church, my brothers and sisters in ministry, and their churches, as wolves was incredibly disturbing to me. What is even more disturbing is that the author has not apologized to me, The Bridge, or, to my knowledge, any of my brothers and sisters who are listed in this essay. How is it that this individual still has a license and a post as a senior pastor in the BIC? It would seem they've been provided a variance of some kind.

While I admitted that my beliefs didn't perfectly align with BIC theology, it became evident through my experience that individuals were allowed much more theological leeway if their divergence from theological purity didn't relate to matters of human sexuality. This intentional inconsistency remains a source of deep concern for me. It seems terribly unfair to remove one pastor's credentials for being misaligned with the denomination on this one particular "issue" while others are allowed to minister freely despite being at odds with some of the church's most central beliefs and values.

About a week later, the bishop informed me of the following motion that had been taken by Leadership Council (LC).

> **Motion:** Leadership Council, having met and prayerfully dialogued with brother Justin Douglas, upholds the decision of Leadership Council on March 14, 2019 to revoke Justin's BIC U.S. ministerial credentials because of his stated views that same-sex behavior within a loving, committed, monogamous relationship is not necessarily sinful but can be blessed by God and affirmed by the Church. However, because of our commitment to brotherhood,

community, and restoration, if Justin is willing to enter a process of engagement with BIC U.S. concerning the counsel of the Church regarding same-sex behavior, and if he is willing to communicate to The Bridge and to his electronic followership that he is entering such a process of engagement, and that during this time he will not teach doctrine contrary to the understanding of the BIC U.S., we will extend his period of appeal to August 15, 2019.

Around the same time, on May 23, 2019, The Bridge Strategic Leadership Team received a letter written on behalf of LC. A portion of this letter reads as follows:

> After listening to what you shared and discussing together, the Leadership Council has decided to affirm its original decision and not enter into a different type of relationship with The Bridge Church. . . .
>
> However, as was stated at the outset of the meeting, the BIC U.S. does desire for The Bridge Church to remain a congregation within our family of congregations if you as leadership desire to continue as a BIC congregation under the polity of the BIC U.S. The single biggest impediment to that happening is not the values of the church or your desire to love all people as Jesus would, but that your present understanding of how that should be expressed within ministry to the LGBTQ community is an "affirming" or "Side A" theological understanding. That understanding of Scripture is contrary to the MDG of the BIC U.S. and thus cannot be held and expressed by a BIC congregation. If you as a leadership group would choose to re-consider your beliefs around that subject, as well as how you teach and lead people to follow Jesus in that way, the LC would be glad to move forward in relationship together with you providing vital leadership for the church moving forward under the polity of the BIC U.S.
>
> If that is not your desire, we wish you well in any ongoing ministry you desire to undertake together or individually as you follow Jesus and desire to share his love with those around you. We desire

the same and the Atlantic Conference of the BIC currently plans to continue the ministry of The Bridge Church with different leadership. The planned date for that leadership transition is Sunday June 9, 2019. . . . Our hope is that we can do that as brothers and sisters in Jesus expressing mutual love and respect for one another.

I was open to additional discussion and prolonging the appeal process until August. I genuinely thought that this extension could afford the time that wasn't initially granted and potentially broaden the conversation. However, when I indicated my willingness to participate in this extended dialogue, I was informed that it was only an option if I anticipated a change in my stance. Essentially, the extension was conditional on my willingness to ultimately alter my position, with no reciprocal openness from their side to reconsider their stance.

Why am I sharing all this with you? Because this narrative exemplifies the lengths the denomination has gone to avoid engaging in this essential conversation. If you're reading this book, and any of the books and articles suggested in the "Resources for Further Study" at the end, it's likely that you are open to discussing the intersection of theology and sexuality. However, in my deeply personal experience, I did not witness a willingness within the BIC leadership to embrace such a conversation openly. Instead, I observed a desire to tightly control the discourse and to silence any voices or perspectives that deviated from the norm. This approach starkly contrasts with how we handle other theological beliefs, even those considered fundamental to our Core Values.

The Bridge Church faced erasure. All of our assets were seized, including bank accounts, properties, computers, guitar cables, and more. We weren't even allowed to retain our name, website, or the carefully cultivated social media presence we had established. Upon my dismissal by the denomination, there was no offer of a severance package, and my family and I were required to leave the parsonage, which had previously been The Bridge's property and was regarded as one of my benefits.

I'm sharing this because some of you may be determined to work for full inclusion of LGBTQ+ people in the BIC Church. I commend your commitment. But I warn you to be prepared for an arduous journey. Leaders within the denomination seem willing and ready to do whatever is necessary to maintain what they deem to be "correct" theology about same-sex relationships. The path toward greater inclusion, or even toward fostering an environment for genuine conversations where a variety of voices are heard, seems to be a considerable distance away. The journey ahead is lengthy, and though I've reluctantly passed the baton, I'm grateful that individuals are stepping up and tirelessly advocating for inclusion within the BIC.

I offer this heartfelt blessing for BICers who continue to strive in their pursuit of inclusion:

> May you find the courage to speak boldly to BIC leadership, not out of a sense of theological superiority, but out of compassion for those they have overlooked, who suffer because of the theology they uphold.
>
> May your presence bring solace and healing to people wounded by the harsh judgments and shame they've endured.
>
> May you nurture your own well-being, discovering joy, forgiveness, and hope amidst the inevitable challenges and frustrations that arise in your pursuit of justice.
>
> May God bless you and keep you!

Justin Douglas *serves as the Founding Pastor at The Belong Collective (Harrisburg) and is a Co-Founder of Pride Hershey. Justin was recently elected as a Dauphin County Commissioner and is using his leadership skills for public service as he strives to make a positive impact on his community. Justin lives in Central Pennsylvania with his wife Brittney and their three children.*

I Once Was a Minister in Good Standing

Jay McDermond

A former Brethren in Christ minister shares the painful story of having his credentials suddenly removed because of his views on same-sex relationships.

Swedish author Fredrik Backman begins the first book of his Beartown trilogy with these words:

> Late one evening toward the end of March, a teenager picked up a double-barreled shotgun, walked into the forest, put the gun to someone else's forehead, and pulled the trigger.

> This is the story of how we got there.

The stories are told from the perspective of an omniscient narrator, and the volumes are, like most novels, about human failings and triumphs and all the painful complexities of life. We assume the narrator is essentially accurate in the telling of the story, but elements may have been missed, while others are starkly accurate and stand out.

My contribution to this collection of essays certainly doesn't rise to the level of Backman's storytelling. However, it is complex; it has a certain degree of failure at its core, and, like the first novel's ending, the story is unresolved. Or, at least, I would hope I am not telling you a story that is completed and final. I do not claim to offer it to you as a document that might pass the scrutiny of a trained historian's evaluation, but I am endeavoring to avoid inaccurate embellishment, and I have done my best to refrain from any intentionally vindictive prose.

At the same time, there are elements that are seared into my memory, and these elements include the general timeline, very specific incidents, and a few specific words uttered during its unfolding. This is the story of how I got to where I am with the Brethren in Christ (BIC) Church. Part of me hopes there is another volume to be written. Another part of me wonders if that is even possible, given the first volume.

My journey with the BIC began in the fall of 1972 when I registered as a first-year student at Messiah College. Roughly a year earlier, I had experienced an unexpected conversion at a Dave Wilkerson rally in Harrisburg, Pennsylvania. Wilkerson told me to go home and read the Bible, starting with Matthew. I did as instructed, and it didn't take very long before I realized I was in trouble. As I read the Sermon on the Mount, I knew I had to decide: follow Jesus or follow my family. All the men in my family had served proudly in the military, and here was Jesus calling me along another road. I opted for Jesus. I thought I had stumbled onto a new and unique way of being a Christian. I was a pacifist. I thought I might be the only one. I was very young and naïve.

At Messiah, I met Martin Schrag, a faculty member of the Religion and Philosophy Department. He taught me about an element of the church I had never imagined existed: Anabaptism. Furthermore, he told me that the BIC viewed this theological stream as a basic portion of its identity. He encouraged me to consider joining the church.

I began looking for a BIC congregation near my hometown. The closest was the Roseglen congregation located in Duncannon, Pennsylvania. Simon and Betty Lehman served as the pastoral couple. They introduced me to a second stream of the BIC Church: Holiness. The Lehmans were an infectiously loving and warm couple. It was obvious they loved Jesus. They loved the people around them, and they deeply desired to be as holy as they could with the Spirit's help. I came to respect the holiness tradition because of them. Simon encouraged me to apply for a "lay license," which enabled me to minister with him at that congregation, and I did.

After Messiah I attended Associated Mennonite Biblical Seminary in Elkhart, Indiana, and worshipped at Nappanee BIC Church. It was at this time I became a licensed minister in the denomination. This allowed me to be a summer interim pastor in that congregation and eventually led to being called as their pastor from 1979-1982.

From 1982-1987 I did post-graduate work in the United Kingdom, then returned to the United States to teach at Messiah in the Biblical and Religious Studies Department until I retired in May 2016. During that time, I was ordained (in April 1994), and I actively contributed to the denomination's newspaper, *The Evangelical Visitor*, and to the denominational journal, *Brethren in Christ History and Life*. I wrote the chapter on prayer in *Focusing our Faith: Brethren in Christ Core Values*. I served on two interim preaching teams (Carlisle and Manor congregations) and on a sabbatical preaching team at Harrisburg BIC, my home congregation at the time.

And then, unknown to me, the wheels began to fall off my church vehicle. Five days after I retired, I received an unexpected call from my bishop. He asked if I would serve as the interim pastor at Engage Community Church, a relatively new and somewhat struggling church plant in Carlisle, Pennsylvania. I agreed. As part of my assignment, the bishop wanted to know if this congregation had a future. We met after three months on the job, and I said I thought they did. The search for a new pastor began, and I eventually agreed to be Engage's pastor.

I cannot provide specific dates for all the incidents that I am about to share, but I do know the beginning: June 12, 2016. That was the day Omar Mateen entered the Pulse Nightclub, a popular LGBTQ+ venue in Orlando, Florida, and proceeded to kill forty-nine and wound fifty-three. Engage had planned to have a worship service the following day in a park near where we worshipped. When we arrived, Christine, a transgender woman, was already at the pavilion. Clearly, she was struggling with the news from Orlando. I and others from the congregation spent time with her. She stayed for the service, and at the end, I told her where and when we met, and I encouraged her to consider worshipping with us.

A few weeks later, I did something I very rarely do. I abandoned my sermon notes, and I spoke about Christine. I recall encouraging the congregation to consider the deep needs of Christine and other LGBTQ+ people living in Carlisle. I also encouraged those present to talk to me if they were offended by my closing comments. I knew this was a hot topic. No one stepped up to admit concerns. However, one person cornered me to say he was thankful I said it. This brother is gay and a Christian living in another town. Because he is gay, he didn't have any congregations that would accept him.

These two incidents caught my attention. Was our small struggling congregation being called by the Spirit to be a church that welcomed and embraced people from the LGBTQ+ community? I certainly thought we were. And more evidence gradually appeared.

Despite my optimism about Engage's viability as a congregation, the attendance numbers dwindled. We moved from our original meeting place to the local Seventh Day Adventist building to save money. At that time, two adult couples started worshipping with us. They were parents of gay adult children. Their home congregations (both BIC) struggled to address their concerns about caring for people in the gay community. Their presence and concerns were noted, and I was 90% sure this was to be Engage's focus.

We hired a consultant to help us process our sense of focus and ministry in Carlisle. The two leading foci were the LGBTQ+ community and Dickinson College students. We started discussion groups around needing to learn more about the gay community and how Christians interacted with that group. In the "feedback" time after the sermon one Sunday, a regular attender said we really needed to start this ministry to the gay community. That Sunday, one of our occasional attenders was present and he asked me if we could meet. He said it was rather urgent, so we arranged to meet the following evening. I then learned he was a gay man married to a woman, and their marriage was disintegrating due to his orientation. He wanted someone to talk to about this upheaval in his life.

It was clear to me that the Spirit was calling Engage to reach out to this group of people.

As our attendance numbers continued to fall, I and two other people from our congregation began dialoguing with our current bishop. We wanted to know if we would receive denominational support for where we thought we were being called. We knew the BIC policy: ministers can't officiate at a same-sex marriage ceremony, and no BIC congregational building could facilitate a same-sex marriage. I went out of my way in the meetings with my bishop to make it clear I would not violate that policy. My assurances were a reaffirmation of what I had written on my renewal application for ordination in January 2017. In that re-application I wrote the following at the end of the document:

> While I am very much in broad agreement with the BIC doctrines and concerns for Christian life and practice, I believe I have a theological difference on one point. The point is not one of personal practice, but does relate to the matter of homosexuality. I would describe myself as a person who affirms marriage equality; and, therefore, I do 'wonder' about Article XVIII, Section 1.C regarding the practice of homosexuality and Section 2.A's affirmation that marriage is between a husband and wife. Since I am pro-marriage equality the language in these sections are [*sic*] 'interesting' (1.C) and disagreeable (2.A) to me. Having said that, I did attend the gathering on LGBTQ matters, and I understand the denomination's stance.

The July 3, 2017, Commission on Ministry and Doctrine (CMD) cover letter, accompanying my renewed ordination card, read, in part, "Thank you for your response to the review questionnaire. The church is pleased to note your commitment to the high standards of vocational Christian ministry described in the questionnaire and your promise of fidelity to the community of believers we know as the Brethren in Christ."

By the spring of 2019, it was clear that Engage Community Church needed to close. I had been meeting with my bishop to process this reality. We set March 31, 2019, as the last service for the congregation. I met with him on Monday, March 25, to finalize the details. At that meeting, I mentioned that I wanted him to know I was open to serving the conference in any way that might be needed. He replied that Leadership Council (LC) had decided to remove my credentials because of my views on homosexuality.

I was utterly and totally blindsided.

I was never told this consideration was in the works. I was never given a chance to dialogue with LC. I was simply told it was done. Insult was added to injury later that day when I met with the National Director of the denomination, and he informed me that LC knew this decision was "inconsistent and unfair, but they didn't know what else to do." I remember those words because I thought to myself, "You could have tried harder to do something consistent and fair."

I was given an opportunity to meet with both LC and the CMD in mid-May. On May 15th, I submitted a three-page clarification of my position on same-sex marriage, and we met in person shortly thereafter. On May 23, 2019, I received a communication from the National Director that the following was decided:

> **Motion:** Leadership Council, having met and prayerfully dialogued with brother Jay McDermond, upholds the decision of Leadership Council on March 14, 2019 to revoke Jay's BIC U.S. ministerial credentials because of his stated views that same-sex behavior with in [*sic*] a loving, committed, monogamous relationship is not necessarily sinful and can be blessed by God and affirmed by the Church. However, because of our commitment to brotherhood, community, and restoration, if Jay is willing to enter a process of engagement with BIC U.S. concerning the counsel of the Church regarding same-sex behavior, we will extend his period of appeal to August 15, 2019.

I responded to this communication asking for clarification. Was this process to be a dialogue or an attempt to convince me I was wrong for my current position? I was informed that dialogue was not the end goal.

I did not accept the option of counsel, and I am now a former minister of the Brethren in Christ Church. For a number of years after this, I ministered part-time with a small local United Methodist congregation.

What you just read is "the story of how we got there."

At the end of *Beartown*, the reader realizes there were no shells in the shotgun when the trigger was pulled. The "shooter's" intention was not to kill or inflict harm. Rather, she wanted her assailant to be held accountable for what he did.

Likewise, I do not wish harm or injury to be visited upon anyone in denominational leadership. I do, however, believe accountability is in order. For me that accountability might involve a public admission that these events occurred. Furthermore, I think a public apology might be in order. In my most optimistic dreams, I would be open to an invitation to engage in a denominational conversation about how the BIC Church is being called to reconsider its approach to people in the LGBTQ+ community who are part of our congregations.

Jay McDermond is retired from both teaching and pastoral ministry. He taught at Messiah University for twenty-nine years and was Professor of Christian Spirituality at the time of his retirement. Recently, he began his "dream job," working part-time at a hardware store. He is married to Wanda Thuma-McDermond, and they have two adult sons. He is a casual bird watcher and an avid fan of the English Premier League. His favorite team is Newcastle United, but he likes Nottingham Forest and Luton Town, as well, because "God seems to like underdogs."

Full Inclusion

Keith Miller

A pastor leading a BIC church informs his bishop and Conference Board that he believes in full inclusion of LGBTQ people in the life of the church.

Editor's Note: We have published the following letter exactly as written and have not edited it (with the exception of removing a name in some places). For more of Keith's story about what led to the decision to become fully inclusive, see his earlier essay in the book titled "A Moment of Clarity."

The Letter

Dear Bishop and members of the Atlantic Conference Board, 11/26/2022

Over the past 8 years, I've been wrestling with how I relate to my neighbors who identify as LGBTQ: as a pastor, a BIC leader, and a disciple of Jesus. I have studied relevant scripture passages and learned about their cultural context. I have met with people, read books and articles from various perspectives, and prayerfully reflected. I have had countless conversations, many of them with some of the members on this conference board.

For years I have been comfortable being "in process" about my views on homosexuality, and would explain this to those who wanted to know what stance our church held. However, I always struggled to find the words, because I was aware of the damage that Christians have done to many in the LGBTQ community. But in addition to that, something deeper did not sit right in my spirit as my conversations continued. It was not until recently, when I received an email from a couple who found our website and resonated deeply with how we follow Jesus and express his mission, that I reached a turning point. They asked, as a same-sex married couple, if they would be welcomed to worship Jesus and share in his mission in our community. Their gentle, hopeful spirit was beautiful and so clearly reflected Jesus. And I realized for the first time that I could no longer draw a line that would inhibit them from fully participating in the work Jesus is doing here. As I got to know them, my convictions were solidified.

I do not claim to see truth beyond a glass dimly lit. But I have come to a theological position of peace and hope in the full inclusion of faithful LGBTQ disciples in the life and ministry of the local church. I do not believe that expressing a natural desire for intimacy in a life-long, Christ-honoring same sex marriage relationship disqualifies an individual from the body of Christ in any way, including both serving and leading. I believe that the scriptures that are used to absolutely prohibit any expression of natural same sex attraction leave far too many linguistic and cultural questions for absolute certainty. I also do not believe that they describe the character and situations of the individuals that I am pastoring today.

For me, it has become significant to acknowledge that in most of the cited passages, "homosexual" activity is mentioned as an outflow of idolatry, pagan worship, denying God, disobedient lives, giving of oneself over to uncontrollable lust and evil, and a host of other clear indicators that these individuals had hearts that did not desire to follow God. Homosexual behavior as an outflow of those attitudes, much like heterosexual behavior not grounded in self-control and commitment, are sinful. But when I meet thoughtful gay Christians who are unquestionably trying to be faithful and follow Jesus with agape love in lifelong relationships, it seems very different from Paul's words, and needs renewed discernment for our times.

Furthermore, I bear witness to the fruit of the Holy Spirit among LGBTQ persons in my life who are in same sex marriages and following Jesus with their whole selves. Some have arrived at this point themselves only after decades of wrestling, praying, embracing celibacy for years, and walking with humility and gentleness into their convictions. I fully trust that they are hearing from God as they follow Jesus, too. I see goodness and freedom in Christ emerging out of same-sex relationships that keep Jesus at their center.

As I have been a lead pastor of 12 years building relationships in Northern Delaware, I am connected with my greater community and I have seen the missional loss that a restrictive stance has brought to individuals who were initially drawn to follow Jesus alongside us at LifePath. This particular issue has limited our ability to express full love and welcome in our neighborhoods time and time again. Some amazing gifts have been missed out on in the Body of Christ. My experience is that a "third way" approach (welcoming, but not affirming), does not look or feel like the way of Jesus to those we are seeking to love.

I have spoken at length with my bishop, and I'm aware that there is not space for this theological viewpoint among BIC pastors. I have accepted this reality and I am aware that my ministerial license will be removed at a date that the Atlantic Conference decides. I will not seek to create conflict or resist that revocation. I would also like the conference to know that I did not suggest or direct my church to move toward dissociation. When I shared my convictions with our Vision Team, I did so with the acceptance that my employment could be terminated. The board met without me and independently chose to move toward dissociation. I was not seeking to cause division within the BIC or the Atlantic Conference. That has never been my heart. I have loved and pastored in this family for over 17 years. My heart as an anabaptist has not changed, nor has my desire to be faithful to Jesus and take the scriptures seriously. In fact, my convictions here are a direct outflow of those foundations. I grieve that our BIC doctrine requires the parting of ways over this single issue.

I'm grateful for the relationships and support of the BIC over these past years, and I'm grateful for the opportunities to serve the BIC by speaking at events, writing in publications, training and coaching others, and being a friend and encourager alongside a lot of wonderful pastoral colleagues. I'm hoping those relationships can continue in some way, though I know they will be different. There is sorrow, without question. But, I am filled with joy when people on the edges of our community share tear-filled gratitude, because they finally feel the freedom to walk toward Jesus with us.

Invitation to Conversation

Since our church voted on this transition, I have tried my best to lead us through it in a way that reflects the character of Jesus and the commitment that we have to live in love as siblings in Christ with the BIC. I acknowledge how complicated of a theological issue this can be, and I know how much vitriol can exist in either direction toward many who are genuinely trying their best to be faithful. These conflicts can be ugly and dishonoring to Jesus. I am committed to doing it differently, with gentleness and love at the center, even in moments of separation. The people at LifePath do not feel ill-will toward the BIC, and I do not either.

I did not want to use this letter primarily to defend my theological position or convince anyone of anything. I don't believe that is helpful at this point in time. However, I am more than willing to dialogue about my journey if there are remaining questions. My bishop and I have talked and written back and forth many times, and he can share more insight regarding my theological journey.

I honor the wonderful work that the BIC is doing in so many areas of discipleship and mission. I hope that this family continues to lean into the radical love of Jesus with all its heart. I will do the same. Thanks to all of you on the board for the time you give to leading our family of churches. I am especially grateful for my bishop and his desire to walk through this process with me with gentleness and respect. It has been an emotionally overwhelming few months. I love the Brethren in Christ and I am thankful that I have been formed in so many ways as through its people.

In Christ,

Keith Miller
Lead Pastor, LifePath Church

Keith Miller *has been the Lead Pastor of an incredible collection of disciples at LifePath Church Delaware in Newark, Delaware, for thirteen years. His extra time is spent running ultramarathons and coaching his cross-country team. When he's not moving, it's probably because he's watching a migrant at his backyard bird feeder because he believes that God's wonder is everywhere.*

I Don't Want to Have a Gay Policy

Rod White

A former BIC pastor reflects on the challenges of stating what the church believes about same-sex relationships and about his disappointment with the denomination he served for many years.

In 2001, when I was pastor of Circle of Hope Center City, the church was exiled to Ben Franklin High School until we figured out how to satisfy the sound ordinance at our location on Tenth and Locust Streets. In that echoing auditorium, I made my first speech about our "gay policy" and why we did not have one. I suppose a main reason we did not have one was because the pastor (me) didn't really want one. I had an abiding fear of turning the gay people in our church into objects of policy rather than treating them as brothers and sisters. Here is my summary statement from the speech.

> I don't want to have a gay policy, because it would then appear as if life were about making policy. I don't have much faith in the policies the philosophers and governments are coming up with right now. I wish them well and I want to participate, but when it comes down to it, I don't have a lot to offer if it is not based on my total reliance on what God did for me in Jesus. Even in the case of the most powerless, and often homosexuals *[sic]* feel powerless over their sexuality and disempowered by the society, even then, about all I can say is that Christ is the power and wisdom of God. Other

solutions are end points, not beginnings, and I can't say that I can go along with them.

I should have predicted that people would think "no policy" was the same as a negative statement because we were not making a positive statement. I was relying on traditional Christian deeds to do the talking for us. But our no-stance stance became more of an indecipherable nuance than a real option as our society became increasingly polarized.

I thought creating coercive and combative stances was far removed from strategies in the Bible for being and doing church, especially when it came to Paul's instruction. I began to teach more explicitly about the premier church planter's "two-tiered" approach to theology. Paul's primary tier is more absolute. The secondary tier is more provisional and reflects local issues in his developing mission. (For a summary of the two tiers, see https://rodwhite.net/info-and-articles/pauls-two-tiered-theology-and-social-action/).

I thought this interpretation was kind of obvious, but I found many people had been taught the Bible as if it were a textbook divided into chapters about the same subject instead of a story or a mission manual with a lot of diverse elements and many moving parts. I did not really think we needed Paul to talk about these two tiers since we acted them out all the time ourselves. Christians worldwide generally agree on the truths and behaviors that make us Jesus followers. After that, we have thousands of variations and applications of the truth, which change and develop over time and according to circumstances.

When it came to "gay policies" and proving whether we were "open and affirming" according to the most recent standards, I thought we needed to rely on tier one and not fruitlessly and divisively sort out tier two since what people hate most about the church is how we fight. It is so hypocritical to state a principle like "hate the sin, love the sinner" when no sinner ever felt loved when they heard that (as far as I know). Rather, they feel otherized. Most unbelievers know Christians are supposed to be all about love, so it is shocking to unbelievers to watch Christians take each other out and denigrate whole classes of people.

We were doing careful, practical theology, but doing it in a society (and church) progressively intolerant to dialogue. So eventually I, along with our church's leadership, decided we needed to provide a better statement to satisfy people who just could not get what we were trying to do. They kept saying "You seem to be open and affirming, so why not put out a gay flag?"

In about 2014, I wrote up the essence of a long dialogue we had about LGBTQIA+ "issues." The country was on the way toward *Obergefell v. Hodges*, which would give same-sex marriages full recognition under the law. I personally was very much in favor of this as a legal improvement since everyone who gets tagged as a "minority" in the U.S. is perpetually stigmatized and discriminated against. I don't think being legalized always helps the marginalized, but it is a lot better than being invisibilized. In light of the Supreme Court decision, our first "gay policy" statement ended up being about marriage. We called it *Marriage in the New Creation*. (For an early rendition, see https://rodwhite.net/marriage-new-creation/.)

The statement (slightly edited here) starts with two "tier one" truths.

- Love is bigger than anyone's identity. "The only thing that counts is faith expressing itself through love," and "what counts is the new creation" (Galatians 5:6, 6:15, NIV).

- Marriage is not the ultimate expression of love and commitment; relating as the body of Christ is. Within that inspired and diverse body, composed of everyone who can name Jesus as Lord, "there are different kinds of gifts, but the same Spirit distributes them. There are different kinds of service, but the same Lord. There are different kinds of working, but in all of them and in everyone it is the same God at work." Every Jesus-follower is honorable and must be honored because each is given "the manifestation of the Spirit . . . for the common good" (1 Corinthians 12:4-7, NIV).

The statement moves on to two "tier two" interpretations for the present moment.

- The church has rarely been a safe place, historically, for sexual nonconformity. Many people have been oppressed and injured. So, we must be even more careful to welcome every person as they are, no matter where they are on their journey of discovering the fullness of what God has for them.

- Love requires personal effort and commitment, not just careful adjudication or implementation of regulations. As Jesus-followers, we need to love real, complex people with an unfolding future, not just organize identities as if we were the Social Security Administration.

Knowing these general statements only went so far for many people, we tried to answer the questions people often had about us. I think this is the most interesting part of the statement, so I'll quote it in full:

What about the pressure to choose a sexual identity? Sexual arousal is a characteristic of a person, not their identity. How we respond to our arousal and the feelings themselves tend to be fluid and are subject to the same temptations and maturation as are all our ways. Jesus is Lord of all our feelings and ways. We seek to honor each person as they experience their feelings and find their way along their unique journey as a member of the body of Christ.

What about the increasing experience of living together as sexual partners before marriage? Generally, sexual expression should happen within a relationship founded in a marriage covenant. Couples who cohabit as sexual partners without a public commitment should consider themselves married. Likewise, if they break up, they should consider themselves divorced. The rights the nation gives or withholds regarding marriage and other relationships are superseded by our life in faith as part of the new creation.

What about "same sex attraction?" Jesus followers who desire sexual relations with people of their own gender are no less honorable than anyone else. They are going to work out their sexuality in a variety of ways, as they are convicted and gifted.

- Some will choose celibacy and struggle alongside Jesus and Paul.

- Some will choose to have a committed relationship that can be a faithful response to their desire.

- Some will marry a person of the complementary gender and not express their other attractions, as all married couples are called to do.

There does not need to be one approach to marriage and sexual expression that supposedly meets the needs and aspirations of all people. All approaches to marriage do not need to be seen as equal in value or validity. The key to unity in diversity is the work of grace that enables disparate people to manifest the Spirit for the common good. We all experience brokenness, sin and loneliness in our loves; so we will bear one another's burdens and so fulfill the law of Christ (Galatians 6:2). What counts is the new creation.

The church kept tinkering with the statement, of course. I'm not sure what it says now.

I am not sure why the Brethren in Christ (BIC) ignored our *Marriage in the New Creation* statement. I can't remember hearing from them about it. Maybe they were ignoring us in general. Maybe they thought we were making an accurate statement. Maybe we were in Philadelphia, and they still did not know what to do with urban people. I suppose I could have helped get us thrown out in 2014 if I had led us to pick a fight. I did not think such a fight would help gay people or anyone else and, besides, a trans man was in my cell group at the time, transitioning. They needed to be loved and to grow their lively new faith, not get embroiled in an argument with angry white men from the interior.

In May of 2020, George Floyd was murdered in front of our eyes by Derek Chauvin, the world was upended by a pandemic, and people were done with weak responses from institutions. Our statement above seemed much too timid to many people. Ironically, the most "liberal" members of many congregations, including ours, decided to "go biblical" and apply their judgment of society's sins to the church first (1 Pet 4:17). Their witch-hunt found racists and homophobes like Joe McCarthy found "communists."

Intrinsically antiracist and open and affirming people were thrown out like babies with the bathwater based on their mere association with a suspicious institution. The church has yet to recover.

A similar effort, pointed in the opposite direction, had been working its way through the BIC Church for many years prior. I grew increasingly confused about the direction of the BIC during my last years as a pastor. I had some strange experiences that felt surprisingly authoritarian. Dialogue essentially ended, but careful theology from the top rarely replaced it. I am not sure what was going on, if the leaders were simply giving up as they faced increasing distrust of institutions.

I did hear that a couple of church leaders went on a speaking tour about human sexuality (see *In Part* [Fall/Winter 2015]). I was glad I did not get to hear their presentation. I think it helped preserve my affection for the presenters. A few years after their tour, after I was gone, people in Circle of Hope found the BIC stance so intolerable, they disaffiliated. The denomination gave notice it was seizing their buildings. I'm not sure about all the negotiations—one of my old colleagues who started the dissolution was already gone. But as of November 2023 the denomination owned all the assets, including the name, and the main congregations disbanded. Other BIC pastors and whole churches have also evacuated or been thrown out for having "pro-gay" policies.

I have always been "pro-gay" about individuals, especially when I met up with "anti-gay" people. I think that is why I gravitated back to my original "no policy" stance when I became acquainted with more queer authors, especially Pamela Lightsey. Many LGBTQ people would like to be as unlabeled as everyone else and would like to stop being an object of policymakers and divisive rhetoric (see the section titled "Unlabeled sexuality" at https://en.wikipedia.org/wiki/Sexual_identity, or hear Pamela Lightsey at https://www.youtube.com/watch?v=b4k8yZ6iBds.

After all the church planting and growth that happened in Circle of Hope in Philadelphia, all it took was a hardline policy toward LGBTQ+ people and a doubling down by the denominational leaders to set in motion a series of events that disassembled the church for the next generation. Unfortunately, that is not a new phenomenon for the church.

When I was becoming an adult Christian in California in the 1970s, there was division over the "praise and worship" music emanating from the hippies down at the beach in Costa Mesa, which I considered part of my homeland. Lonnie Frisbee was the first super influential worship leader at Calvary Chapel, and one of his signature songs was "Seek Ye First." [Greg Laurie's tale: https://harvest.org/resources/gregs-blog/post/the-long-strange-trip-of-lonnie-frisbee/]. Frisbee's music was "wild" back then. Some people found it unholy. Now it is probably in your hymnal. Lonnie died of AIDS in 1986, but he's kind of in your hymnal, too.

Rod White *is a former pastor and development pastor for Circle of Hope, a BIC-affiliated church in Philadelphia. He now practices psychotherapy and spiritual direction, travels with anyone who will go with him, records Smule songs for his sister, writes stuff, and revels in the wonders of his wife and clan.*

Part V

Allies Call For Full Inclusion

Biblical Considerations

A Biblical Journey Toward Loving, Committed, Same-Sex Unions

Fred Miller

A former BIC pastor describes key principles for reading the Bible that led to his affirmation of same-sex relationships and that freed him theologically and spiritually in other ways as well.

Some time ago, I was in a church home group where we decided to discuss a controversial topic together and see if we could practice the biblical quality of *gentleness* with one another. The topic was homosexuality—and we pulled it off! We all left as friends. But one thing disappointed me. Most of those who held a traditional view of marriage had no idea how someone could affirm gay marriage and still be biblical. In fact, a number of people in the group were affirming only because of the gay people they knew. They were still conflicted because of what they *thought* the Bible said about this matter.

In this essay, I consider a number of principles that are useful for reading and interpreting the Bible well. After explaining each principle, I will then describe how it should inform our views about LGBTQ+ people and same-sex relationships.

1. The Principle of God-Directed Worship

The Bible and its words are not God. We don't need a perfect Bible to encounter and worship a loving and holy God who wooed the people he created in his image long before written materials were invented.

Invitation to Conversation

To put it simply: God is bigger than the Bible. God's revelation is not confined to this source. Before there was a written Old Testament and a written New Testament, God was *already* speaking to humanity in love. According to Romans 1-2, we can know God sufficiently through creation and our conscience. In fact, the greatest revelation of all was *not* a book, but a *person*—Jesus, the "Word" (John 1:1). Furthermore, millions of people throughout history have been illiterate, yet God still reached out to be known by them. Through the Spirit, God continues to guide us collectively into all truth.

But even *with* a book to guide us, history shows that Christian groups rarely agree with one another. Therefore, we must approach this process of reading the Bible cautiously and humbly. Christians throughout the ages have been convinced their interpretations were right, only to eventually conclude they were wrong at points. For example, Galileo's thesis that the earth orbited around the sun caused the church to label him a heretic because the Bible "clearly" said that the sun "rises" and "sets." And thousands of preachers and Christians in the United States used two hundred passages about slavery in the Bible as evidence that God endorsed slave trafficking.

LGBTQ+ application
We need to read our Bibles humbly. We should humbly listen for the word of God to us and humbly worship God (as we best understand God) in love. This may mean that views we once held to be true should no longer be regarded that way.

2. The Principle of Context

As with any kind of literature, the Bible must be understood in its literary and cultural setting.

When reading the Bible, we must remember that it was not written *to* us but *for* us. Commands given *to* Israel are not necessarily given *for* us: we don't stone rebellious youth (Deut 21:18), kill neighbors who might contaminate our faith (Deut 20:16), or prohibit wearing clothing made of different types of material (Lev 19:19).

The Bible is an ancient book. This means we must try to understand how a person living in the ancient Near East might understand it. People in antiquity did not value historical and scientific accuracy the way we do today. Rather, they wrote to convey a message. Hyperbole, figures of speech, metaphors, and parables were common means of getting their message across.

LGBTQ+ application
Statements about same-sex behavior in the Bible must be understood in cultural context—where same-sex sex might be viewed as problematic because it was exploitative or regarded as sexual excess—and in the broader historical ancient Near Eastern context where people had no awareness of the concept of sexual orientation.

3. The Principle of Using Jesus as Our Interpretive Guide
All Scripture should be interpreted in light of Jesus' life and teaching.

Looking at how Jesus lived and taught is the clearest means we have of knowing who God is. Jesus said, "Anyone who has seen me has seen the Father" (John 14:9, NIV). And Hebrews 1:3 says Jesus is "the exact representation of his [God's] being." So it makes sense that we look to Jesus for guidance on morality and ethics.

Jesus taught that he had come to fulfill the Mosaic Law. This meant that some Old Testament laws would get a face-lift by going deeper into the heart of the law. In Matthew 5, Jesus used the formula, "You have heard that it was said . . . but I tell you," to teach against both murder *and* hatred, both adultery *and* lust, and both divorce *and* unfaithfulness. And he taught love for both neighbors *and* enemies.

Jesus revised the rules of the Old Testament sabbath law, making it more flexible to benefit people. He also overruled the law of stoning a woman caught in adultery because he said her accusers were also sinners and the woman needed mercy. And he touched "unclean" people and ate with well-known sinners. These are all examples of teaching and acting *contrary* to clear Old Testament commands. Scores of other Mosaic laws were superseded by his laws of love and mercy. It is love for God and love for neighbor, after all, that Jesus said are the greatest commandments (Matt 22:36-40).

LGBTQ+ application
Jesus is our moral compass, and he is silent on same-sex relationships. This is most likely because it was not a major issue facing people at the time. But we do see Jesus emphasizing a deeper ethic flowing from the heart of the law. It shouldn't surprise us, then, if Jesus might later affirm something new that taps into this deeper ethic to promote loving relationships.

4. The Principle of Love

Acting compassionately in the best interests of others is foundational to all of God's ethics.

Both Jesus (Matt 22:39-40) and Paul (Rom 13:9-10) affirm the principle that all morality is summed up in the command to love. So when asking ourselves if some behavior is right or wrong, asking "Is it loving?" is a primary way to discern this. Of course, love requires us to ask what *really* is in a person's best interest, and there may be differences of opinion, especially if we acknowledge the need to sometimes use "tough" love. But in the end, our motives must be ruled by love as we best understand it. When self-giving, servant love is shown—the kind of love described in 1 Corinthians 13—relationships bear good fruit.

Over the years, many issues have undergone changes in ethical judgments because of love, the kind of love that "does no harm to a neighbor" (Romans 13:10, NIV). For example, biblical interpretations about divorce and remarriage, interracial marriages, and freedom for slaves have all been shaped by Jesus' core ethic of love and grace.

LGBTQ+ application
When LGBTQ+ individuals have been freed to love one another in a committed and exclusive way—and when the church has loved them as they are—peace, kindness, and compassion have followed. This "good fruit" is Jesus' ethical

criterion to determine what is right and wrong (Matt 7:16). "Bad fruit" often results from the harm inflicted on members of the LGBTQ+ community when they are judged and ostracized by their Christian brothers and sisters.

5. The Principle of Progressive Revelation

Since God has self-revealed in increasingly fuller ways over time, all parts of the Bible are not equally authoritative and should not be treated as such.

The Bible is not "flat." In other words, some parts are more authoritative for us today than others. Unfortunately, many Christians behave as though everything in the Bible is equally relevant to us today. But this is clearly not true. Since Christians live under the new covenant, certain aspects of the old covenant no longer apply. For example, circumcision is not required of Christians (Galatians 5), despite the fact that it was required of ancient Israelites (Genesis 17). Further, dietary restrictions found in the Old Testament (Leviticus 11) have been lifted, allowing Jewish followers of Jesus to eat with Gentiles (Acts 10). These are both examples of past revelation being overturned by the Spirit of God. This means the Bible is not an equally weighted book because God, and the people of God, are telling an ever-developing story.

LGBTQ+ application
Since God has progressively revealed himself throughout history, God is continuing to do this even up to the present time. This could certainly mean that God is doing something new among us regarding same-sex relationships.

6. The Principle of Interpreting the Bible on a Trajectory

God's progressive ethical revelations give us reason to believe that this process did not stop just because the New Testament was written. Rather, it continues to this day.

God has always been on the move. Sometimes, it's because new situations and cultures require something new. Other times, it's because God is moving people to something deeper and fuller, something more in line with God's loving designs. This means that the New Testament writers did not convey God's final words to people. The Spirit of God still speaks today. This is easy to demonstrate by considering some historical examples.

Let's return, for a moment, to the issue of slavery. Although slavery was accepted in ancient Israel, and even though the Bible contains over two hundred verses affirming it, Christians no longer condone it. Yet it wasn't until the nineteenth century that the church led a movement to abolish it. The Spirit was speaking in new and fresh ways to Christians long after the final words of the Bible were written. Another example would be corporal punishment of children. Mosaic law called for stoning rebellious children (Deut 21:20-21). Later, the Bible advises using physical force to discipline children (Prov 13:24; 23:14). But today, most Christian parents use other means of discipline whenever possible, and some completely reject spanking since it is a form of physical violence. Many people would also see the affirmation of women in church leadership as interpreting the Bible by following the "trajectory" of the Bible. As Jesus said in John 16:12, "I have much more to say to you, more than you can now bear" (NIV). Each generation must listen for these additional words of Jesus that the Spirit is speaking to the church.

LGBTQ+ application
God is always moving in a redemptive direction, guiding the world toward justice and goodness. Although Scripture does not address committed, loving, exclusive, same-sex marital relationships, if we understand love to be central to the biblical story—and if we follow the trajectory of the Bible—it is not difficult to conclude that God rejoices in and celebrates relationships like these.

Conclusion

I'm a child of evangelicalism and have been nurtured theologically by many who have gone before me. Yet I have undergone a kind of deconstruction of my understanding of the Bible. I no longer demand that it be error-free, internally consistent, or straightforward. I do expect the Bible to be a way that God speaks to me. And I do expect that God is big enough to do that with a messy Bible, a loving Jesus, and a revealing Spirit.

If I had to narrow down my reasons for moving to an affirmation of LGBTQ+ people, it would be that *love trumps all, and the Spirit still speaks.* Given the way Jesus modified Old Testament laws, I believe same-sex relationships and marriage seem like things that Jesus would affirm if he were among us today. Therefore, I would urge those who hold traditional views to reconsider the way they read and interpret the Bible so they can understand it in a way that allows for full welcome and affirmation of LGBTQ+ people. Only then will the church be a place where love truly wins.

Fred Miller *served for eighteen years as senior pastor of Cumberland Valley BIC Church in Dillsburg, Pennsylvania. He likes reading, perennial gardening, coaching youth lacrosse, and movies (especially with his wife). He is married to Cathy (for 50 years!) and is the joyful father of three adult children and nine grandchildren. He currently lives in Annapolis, Maryland, and is active in a progressive church there.*

Healing the Bible
How the Bible Became a Weapon—
and What to Do about It

Jeff Miller

A former BIC pastor emphasizes the crucial role experience can play in moving the BIC Church toward full inclusion of those who identify as LGBTQ.

The Bible as a Weapon

Growing up, the Bible always had a special place in my life. Its stories guided me. Its heroes inspired me. Its truths instructed me. Its pages introduced me to Jesus and shaped much of how I see the world and who I am today. But as I got older, I started to see that there was a dark side to the idea of a holy book. Instead of bearing good news that brought life, love, and transformed hearts, I saw how the Bible became a weapon. Armed with Scripture, Christians killed and oppressed people throughout history. "But thankfully, those things do not happen today," I told myself. "We have learned. We have evolved. Right?"

As I served as a Brethren in Christ (BIC) pastor for seventeen years, I began to realize this was not true. I was awakened to a new kind of violence that was happening everywhere and continues to this day. Around the country and around the world, vile name-calling, taunting, utter disdain, physical abuse, shame, exclusion, and threats of hell were all directed toward one particular marginalized group—the LGBTQ community. And, like any act of violence, there were casualties. A deadly cocktail of self-hatred, mixed with exclusion, led to skyrocketing rates of depression and suicide. Families were split. Faith was lost.

It was especially heartbreaking to realize that the church not only contributed to these violent acts and attitudes but was often leading the charge. Why? What was causing the church to behave this way? In addition, why do we see a recurring pattern of Christians using the Bible to harm, oppress, and exclude others throughout history? Is it simply the result of misreading the biblical text, or is it a deeper issue? Most important of all, what is the antidote?

Sola Scriptura?

To try to address some of these questions, let's start in the 1600s. In the midst of a corrupt religious system, Martin Luther and others led a religious revolution we now call the Reformation. Faced with church leaders who advanced dubious interpretations of Scripture or who ignored the Bible altogether, the Reformer's mantra became "sola scriptura" ("Scripture alone"). They believed Scripture was the primary authority and should be used to make determinations about theological, ethical, and cultural issues. Despite the merits of this approach, it has certain inherent problems as evidenced by the fact that these same Reformers used Scripture to persecute and kill fellow Christians.

Rather than seeing the Bible as a rule book that supplies answers to all our questions, it is better to understand it as a guide that can help us cultivate wisdom (see Peter Enns, *How the Bible Actually Works*). This might sound like a small shift, but it has huge implications. If wisdom is a chief goal, we should ask ourselves what else can lead us to it. What else can teach us the deep truths of life and how to live? One such thing is experience since experience is a key to wisdom.

As a BIC pastor, I was taught about experience from the Wesleyan Quadrilateral. Derived from the work of John Wesley, this idea states that our theology, doctrine, and practice are best discerned through four sources: Scripture, tradition, reason, and experience. Initially, this sounded positive to me, but I soon realized that in practice (in the BIC and many other traditions) Scripture was in the driver's seat while the other sources seemed more like mere passengers along for the ride.

However, we should not underestimate the power and importance of experience in shaping our beliefs. After all, God used people's emotions, opinions, experiences, and biases to shape *how* the Bible was written. Plus, our clearest picture of God comes to us experientially through the person of Jesus, the Word of God. One wonders why Jesus never chose to write anything down. Could it be that he had seen how Scripture could easily be twisted and could keep us from hearing the Spirit of love speaking afresh to us?

Discerning the Spirit through Experience in the Book of Acts

In the Book of Acts, we read a fascinating account of how experience dramatically changed Peter's theology and practice. In a mystical vision, Peter is instructed to eat food that was unclean for Jews (Acts 10:9-16). He refuses to do so since partaking of this food would be an "abomination" according to the law (see Leviticus 11). His refusal is met with this admonition: "What God has made clean, you must not call profane" (Acts 10:15, NRSV).

This experience prepares Peter to do something else that was forbidden for Jews. At the Spirit's prompting, Peter enters the home of Cornelius, a Gentile, even though this was "unlawful" (Acts 10:28, NRSV). Faced with a dilemma, Peter breaks with tradition and decides to listen to the "subjective" voice of the Spirit. The *experience* he has in the home of this Gentile named Cornelius changes him forever.

Fast forward to Acts 15. At the council in Jerusalem, Jewish leaders accuse Peter of not following the law. They insist that the Scriptures are clear and their meaning indisputable. Peter stands up and says, in effect, "I know what the Bible says. But my *experience* is telling me something different." Peter was on to something important. He was saying that we need to take seriously our lived experiences because they can be vital and authoritative ways by which the Spirit speaks, even if that sometimes runs counter to what Scripture says or to what we think it means.

Invitation to Conversation

Listening to Experience Throughout History

This way of listening to God's direction was not only stunning to the religious Jews of the first century, it was transformational to the whole trajectory of the Gospel. And as we explore Christian history, we see a similar pattern of people allowing the Spirit to speak authoritatively through experience.

For example, when it came to the most troubling chapters in our nation's history, the bondage and enslavement of black and brown people, Christians had a fierce debate. In his landmark book, *The Civil War: A Theological Crisis*, Mark Noll demonstrates that those who claimed to have a "high view" of Scripture, one that emphasized literalism and that saw the Bible as a set of definite laws, were the ones who supported slavery. In contrast, those who were accused of having a "low view" of Scripture, a view that emphasized how God was speaking to their consciences through their experience, were the abolitionists.

The same kind of thing happened with other issues such as women in ministry and divorce and remarriage. Why? Because Scripture changed? No. But people's *experiences* made them wonder if perhaps they were misreading the Bible. Perhaps something bigger was happening. It seems the Bible was written with a comma rather than a period, and the Spirit was speaking afresh.

Learning from the Experiences of LGBTQ People

When I was in college, I was convinced that homosexuality was a sin. It was black and white to me, and I remember trying to convince a few of my friends who were backsliding into liberalism. I had been taught that same-sex attraction was simply the result of certain types of unhealthy parental relationships and could be healed by choice and prayer. And since I didn't know any gay people, there was really no reason for me to question these views.

That changed the year after college when one of my college classmates came out. I was shocked. My friend didn't fit any of the stereotypes I had come to believe were true. This shook me. As time went on, my stereotypes were challenged by reading more and, most importantly, by meeting more people who were gay in my church and through my youth ministry. Instead of gays being "them," people I judged and condemned, they fast became people I knew and cared for.

And their fruit was telling a different story.

In the Gospels, Jesus says Christians are expected to bear fruit (John 15:1-17) and that people will identify them as his followers by the fruit they produce (Matt 7:15-20). The Gospel is not just about having correct beliefs; it is about producing good fruit. We can evaluate the health of a tree by its fruit.

As I listened and learned, two things became clear. First, the theology on sexuality that taught that same-sex attraction was a sin was producing some rotten fruit, such as intense shame, depression, self-loathing, and a real inability to feel God's love. Yet sadly, BIC church leaders often ignored this or explained it away. Second, my experience showed that those who embraced God's love for them in their queerness produced healthy fruit. Their "sin" was supposed to bring about pain, harm, and brokenness. Instead, it brought about joy, freedom, life, wholeness, and health.

Leading Us to a Love That Does No Harm

In Romans 13:9-10 (cf. Gal 5:14 and the words of Jesus in Matt 22:36-40) Paul says all the law and the commandments "are summed up in this one command: 'Love your neighbor as yourself.' Love does no harm to a neighbor. Therefore, love is the fulfillment of the law" (NIV). In his book *Disarming Scripture*, Derek Flood helps us understand the implications of this for interpreting the Bible. He writes:

> If we recognize that a particular interpretation leads to observable harm, this necessarily means that we need to stop and reassess our course. To continue on a course we know to be harmful, simply because "the Bible says so," is morally irresponsible. . . . Scripture is not our master, Jesus is, and the role of Scripture is to serve a servant function leading us to Christ. Here experience is central . . . in evaluating the merit of a particular reading as to whether we are reading it so as to lead us to love and life, which is the aim of Scripture (pp. 234-235).

The Bible remains a wonderful gift that has power to shape our hearts and lives toward love. It is a gift we need to cherish, listen to, and trust. But as the heartbreaking stories of LGBTQ Christians tell us, it was never something that we should use *alone* to discern God's voice. When we do, we are prone to misuse the Bible as a weapon to harm others.

Instead, the Bible needs living partners. It needs people whose experiences can help us interpret it responsibly as culture and contexts change. It needs the Spirit's wisdom and guidance. By paying attention to our lived experiences and seeing how our theology and practice is incarnated, we apply the antidote that can heal the pattern of harm that people do in the Bible's name. We need to listen to the stories and experiences of others and allow the Spirit to move in our hearts. This is certainly true of the BIC Church.

Sadly, I did not see this happening during the years I served this denomination. Even when I and others tried to amplify these stories, they were often ignored, sidelined, and even feared. Personally, this led to conflict with leadership, and over time it led to a mutual parting with the church (The Meeting House) and denomination I loved serving for seventeen years. But my hope is that more and more BIC leaders and lay people will have the courage to let experience speak. When that happens, I'm convinced we will stop using the Bible as a weapon of exclusion and death and will instead allow it to be used in ways that bring life, hope, good fruit, and healing to all.

***Jeff Miller** is a former BIC pastor who spent seventeen years serving at Cumberland Valley Church BIC and The Meeting House (Dillsburg). He is now a fun-loving fifth-grade teacher who loves sports, music, movies/shows, and listening to audiobooks and podcasts. He lives with his wife and three kids outside Carlisle, Pennsylvania, where they are part of an inclusive church in Harrisburg called The Belong Collective.*

God's Love Wins

George Payne

The Bible does not prohibit same-sex relationships—neither should we.

Over the past five years, I have published a blog titled "God's Love Wins" that has been devoted to exploring how the Bible can be used (and misused) to inform discussion about LGBTQ+ people and same-sex relationships. As a result of that study, it became clear to me that biblical passages used in this conversation can be grouped into three categories: (1) passages that are not relevant to the conversation, (2) passages that are indirectly relevant, and (3) passages that are directly relevant. What follows is a brief analysis of passages in each of these categories. For a more comprehensive discussion of these verses, see my blog at towelbasin.blogspot.com.

Passages That Are Not Relevant

The destruction of Sodom and Gomorrah (Genesis 19) is one of the most frequently used passages in discussions about the Bible and "homosexuality." But it is not relevant to contemporary conversations about being gay or about same-sex relationships. The account is about the wickedness of people in two cities that is expressed by a gross breach of hospitality.

We are told that all the men of the city attempt to rape the men/angels God sent to Lot (Gen 19:4-5). But clearly, not every man in the city could have been a "homosexual." Moreover, there really is no connection between this attempt to engage in a heinous act of sexual violence and the experience of two people being in a loving, monogamous, same-sex relationship. Any effort to connect the two is a damaging, distorted use of Scripture.

Passages That Are Indirectly Relevant

Many arguments against same-sex relationships and gender nonconformity appeal to Genesis 1:26-28, where God created male and female in his image, and Genesis 2:23-24 where Adam and Eve unite in "marriage" to become one flesh. Because a gender binary and heterosexual expression are assumed in this narrative, some conclude that this indicates God's divine design for all creation. But that is only a deduction since the story is not about these matters.

The central message of Genesis 1-2 was that the created world did not consist of gods to be worshipped but that all creation was instead spoken into being by the one true God. Furthermore, humankind was not an afterthought created to serve the whims of childish deities. Rather, the *adam* (human being) was the pinnacle of creation and the only created thing God made in God's image. So that God's creation could be stewarded by God's image through the human, God made them as male (*zachar*) and female (*neqevah*) to multiply and care for all creation. That was the point.

It is also frequently argued that Jesus himself used these two verses from Genesis to confirm that heterosexual marriage was God's intention "from the beginning" (Matthew 19:3-12; Mark 10:1-12). But was that what Jesus intended by citing these verses? The context indicates Jesus was not using these verses to define marriage as heterosexual but to speak about divorce.

Jesus was responding to a question about whether there was any reason for a man to divorce his wife, a privilege that only men, not women, had at that time. The reason Jesus references the passage in Genesis that speaks about God creating them male and female was not to emphasize their heterosexual gender but to show that the two who were made by God are also made one by God (Gen 1:27; Matt 19:4). So, Jesus concludes, what God made into one should not be broken into two by using Moses's law of divorce because "from the beginning it was not so" (Matt 19:8, ESV).

Passages That Are Relevant

The most relevant biblical passages referring to same-sex sex are two verses in Leviticus and one passage in Romans. We'll start with Leviticus.

> You shall not lie with a male as with a woman; it is an abomination. (Lev 18:22, ESV)

> If a man lies with a male as with a woman, both of them have committed an abomination; they shall surely be put to death; their blood is upon them. (Lev 20:13, ESV)

These verses prohibit one man from having sex with another man. The act was referred to as an abomination. The word abomination (*toevah*) is used 117 times throughout the Old Testament for various taboos and offenses. It is used to describe how Egyptians felt when eating with Hebrews (Gen 43:32), to refer to certain kinds of birds that Israelites were forbidden from consuming (Lev 11:13), and to refer to a broad range of sexual practices that Israelites disapproved of (Lev 18:26), to list a few examples.

The word abomination means morally "gross," as in viscerally nauseating or revolting. The taboo is expressed in terms of a common gut reaction and the heterosexual norm. The prohibition against homosexual intercourse is followed by a prohibition against bestiality, which could suggest Israelites thought this form of sexual activity crossed "natural boundaries." This same type of reasoning seems partly responsible for the way Israelites determined which animals they could or could not eat by dividing them into categories and proclaiming them "clean" or "unclean."

The most relevant passages in the New Testament are Rom 1:26-27, 1 Cor 6:9, and 1 Tim 1:10. Since the latter two employ obscure Greek terms for same-sex behavior, I will leave those to my blog and focus here on Romans 1.

> For this reason God gave them up to dishonorable passions. For their women exchanged natural relations for those that are contrary to nature; and the men likewise gave up natural relations with

women and were consumed with passion for one another, men committing shameless acts with men and receiving in themselves the due penalty for their error. (Rom 1:26-27, ESV)

In Romans, Paul describes the Hebraic worldview of the fall of the Gentiles (i.e., idol-worshipping nations). The Gentiles willfully worshipped creation rather than the Creator and, by so doing, twisted nature (1:19-22). As Paul sees it, God therefore released them along the path of un-naturing, and as a result, their bodies un-natured (1:26-27) as did their minds (1:28-32). In other words, the whole person was corrupted away from God's created or natural purpose. Their same-sex desire was more than eros; they were "consumed with passion," a hypersexualized longing.

Yet if a monogamous same-sex couple reads Romans 1:26-27, they will not see their attraction, sexual expression, and commitment reflected there. Same-sex partners love one another the same way heterosexual partners do. Whatever Romans 1 is talking about, it is not this. *Having a same-sex orientation, or having same-sex sex, is not unnatural.*

Has the BIC Been Consistent on This Issue?

I do not think our denomination has been very consistent about the way it understands the role culture plays in the interpretation of Scripture when it comes to this matter. For instance, with respect to the role of women in the church, Paul used Genesis to justify the patriarchal order (1 Tim 2:13,14). The Church Fathers also wrote about women in ways that echoed the inherent patriarchy found in the Bible. And the predominant view of much of today's worldwide church reflects the same. Yet our denomination rightly argues that cultural considerations must be taken into account when interpreting verses that seem to restrict women from ministry. We are not bound by the patriarchal culture in which these texts were forged. Instead, we encourage and affirm women in ministry.

Yet when it comes to same-sex marriage, the BIC Church seems to neglect the role culture plays in interpreting these passages. It seems to take these texts as being prescriptive for sexual ethics today without considering their cultural context and meaning. Some might believe this is appropriate since there is a preponderance of biblical passages to support egalitarian understandings of women in ministry, while there is nothing like that for affirming same-sex relationships. But it would be unreasonable to expect to find explicit biblical affirmations of same-sex relationships given the time period in which these texts were written. In ancient times, as today, women made up roughly half of the population. This assured their representation in biblical narratives. On the other hand, non-heterosexuals likely represented less than five percent of the population. It is unsurprising that they do not feature largely in the biblical story.

Our current theology and practice are also inconsistent in another matter. We are heterosexually biased, at best, and hypocritical, at worst, when it comes to heterosexual "adultery." Importantly, the passage that some use to claim Jesus' exclusive support for heterosexual marriage (Matt 19:1-9) also states that those who remarry commit adultery. For over a century, our denomination taught, and still teaches, that remarriage after divorce is adultery. The Brethren in Christ went from not granting membership to granting association but not membership to finally opening membership at General Conference in 1974 to persons who remarry. Remarried divorcees are also allowed ministerial credentialing, and they can perform marriages of divorcees. Furthermore, pastors are not decredentialed if they disagree with the denomination's theology that divorce and remarriage is sin. But this is not the case when it comes to same-sex relationships. Even if pastors are willing to abide by the church's policy in this regard, those who do not agree with the church's position about same-sex marriage have been—and will be—decredentialed on the basis of their beliefs alone. This is inconsistent.

To be clear, I do not fault our denomination's practices surrounding the treatment of those who have divorced and remarried. We have followed Jesus as a community over this. We understand that it does not work to have second-class citizens in terms of membership. Moreover, and most of all, we have seen God's grace and fruit in our sisters and brothers who have remarried, and we affirm the Holy Spirit's witness in them. In the same way, we should not have second-class citizens when it comes to same-sex couples who are committed to following Jesus and serving the church.

Maybe you think Jesus is saying that remarried divorcees live in adultery. And maybe you believe same-sex couples miss the mark if they marry rather than remain celibate. Or perhaps, like me, you may think there is more to what Jesus is saying about divorce and remarriage than what some understand, and you may believe that same-sex marriage is not a sin in God's eyes. Either way, we cannot deny the plain truth that many remarried divorcees and married same-sex couples exhibit the fullness, sanctification, and graces of God's Spirit. That, in and of itself, would seem to indicate that God has settled the matter.

God's Spirit teaches us what is true and right. God's Spirit reveals that age-old Bible prohibitions about eating unclean foods and receiving unclean Gentiles into spiritual fellowship are no longer relevant. God's Spirit shows who is clean and who is acceptable by baptizing them with the fruits and gifts of the Spirit. If you are blessed to know saints of God who have been divorced and remarried, and if you have been blessed by the fellowship of same-sex couples full of the fruits of God's Spirit, then "do not call something unclean if God has made it clean" (Acts 10:15, NLT).

George Payne *has worshiped and served in the Brethren in Christ denomination for over thirty years and is currently a member of the Harrisburg BIC congregation.*

Evolving Faith and Revolutionary Love

Kimberly Tucker

*Christian faith is not static but has evolved through
the centuries, and even during our own lifetime,
with revolutionary love as the by-product.*

Our older son told me he was gay the day I moved him out of the dorm after the completion of his freshman year of college. I was devastated, and I was scared. I had been taught by every church that I was ever a part of that being gay was a sin.

Fast forward a few years.

I went to a Wild Goose Festival in 2008, looking for Christians who were kindred spirits in the realm of social and environmental justice. Since my husband had embraced atheism a few years prior, I found myself a "lone ranger" within my own congregation as I attended several protests and marches in Philadelphia, Washington, D.C., and Harrisburg, Pennsylvania against the Keystone XL pipeline, racism, gun violence, and poverty. Though Christian kindred spirits were abundant at Wild Goose, I unfortunately did not develop friendships with anyone.

To my surprise, there were several workshops led by Justin Lee, the founder of The Gay Christian Network (now Q Christian Network). I listened. I watched. And I purchased their instructional video titled *The Bible and Homosexuality: How the Scriptures Changed My Mind*. As I viewed this at home, it quickly became apparent to me that the core problem with the church's stance on queerness was how we interpret Scripture!

Invitation to Conversation

I do not claim to be a theologian, but it seems to me that Scripture can be used to defend or refute any issue you want to defend or refute. For example, Scripture has been used through the ages to defend slavery *and* to defend the abolition of slavery. The Great Commandment soon became my daily guiding Scripture passage.

> "Teacher, which commandment in the law is the greatest?" He said to him, "'You shall love the Lord your God with all your heart, and with all your soul, and with all your mind.' This is the greatest and first commandment. And a second is like it: 'You shall love your neighbor as yourself.' On these two commandments hang all the law and the prophets." (Matt 22:36-40, NRSV)

Loving everyone just makes sense. As Richard Rohr observes, "When we are allowed to name certain individuals as 'bad,' persecution, scapegoating, and violence almost always follow. When we too easily presume that we are one of the 'good' people, we largely live in illusion and prejudice" (https://cac.org/daily-meditations/we-dont-need-to-know-2022-12-04/).

When I look back at my faith journey, I see that my faith has evolved just as other parts of my life have. Who I am today at sixty-five years old is not who I was at twenty-five. At twenty-five, life seemed pretty black and white. There were right answers and wrong answers to life's questions. There was a correct path to follow and an incorrect path to follow. I did the "do list" and didn't understand people who chose the "don't do list."

At sixty-five, life looks very complicated. There are fewer issues that are black and white. Things look gray. What I do know is that I'm a more gracious person. And I am more convinced than ever that the Beatles were right when they sang in 1967, "All you need is love!"

Just as my faith has evolved, I believe our denomination has evolved. A century ago, members of the Brethren in Christ (BIC) Church thought it was sinful to have life insurance, play cards, or allow women to preach during a worship service. Now look at us! Most of us believe that life insurance is a financially responsible thing to do if you have a young family. No one would think twice about playing cards. And the Susquehanna

Conference has a woman bishop who "oversees her husband" and is a pastor in the conference.

This kind of change should not be surprising, and it is certainly not unexpected. As Brian McLaren observes in his book *The Great Spiritual Migration*:

> For centuries, Christianity has presented itself as an "organized religion"—a change-averse institution . . . that protects and promotes a timeless system of beliefs that were handed down fully formed in the past. Yet Christianity's actual history is a story of change and adaptation. We Christians have repeatedly adapted our message, methods, and mission to the contours of our time. What might happen if we understand the core Christian ethos as creative, constructive, and forward-leaning—as an "organizing religion" that challenges all institutions (including its own) to learn, grow, and mature toward a deepening, enduring vision of reconciliation with God, self, neighbor, enemy, and creation? (p. 3)

My evolving faith has led me to revolutionary love. To quote McLaren again:

> By revolutionary love, I mean *love beyond*: love that goes beyond myself to my neighbor, beyond my neighbor to the stranger, alien, other, outcast, and outsider; beyond the outsider to the critic, antagonist, opponent, and enemy; and even beyond the human to my non-human fellow creatures. In short, revolutionary love means loving as God would love: infinitely, graciously, extravagantly. To put it in more mystical terms, it means loving *with* God, letting divine love fill me and flow through me, without discrimination or limit, as an expression of the heart of the lover, not the merit of the beloved, including the correctness of the beloved's beliefs" (*Faith After Doubt*, pp. 116-117, emphasis original).

This is what I believe God wants for everyone as individuals and for the corporate body of Christ—evolving faith leading to revolutionary love!

Invitation to Conversation

The BIC developed Project 250 as a set of five priorities, or objectives, established to guide the denomination as it moves toward its 250th anniversary in 2028. The fifth objective of Project 250 is "growing to reflect the demographic realities of our communities." While this objective specifically focuses on "women and people of color," every community has people who identify as LGBTQ+. If our congregations are to reflect the demographic realities of our communities, then we need to be fully affirming of our LGBTQ+ siblings.

Kimberly Tucker *is a Christ follower whose passion is shalom. She is a nurturer who loves to care for people and the environment. She deeply desires that people live their lives glorifying and worshipping God. Kimberly is also the wife of Paul Tucker, mother of three adult children, and Nana (grandmother) to six grandchildren. She is a member of the Dillsburg BIC Church and works as a pediatric physical therapist.*

Part V
(continued)

Allies Call for Full Inclusion

General Reflections

A Fountainhead of Justice

John Alfred

The author suggests that our Anabaptist heritage and the practice of contemplation can help shrink the gap between the church's current exclusionary practices and the full inclusion of queer people.

The story of my connection to the Brethren in Christ (BIC) began about a year after I was married. My wife and I were drawn to the BIC with a group of friends with whom we shared life-giving Christian community. Almost forty years later, we're still members of this denominational family and of the same church in Riverside, California. When we were exploring the opportunity to join this denomination rooted in Anabaptist Christianity, we read, talked, dreamed, and prayed together about how God might be leading us. As I reflect on the years of my faith journey with the BIC, I'm also led to consider aspects of my personal spiritual life and the intersections between them. One place they interconnect is in my experience with family, friends, and neighbors who are part of the LGBTQ+ community. My intention here is to offer a contemplative perspective that might lead us to a different, inclusive way of seeing other people, one that challenges the institutional exclusions of gay and queer people in the church.

My BIC Journey

In the autumn of 1984, we began meeting as Riverside BIC Church. We sensed that we had embarked on a journey with kindred spirits. Many attributes, convictions, and traditions of BIC life and faith were so compelling to us: sharing life together in Christian community, seeking peace between one another and in the world at large, living simply instead of caving into the surging materialism all around us, and reading Scripture together to listen for how God might be moving in our time and place. These things provided a framework for regular faith and life from the early years until now as we continue on, now as Madison Street Church. By way of our connection with the BIC, we have received so many pragmatic and faith-full channels for expressing love to the wider world through agencies such as Mennonite Central Committee (MCC), Mennonite Disaster Service, and MCC's International Volunteer Exchange Program (IVEP), to name a few.

Our hearts and souls were drawn to various other practices and experiences of faith and spirituality that resonated with the ways we were seeking to follow Christ in daily life. We adopted foot washing as an expression of living into the Jesus way, and we knew we were part of a larger church family that honored, even savored, this manner of following Jesus's example of humble service. We incorporated the basin, towel, and dove logo as a marker of our new direction, and we sought to let it symbolize who the Holy Spirit was making us to be, both individually and corporately. We held regular love feasts to celebrate our faith walk together as we learned to love and care for each other like God cared for us. All this and more shaped us slowly, surely, and deeply in our early years, and it continues to flavor the life of our faith community. The lessons and formative experiences from Anabaptism and our BIC family have aided us through difficulties and joys, and they continue to influence our congregation as we seek to follow Jesus where we live, work, play, raise families, make friends, and serve in Christ's name.

The Value of Contemplation

Along with these influences from the BIC Church, I also found myself being drawn into more contemplative forms of Christian faith. They felt like partners in faith formation. Merriam-Webster's Dictionary defines contemplation as "a concentration on spiritual things as a form of private devotion;"

"a state of mystical awareness of God's being;" "an act of considering with attention." Reading contemplative authors and developing new habits of prayer, silence, meditation, and more surrender to God's presence in all life's moments has led me into deepening glimpses of how much God loves me and everything that God has made. We know from Scripture that God already loves us beyond anything we can imagine or control, and we all may sense, on some level, that the purpose of our lives is accepting, even falling into, that love for which words are never fully adequate. Contemplative faith is simply the ongoing process of waking up, more and more, to God's immeasurable love for us and everyone around us. Contemplation is a posture of expanding our communion with God.

Contemplation is not, however, just for our well-being, though it does lead us in that direction. Theologian Wendy Farley says that contemplation is the fountainhead of justice. She says, "Contemplation is this reawakening of the desire to return, consciously, to what's already the case; God's devoted, zealous love for us. I don't mean we don't do things that are inappropriate, perhaps even quite destructive to one another, but they don't really have to do with God's relationship to us, they only have to do with our relationship to God. What has to be healed is that, our side of the relationship" (Mike Morrell, "Contemplative Prayer, Queer Theology, and Aroma of Beauty with Wendy Farley," January 26, 2022, https://mikemorrell.org/2022/01/contemplative-prayer-queer-theology-and-aroma-of-beauty-with-wendy-farley/). Cultivating a life of falling more fully into the arms of our loving God is part of that healing process. It is also that which may bring us to new understandings of what it means to love God with all our heart, mind, soul, and strength and to love our neighbor as ourselves (see Matt 22:36-40). It is this that transforms us into pathways, or fountainheads, for God's grace and mercy to be at work in the world.

Addressing the Exclusion of LGBTQ+ People from the Church

Today, we find ourselves gripped in a struggle between the institutional exclusion of queer people from the church and God's all-inclusive and pervasive love, pouring unstoppably outward and into all of God's creation. Reflecting on my journey of faith, I'm cognizant of the real relationships I have with family, friends, and neighbors who are queer. These relationships have lasted many years, ranging from acquaintances to dear loved ones. These relationships have not led me to be fearful or self-protective but have encouraged an openness to look for God's presence and work in the places where I was not taught to look for God. It is in this space between the position of the church and the realities of the people I know—people who have been marginalized and hurt by the church's position—that I hear an invitation to use both the Anabaptist faith story and the wells of Christian contemplation to listen and look for God at work.

As a people who were once persecuted, Anabaptists could lead the way in caring for those who are labeled as "outcast" or "other." In doing so, they would be following the example of Jesus, who sought out those people who were pushed to the margins of society, stigmatized, and excluded from full participation in the community. These were the very people Jesus connected with, served, healed, and reunited with God and with those around them. We, too, should follow Christ's example of selfless surrender and care for the well-being of the "other."

Contemplative perspectives and postures are ways of putting ourselves, individually and collectively, in new places where God can cultivate a love within us that doesn't merely "include" gay and queer people but that also may open us to allowing God to teach us through "the other." One specific element of contemplative wisdom I suggest we place into the breach is the idea of liminal space. The Latin word *limin* means threshold. Liminality is the space between things. Contemplative language describes times when we find ourselves in unresolved places, like leaving one room but not quite being in the next one yet. This is uncertain territory for us.

As modern Westerners, we're deeply trained to have calculating minds. We unconsciously pursue certainty, security, control, and comprehension in all our endeavors. Calculating is appropriate for many endeavors, but it is restricting in matters of spirit and soul. When events and circumstances arise in our lives that push the calculating mind to its limits, and we can't enforce or ensure the outcomes we think are right, we experience suffering. We suffer when we cannot fix, control, or understand something. Suffering jolts us into liminal spaces where outcomes are unclear. Richard Rohr describes liminal space this way:

> You've lost . . . one set of certitudes, a clarity that held you together, your boundary and your boundary markers that told you you're right and best and safe and secure and superior; all the things the ego wants. For whatever reason, God in God's grace has been able to take that away from you (Richard Rohr, *How Do We Get Everything to Belong?*, Generic, 2005, compact disc).

Job's trials and Jonah in the belly of the fish are biblical images of liminality. The breach we face in the church is such a liminal space.

One line along which the breach between inclusion and exclusion seems to form is whether we are liberal or conservative. Regardless of where we fall on that spectrum, when we find ourselves in liminal territory, God may be providing a new way of seeing rather than simply leaving us to fall into whatever camp our instincts draw us to. Rohr says:

> You can be an ego-centric conservative and you can be an ego-centric liberal. . . . They're two different hiding places and don't make one natural holiness and don't make the other natural evil or sinfulness. . . . It doesn't address the real problem. . . . What God's work is . . . is to teach people how to stay in liminal space, how to wait there, how to not get rid of the pain until you've learned its lessons. . . . It's always, brothers and sisters, what you do with your pain (Richard Rohr, *How Do We Get Everything to Belong?*, Generic, 2005, compact disc).

There is pain on both sides of the inclusion-exclusion divide. It is painful to feel a threat to your heritage, to traditions and/or to heartfelt convictions about what you believe is normal or right. Likewise, it is deeply damaging to be treated as an outsider, sinner, or deviant for what you can't deny as part of your personhood.

Let us reflect on the streams of our Anabaptist faith, and let us consider the beauty and mystery of God's ineffable love for all of us, as expressed and experienced in the many forms of Christian contemplation. Let us open ourselves more to God's presence and to God's work in us and in everyone we encounter. As we do, may we become participants in all the ways God's unending love can touch and heal the separations experienced in the gap between the inclusion of queer people living out their faith in the common life of our denomination (and the whole church), and the exclusion of them as full, fellow members of the Body of Christ. Even in places of challenge, suffering, and pain, may we see, hear, and act in new ways that bring the healing, forgiving, affirming, and accepting life of Christ into our faith family and beyond. I hope that the touch of God experienced through openness to contemplative perspectives will become a fountainhead of justice in our common life.

John Alfred *works for Habitat for Humanity and is a member of Madison Street Church, a BIC Community in Riverside, California. He loves bicycle riding, reading, time with friends and family, hiking, and other outdoor activities. John leads Madison Street's Taizé worship team and participates regularly in the worship and service life of the church. He and his wife live in Riverside, where they have two adult children and two grandchildren.*

A Last Ditch Letter

Lindsay Barnes

I sent the following letter to the Leadership Council of my church as a plea and demand that a clear stance on LGBTQIA+ people be taken and be done so with urgency.

Contextual Statement

I sent this letter to my church's Leadership Council in August 2020. Yes, it was in the midst of the pandemic, and I received some pushback because of the timing. But when would be better? How long should we neglect to address an issue of equity and justice that, in my opinion, has already been pushed off far too long?

Our family had been attending Madison Street Church, a Brethren in Christ (BIC) congregation in Riverside, California, for a decade, excluding a brief sojourn to the Bay Area. My husband and I had been involved with all parts of congregational life. We helped set up for the service nearly every week. He played in the worship band, and we both served for years on the Leadership Council. Our daughter bounced from lap to lap on Sunday mornings. The church and its congregants were our most frequent and consistent community.

It was with no small amount of trepidation that I sent this letter. But it had reached the point that I felt badgered by my own conscience to insist this issue be meaningfully addressed. I have edited the letter for inclusion in this book, primarily to provide some clarification for those not in this particular congregation and to remove some identifying information to protect people's privacy.

The Letter

Dear Leadership Council,

I am writing this because I hope it will kindle not just discussion, but decision and movement. But if it does not do that, at least I want my decision to be unambiguous.

I love this community. It has been a gift to me and to my family. We have felt welcomed and included from the beginning. We have been celebrated and supported at life milestones. And we are valued for—and encouraged to use—our gifts. So it is increasingly difficult for me to see our church stay silent regarding welcoming and affirming LGBTQIA+ folks.

My husband and I are making a concerted effort to teach our babies to love and value others in all the wild diversity in which humans come, and we don't just talk about that in the context of skin color. We don't know who our kids will grow up to be or to love, and I never want them to feel they can't be their full authentic selves with us or the people with whom we surround them.

Our pastor asked in the sermon a couple weeks ago, "What is the power of welcome in our lives?" Whatever it is, the power is thoroughly undermined if our welcome is predicated on leaving a part of oneself behind in order to be accepted. Lest we congratulate ourselves for being "better" than most Christians by not outright condemning non-cisgender, non-heteronormative people, I think it is telling that, to my knowledge, we have no *out* LGBTQIA+ folks in regular attendance. For me, identifying the difference between "right" and "almost right" is not just the difference between saying "you are beloved" versus "you are beloved insofar as you can conform yourself to fit into this tiny, rigid box." It is rather the difference between "you are beloved" and "you are beloved as long as we don't talk about this significant part of your identity with which we are uncomfortable." "Right vs. almost right" is one of critical nuance, not stark difference.

We say we care about racial justice. However, saying we care about racial justice but failing to acknowledge, accept, and advocate for BIPOC

(Black, Indigenous, people of color) folks who are also LGBTQIA+ is an adventure in missing the point. We say we care about immigration policy. But saying that we care about immigration policy while failing to acknowledge, accept, and advocate for those who come here because they face persecution in their home country *because* they are LGBTQIA+, particularly folks who are transgender, is an adventure in missing the point. We say we care about unhoused people. However, saying we care about unhoused people but failing to acknowledge, accept, and advocate for LGBTQIA+ youth, who comprise as much as 40% of youth experiencing homelessness, is an adventure in missing the point. Can we in good faith really call ourselves a peace and justice church if we ignore or exclude the most marginalized individuals in communities that are already systemically denied peace and justice?

Additionally, potential queer congregants deserve to know where this church stands. It should not require asking someone, or attending for months, to determine a congregation's belief about the whole humanity of a person; it should be crystal clear.

All this is to say that if the conclusion of the congregation is to align with the current BIC position, then I feel obligated to no longer support and participate in this church. If the main concern is that taking an affirming position would risk our meeting house, I would ask us to look seriously at the message that concern sends of valuing property over people. Because of the structure of the BIC, we've been told that our meeting house and property legally belongs to the denomination (a required arrangement if a congregation wishes to join the BIC) even though it was literally built by founding members and obviously paid for by the congregation. Taking an affirmative position would risk the BIC kicking out the congregation and keeping the property, thereby losing the thirty plus years of investment that church members have poured into the space.

I appreciate that either decision has significant repercussions, and these can feel hard to face. But as with matters of racial justice, we have long since reached the point wherein silence is complicity with oppression.

I write this with great angst. We literally moved back to this city, rather than closer to my husband's work, to be near this faith community. Contemplating no longer being a part of this church body breaks my heart.

At the same time, I cannot abide the personal hypocrisy that it would be to categorically align myself with an organization if it adheres to a position so in opposition to my core values.

With love and hope,
Lindsay

Concluding Note

My family and I stopped attending Madison Street Church after well over a year of discussion on this topic resulted in no discernible movement by the church as a whole toward full inclusion.

Lindsay Barnes *is a former member (and current friend) of Madison Street Church, a BIC church in southern California where she attended and served for more than a decade. She is an avid gardener, baker, cook, and reader. She is a stay-at-home, homeschooling parent and jokes that the only thing she's currently using her Political Science degrees for is a slightly better understanding of the news. Lindsay lives in Riverside, California, with her spouse, two young kiddos, a geriatric dog, two enormous rescue pups, and an undisclosed number of chickens.*

Let's Join LGBTQ+ Christians on a Journey toward Holiness

Susan Felix

Since Jesus came to remove barriers, we should do likewise, removing all obstacles that keep LGBTQ+ people from being fully included in the life of the church.

We are called to love one another. We are people made in God's image, deserving of respect and kindness. We are more alike than different, yet each one has a unique set of characteristics and traits. Lesbian, gay, bisexual, transgender, and queer people are all God's creations, and all of God's creations are good.

Few people like to be identified as a single characteristic and put in a box. Yet this is what has been done to LGBTQ+ people. LGBTQ+ people are human beings loved by God. If a person has accepted Jesus and asked for forgiveness of sins, who decides their level of participation in a local congregation? May they be baptized? May they partake in communion? May they serve communion? May they be part of, or lead a Bible study group? May they join the choir or worship team? May they join the local church? Are there restrictions, or should there be, on who holds leadership positions within the church? Today, LGBTQ+ Christians in same-sex relationships are being denied membership and certain leadership roles in the Brethren in Christ (BIC) Church.

Church politics make it difficult to know how to proceed without being divisive and hurtful. What is acceptable and what is not? There are factors to consider on the congregational, regional conference, and denominational levels. From where does change come? Does policy change from the top level down or from the local level up? Or is it perhaps some combination of these? Who is free to interpret policy? Who has the authority to initiate change? It is difficult to change policy when there are strong feelings on multiple sides.

All this calls for difficult conversation. But if we are going to be a peace church, we need to talk. Passivity and inaction will not resolve our disagreements. Our words can communicate love and care for one another and a desire to confront challenging topics. If we can find ways to talk about the hard stuff, it is more likely that others will be more open to joining us on the journey to becoming more like Jesus.

There is no evidence of Jesus speaking against same-sex relationships. Yet, we do have examples of Jesus loving those whom other people despised. He warned us against judging people too quickly. Jesus did not reject people. He loved and continues to love all people. Jesus wants to remove barriers people sometimes erect due to gender, class, disability, ethnicity, etc. Let us not be a stumbling block.

Once we have been forgiven, we embark on a lifelong journey to become more Christ-like. Ideally, members of the church community help and support one another on this journey. Jesus calls us to love, not divide; to accept, not reject. Where do we find common ground? In our common goal to become more like Jesus.

The T for transgender in LGBTQ+ is a bit different since it is not about sexual orientation. Rather, it is about gender identity, about who a person is on a gender spectrum. It isn't about *wanting* to be another gender. It is about wanting to be seen as the correct gender, the gender they already know themselves to be. The majority of trans people do not have an "agenda." They simply want to be true to themselves, not to someone else's idea of who they should be and how they should act.

Being a parent of a trans woman has helped me be more accepting of others not like me. I've been doing some reading to better understand those who identify as trans by learning from transgender authors and gender studies. I attended a gender diversity conference to meet others. I hear conversations differently because I know more trans people. I've moved from theoretical to personal acceptance. A person's character does not change because a different gender is expressed. Sometimes, you won't know someone is a trans person unless they tell you.

I was pleased with the progress our country was making toward accepting LGBTQ+ people. Rights, privileges, and freedom from discrimination were being granted. Lately, there has been regression based on fear.

If we say we accept all children in our midst, do we continue to love them when they tell us that the gender they were assigned at birth is wrong or that they are gay, lesbian, bisexual, questioning, or queer? Are they still welcome in our midst? Does the congregation disown them or continue to love and accept them as they grow to adulthood?

I have much respect for the BIC and our stand on discipleship, personal growth toward holiness, and working toward peace even when it's hard. All of us are people made in God's image and loved by God. We can love those whom the world has rejected. Therefore, I am advocating change: to accept LGBTQ+ Christians as fellow humans on a journey toward holiness. Let's allow all Christians to serve in the church, sharing gifts and talents. I'm opposed to singling out certain kinds of people or denying them membership. We are all on a journey to become more Christ-like.

Let's invite people to come into a welcoming space where we can speak with respect and listen to one another's point of view. Let's walk together in becoming more like Christ. Let's use the Bible as a guide for how God wants us to live, not as a weapon to beat or judge others. Let's use it to draw other people to Jesus. And when we do talk together, as we should, let our language be seasoned with grace.

Susan Felix *is a physical therapist assistant living in central Pennsylvania. She and her husband are parents of a trans woman. Susan enjoys reading and doing word, number, and jigsaw puzzles.*

I Wish the BIC Church Offered Unconditional Love to Queer People

Wanda L. Heise

Following the example of Jesus, the church should welcome and embrace all people, especially members of the LGBTQ+ community who are far too often held at arm's length by other Christians.

I realize I've lived a long time. I am reflecting on a lifetime of living within the Brethren in Christ (BIC) denomination and culture where I was born and raised. One thing I have learned to appreciate is that the patriarchy and legalism of the church I was born into have begun to change. Other things have changed as well. Society has changed. Our medical and scientific understandings of the world have changed. Our climate has changed. The economics of the world have changed. Some of the changes have improved our world; others have made life more difficult for many people.

But God has not changed. In the Bible, Jesus often surprised those around Him—changing water into wine, going to the home of a reviled tax collector, and healing a paralyzed man brought to him through the roof of a house. I especially like the story about Jesus talking to the woman at the well who, in addition to being a woman, was a Samaritan. Shocking in that culture! He was not surprised or stymied by the cultural conditions of His day.

Over the years, I have watched the church wrestle with several societal issues. Some have touched my life directly, others indirectly. As a young girl, my service opportunities in the church were limited even though I grew up in a pastor's family. Music and children's ministries were open to me. And though I participated by becoming an organist, that didn't feel fulfilling to me during my early years. I always enjoyed organizational issues and the many conversations and meetings that were involved. But both our society and our church gave men that responsibility—until more recently. Sometimes, we confuse cultural norms with biblical directives and perhaps miss the main thing—being available to love as Jesus loved.

My uncle and aunt divorced many years ago. They were both Christians in an era where divorce separated people from the church. My uncle was a quiet and gifted man who desired to live a godly life. His dream of doing missions by using his gifts in radio ministry was thwarted as he raised his children. Only after the church allowed divorce and remarriage—through the General Conference discernment process—did my uncle feel restored in the eyes of the church and free to marry a gifted single woman who had served as a missionary for many years. Although years after the initial pain, I believe that God creatively brought these two individuals together through the church. Most of us, at the time of the divorce, could not have imagined how my uncle's life would be redeemed.

Our church has seen fit to study divisive issues carefully. With the Holy Spirit's leading, the church has tried to discern the will of God for our community of believers. But many of our congregants have lived in pain. Some felt judged and left the church, resulting in exclusion from the fellowship that God created to guard and grow us. As these precious children of our heavenly Father have left the church, I, too, have been hurt. Some were family and friends. Others were seeking the support and community that we enjoy as a fellowship of believers. When God wants to draw all of us to Himself, how could we do less? How could we believe that we know better?

One of the current issues our society is struggling with is how to view people who are gender nonconforming or whose gender identity differs from the sex they were assigned at birth. During my professional career in the field of medicine and psychology, I have come to understand the world in non-binary ways, to view people along a spectrum. Much of our world is not black and white. Much of what we know about each other fades from the extremes toward the middle and back again over much time. Introverts and extroverts are examples. Many lives vary on a continuum when trying to define exactly who they are on this spectrum. Girls and boys are called names if they don't exhibit the characteristics that *society* has defined as feminine or masculine. This fails to take into account their unique preferences and personalities. There are girls who like to go hunting and boys who like to stay at home and read. We are different in so many ways.

I have also become aware of genetic and medical differences throughout God's creation. There are many people with a genetic makeup that the medical world has defined as aberrant in the past. Only recently have we begun to understand that some of those differences, such as those on the autism spectrum, represent a different way of perceiving our world. We need to learn to understand them as they teach us about their strengths and experiences.

My husband and I have a Christian friend on the autism spectrum who understands street people and others with differences more clearly than I do. He responds differently to them and, I believe, is often more Christ-like toward them than I am. I wrestle with the decisions that he makes that seem naïve and unwise. And yet, the Lord takes care of him over and over again as he shares his apartment with a street person and tolerates a neighbor with mental illness whose cries often don't allow him to sleep.

There are people whose physical and genetic makeups, experiences (some traumatic), and social and emotional worlds do not permit them to be defined in a binary way as male or female, as these terms have been traditionally understood. I wish Jesus was here to address these issues today. But we are here for this time and in this society. God has placed us here.

I watched a gay childhood friend of our daughters marry his male partner and adopt two daughters. They are Christians and have found a church that accepts them. They are responsibly giving a home and a Christian upbringing to these young ladies who come from unknown circumstances. They are teaching them about the love of Jesus through the church. I bless them for that.

Over the past five years, I have been part of the Court Appointed Special Advocate (CASA) program in Dauphin County, Pennsylvania, where I used to live. CASAs are assigned children to follow through the Children and Youth Court system. Often, the children in this system have been abused, neglected, or traumatized. Most are removed from their biological homes, either temporarily or permanently, if an adoptive home can be found. There is a constant shortage of foster homes and adoptive homes. These children need long-term love, safety, and security to heal and grow into loving adults. Working as a CASA, I've found there is little that can be done other than to support them in the broken social service system through their many home moves and in schools that are understaffed, underfunded, and unprepared to provide desperately needed mental health care.

One of the moments that touched me was when a family cousin and his male partner stepped forward and provided a home and family for five children who were siblings. These five children became part of a home with stability, pets, love, and older siblings who were themselves adopted. *What made me sad was the fact that I didn't feel like I could invite them to my church.* I knew that this family could have benefited from the love and support of our church community, but I didn't feel they would be accepted because the parents were gay. I don't know if they were Christians, but they certainly could have experienced the love of Jesus if the church had welcomed them, embraced them, and supported them as they raised their children.

I also grieve that I cannot offer the unconditional love and acceptance of my church to my Christian sister, who married her female partner and gave up her gifted teaching role in the church's English Language Learning program. She believed that she would not be accepted there anymore.

Why have we, as a church body, found it so hard to understand that Jesus' words about loving others and his example of ministering to those who were marginalized by society are for this time and place? I believe that the lessons we learn throughout the Bible about God's generosity, His faithfulness, and His desire that we embody His Spirit should govern the way we treat others. As a church body, shouldn't we be the ones inviting into our midst people whom society considers unworthy or different?

I watched a young lesbian couple attend our church for a period of time. They appeared to be open and eager to get to know us as believers in Christ, just like they were. And slowly, over time, they quit coming. Is this the way the Lord wants us to minister to young couples trying to make their way in our complicated world? Many heterosexual couples are choosing to live together without getting married. Yet it seems easier to accept them into our fellowship than to accept those of the gay community. Who am I to know what works God will perform, who He will draw to Himself through the gay community if we are faithful?

I pray that we wrestle well and err on the side of love instead of condemnation. May the Holy Spirit guide us.

Wanda L. Heise *is retired from the fields of clinical psychology and nursing. She served as Director of Social Services at Paxton Ministries and as administrative pastor of the Harrisburg BIC Church, where she has served in many roles for over fifty years. She has also served on the Board of Directors in the Atlantic Conference where she was the first woman elected to serve as Atlantic Regional Conference Secretary. She later served on the General Conference Board and became its Chair. Wanda currently serves Paxton Ministries on the board and as a volunteer. She enjoys teaching knitting to third, fourth, and fifth graders at St. Stephen's School and recently completed five years of service as part of the first class of Dauphin County Court Appointed Special Advocates (CASA). After living in Harrisburg, Pennsylvania, for over fifty years, Wanda moved to Messiah Village with her husband, Glen, and two cats, Molly and Leo. Her two daughters and their families are currently serving overseas.*

The Tent Is Getting Smaller—
Let's Enlarge It!

Vernon Hyndman

Historically, the BIC have found ways to stay together in the face of disagreement and should continue to do so, given differences of opinion about the inclusion of LGBTQ+ individuals into the life and leadership of the church.

A Problem

Atrocious abuses have been perpetrated against LGBTQ+ people in the United States (and around the world). The church has often been complicit in its silence, if not proactively supportive, of the abuse. Christians have stood by while our justice system has prosecuted and jailed LGBTQ+ people simply for being queer. Mathematics genius and World War II hero Alan Turing, who cracked the enigma machine and is considered by some to be the father of computer science, was prosecuted and chemically castrated for being gay. During the AIDS crisis of the 1980s, gays were blamed for the disease, and AIDS victims died alone because hospitals did not allow their partners to be with them since they were not considered "family." In 1988, when Matthew Shepard was beaten and left to freeze to death against a split-rail fence in Laramie, Wyoming, the silence from the church was deafening.

This essay explores how the Brethren in Christ (BIC) Church has related to the LGBTQ+ community and then offers a metaphor for a way forward, one that avoids some of the fracturing that is already occurring. Hopefully, by using a new model of staying in relationship with one another despite disagreements, our current connections can be strengthened and maintained, and we can all offer and receive the resulting gifts of the Spirit.

The Need for Inclusion

The abundant life is found in surrender, in offering our lives to Jesus, and in trusting Jesus to make the kind of changes in us that are necessary to follow him faithfully. We cisgender, heterosexual Christians make a huge leap when we assume that change means Jesus will make people look and behave more like *us* instead of understanding that the goal of transformation is to make all of us look and behave more like Jesus. We need LGBTQ+ pastors, leaders, and members among us to clarify and correct unverified assumptions about the queer community, assumptions that denigrate and harm the LGBTQ+ community. We need LGBTQ+ folks who are actively and broadly involved in decision-making in our churches in order to counter the marginalization of this group. We need BIC leadership to educate church pastors, giving their very best efforts to equip pastors and other church leaders to help congregants discern God's ways and challenge misinformation as they consider issues of sexuality.

If we desire healthy, viable faith communities, we cannot exclude an entire group of people from full church membership. It is wrong to encourage LGBTQ+ people to participate in a church community only to have them discover that they will always exist in a sequestered ghetto of sorts, prohibited from certain leadership roles, and unable to fully exercise the gifts that the Spirit of God has given them. We must work toward full inclusion of LGBTQ+ people in the life of the church. We must change.

Maintaining Relationship

In the BIC, issues have often fallen along conservative and progressive lines, reflecting our politicized American culture. We have wrestled with issues like women in leadership/ministry and the ordination of divorced people, and we have come to accept new understandings. For many years, however, when these issues were controversial and under discussion, the BIC stance remained unchanged as conservative members practiced a strategy of "sandbagging." By kicking the can down the road, avoiding resolution, and claiming that the issue was in process, everyone knew that the conservative cohort could prevail indefinitely simply by thwarting a decision. When sandbagging is employed in a group or organization, advocates of change experience pain and exhaustion. Eventually, they may leave the group or organization. This results in further bias of the discussion and often in eventual consensus by attrition.

Instead of repeating mistakes that the BIC U.S. has made over controversial issues in the past, how might we learn from those mistakes when it comes to the treatment of LGBTQ+ people? Instead of sandbagging, could we consider broadening our policies? Could we allow churches that have more fully inclusive views—and that desire freedom to practice them—to stay within the BIC denomination right alongside churches with more conservative views and practices, all the while trusting the Spirit to move in our midst as we continue to discern ways forward together as a family of churches?

After his crucifixion and before his ascension, Jesus promised that the Spirit would empower our transformation and would be our indwelling counselor. How many relationships could be spared and church splits be avoided if we would trust that the Spirit is actively counseling and is powerfully performing the work of transformation within our broad and diverse BIC family of faith? Could we remain in relationship and trust that the Spirit might have different priorities than our own particular concerns? Might gifts of the Spirit manifest themselves within our BIC family of churches in the tension of remaining in healthy relationship while holding different views on this issue as we trust the Spirit to finish the work begun and to guide us as we move forward together?

The Tent is Getting Smaller

The BIC has always had a big tent in which pastors from different theological traditions (e.g., Reformed and Charismatic) could labor alongside one another and enjoy the fruits of encountering differing perspectives of what may otherwise be mutually exclusive belief systems. But the BIC tent is getting smaller. Lately, I've noticed within the BIC a move to tighten up beliefs and build greater conformity. In what once was a confluence of Wesleyan, Anabaptist, and Pietist roots, the American manifestation of Evangelicalism has infected the BIC, demanding conformity to Christian nationalism, under-the-radar white supremacy, suppression of women in pastoral leadership, and homophobia.

Consider how the American Evangelical stance against women in ministry, a stance based on a flat, literal reading of Scripture, might be related to the current stance on LGBTQ+ people in ministry. The first Christian evangelist, Anna, was a woman who witnessed the circumcision of eight-day-old Jesus and "spoke about the child to all who were looking forward to the redemption of Jerusalem" (Luke 2:38, NIV). The second Christian evangelist was the Samaritan woman at the well. Upon hearing her own story through the voice of grace, she believed and subsequently converted her whole town (John 4:1-42). There was no church hierarchy to silence her. She preached to her constituency because they knew her previously, and they beheld her now. The ripples of the Spirit in her life changed their lives, too, and they believed.

Given the respect afforded these and other women ministers in Scripture and in the early church, it is shocking that, until recent years, BIC polity excluded talented and educated women from pastoral leadership. Unfortunately, a similar exclusion is happening with LGBTQ+ persons in general, and with LGBTQ+ persons who are gifted, potential leaders in particular. By writing off the LGBTQ+ community and not developing LGBTQ+ pastors who can speak to these individuals and identify with them, the BIC is unlikely to be effective in ministry to LGBTQ+ communities. In addition, the LGBTQ+ community has gifts that the wider church will not receive as long as it continues various forms of exclusion and discrimination against these individuals.

A Way Forward: Commitment to Jesus and to One Another

We should remember that in the same way *we* come to Jesus just as we are, people who are different from us come to Jesus just as *they* are. If we are bound together by our mutual commitment to following Jesus, then the BIC tent is wide enough and stable enough to include non-traditional BIC beliefs. If the BIC can maintain space, as it currently does, for pastors who affirm the traditional peace position *and* for those who ascribe to the just war theory, it can maintain a place for pastors who adhere to traditional views of human sexuality *and* for those who affirm the full inclusion of LGBTQ+ people. Jesus was very specific about the topics of peacemaking and enemy love. Yet, we have found a way to be unified despite our differing views on the matter. Certainly, the BIC tent is big enough to include non-traditional beliefs on other issues as well.

I would like to offer the metaphor of a tipi as a new way for BIC churches to stay connected to one another even when we do not see eye-to-eye. A tipi is a tentlike dwelling formed by a covering over lodge poles or spars arranged in a circle. If the circle is small, the tipi will be tall and narrow, and it will be susceptible to being blown over. A strong tipi has spars placed relatively far apart. Across from each spar, there is another spar leaned in direct opposition, creating tension. Unharnessed tension within any system can lead to instability, but the tension of the spars of a tipi is harnessed by being lashed together at the top. Thus, it creates stability for the entire structure. Tension is a good and necessary thing here and in lots of other scenarios. A violin with no tension plays no music. An archer's bow with no tension is a stick and a string.

Bringing the tipi metaphor back to the wide network of BIC U.S. churches, might being bound together with Jesus "at the top" be enough? If we remain bound together in our core commitments to the way of Jesus, we are actually stabilized by the tension. What if we could build relationally strong ties with Jesus and with one another while sometimes being in direct opposition to each other on difficult issues?

Could the BIC accept and respect leadership from a wide variety of people, straight and LGBTQ+, if we saw one another as being securely joined in Christ and bound together in his love? Could we trust that the Spirit would work in the hearts of our brothers and sisters even when we disagree on disputable topics? Instead of sandbagging, could we commit to ongoing relationship with different kinds of people with different kinds of ideas, agreeing to stick together for as long as it takes to wrestle with this issue and discern God's way forward for us? Could the BIC emulate the structural stability created by a tipi's opposing spars by allowing churches with opposing views on LGBTQ+ inclusion to remain bound together securely in commitment to Christ with the BIC tent covering spread wide enough to include us all?

I certainly hope so.

Vernon Hyndman *was a licensed BIC minister who served at Engage Community Church, a BIC church plant, from pre-launch through 2016. He is a pastoral interventionist whose diverse background includes biomedical research in anesthesia, internet entrepreneurship, work with incarcerated heroin addicts, pastoring pastors, writing, and helping people find a way forward in the midst of life's train wrecks. Vernon has an undergraduate degree in engineering, a Masters in Entrepreneurial Ministry from Tabor College, and a DMin in Semiotics from Portland Seminary. Vernon lives in Boiling Springs, Pennsylvania, with Shelley, his wife of thirty-eight years, and with four adult children nearby. Vernon is a frequent visitor to Starbucks with his three-year-old granddaughter.*

Table for Few? Why the BIC Needs to Reconsider LGBTQ+ Inclusion

Jackie Inouye

An LGBTQ+ supporter who was a member of a BIC church explains why she and her husband chose to leave their church and seek one that was affirming.

When I picture heaven, I see a giant table around which we all sit and share a meal. God is our host. Everything God gives us is very good and we are all satisfied. These days, as I consider this picture, it seems that there are some chairs missing from that table. There are hungry people, but they haven't been invited. These are our LGBTQ+ siblings. I truly feel that the church is missing out by excluding them. Although I'm not LGBTQ+, I love and support many who are. At this place in history, where we see so many individuals struggling under the weight of rejection and judgment, it's our job as the church to come alongside and remind them that they are loved and affirmed just as they are and that, yes, we want them at our table.

About a decade ago, after a long-distance move, my husband and I decided to attend a Brethren in Christ (BIC) church for the first time. We were drawn to the BIC's stated commitment to reconciliation and peacemaking as well as to the centrality of Jesus. And we were pleased to see that women with pastoral and teaching skills were freely accepted as leaders in the BIC. There was room here.

Invitation to Conversation

Having grown up in churches where there wasn't a lot of space to ask questions, we were also drawn to this particular church because it seemed like a place where we could explore the questions we were thinking about without being rejected by the community. It also appeared to be a church where people with differing perspectives on certain religious topics (pacifism, baptism, evolution, etc.) could come together under one goal: loving others and patterning our lives after Jesus.

At this point, we were already affirming, although I wouldn't say we were advocates. It was more of a quiet, heart-level support of the LGBTQ+ folks we knew and loved. We watched how many of these people were struggling with the need to hide parts of themselves from society, friends, family, or the church in order to be accepted. It was clear to us that being gay, transgender, etc., was not merely a choice they had made but was something as integral to their identity as eye or skin color. After all, who would choose to bring the judgment of others upon them and, in some cases, compromise their own mental and physical safety in this way? Some of them didn't attend church anymore, not necessarily because they had lost faith, but because they felt unaccepted in that community or rejected by God because of the actions and words of churchgoers.

I joined a discussion group outside of the church (though it was with several other church members) that was centered on the book *Walking the Bridgeless Canyon: Repairing the Breach Between the Church and the LGBT Community* by Kathy Baldock. Part of this book explores the history of how the church has treated LGBTQ+ individuals and examines specific Bible passages used to refute being gay/lesbian/bi. It also considers the origin of many of the misconceptions people have about this group of people, the history of LGBTQ+ rights, and research related to the LGBTQ+ community. It further opened my eyes to their struggle of being rejected for simply wanting the things that we all want—a safe space in which to pursue happy lives, families, and careers. And for LGBTQ+ Christians and those interested in the faith, this struggle also includes the pain of being rejected by a church community that accepted them until it learned they were LGBTQ+ and that told them that all were welcome, only to later place limits on that welcome.

As I read through the book, it was difficult to note that, in many ways, the LGBTQ+ community is still facing the rejection and judgment it did decades ago. It was disheartening to witness the reaction of the church and to admit that the same tradition I have been a part of was contributing to the suffering of individuals by not affirming them.

After considering my personal experience with LGBTQ+ friends, in addition to what I had learned in the book discussion and from further reading I did, I knew I wanted to be a part of a church community that was inclusive, where my friends and family would be fully welcome. It was a difficult decision, but my husband and I decided to leave the church where we had served as members for more than six years.

I like to remain neutral on many things. I want to remain open-minded and not choose sides, to find common ground wherever it can be found and to focus on our commonalities rather than our differences. But I've come to realize that as Christians we are called to stand with the marginalized, as Jesus did. And when we stand, we take a side. I want the church to be a safe place for LGBTQ+ people to be accepted and loved as they are. I want to be part of a community that is actively loving those whom the world treats as less than.

Some Christians I talk with say they would like to be able to affirm those who are LGBTQ+, but they don't feel they can because they think the Bible states that homosexuality is wrong. But many of them have never been exposed to research and scholarship that represents other valid views that are affirming. Many Christians lack knowledge about differing interpretations of the "clobber" passages, a handful of biblical texts used to condemn same-sex expression (Gen 19:1-26; Lev 18:22, 20:13; Rom 1:24-27; 1 Cor 6:9-11; 1 Tim 1:10). Likewise, many Christians believe that it's a "lifestyle" one chooses rather than an identity.

When a person has not had a personal relationship with someone who is LGBTQ+, it's easier to dismiss the concerns of those who identify as such. But as Christians, aren't we called to consider the needs of others and to bear one another's burdens? Feeling rejected by your own faith community is a burden. Not feeling safe in the world because of your identity is a burden. In a sense, these people are our siblings, our spiritual family. How can we look the other way when they are crying out for community? They will find it elsewhere if we do not provide an opportunity in the church.

A recent study from the June 2020 edition of the *Journal for the Scientific Study of Religion* (see pp. 379-396) shows that people who identify as LGBTQ+ are more than twice as likely to leave their faith. Other studies reveal significantly higher rates of suicide among members of the LGBTQ+ community than among the population at large, and religious beliefs are sometimes a contributing factor. People look to the church to understand what God is like. If the church rejects them, they feel God has rejected them. Imagine if the church changed course—much like it did with regard to African Americans during the civil rights era—and took a public stand of acceptance and alignment with those who are LGTBQ+. Might that keep them from leaving the church? Might that save lives otherwise lost to suicide?

Let's remember what a blessing it is to have diversity in the church. When heaven is described as a place where every tongue and tribe and nation belong, surely that implies there is room for other differences: those who are neurodivergent, those who have physical differences, those with various giftings, those who are racially and ethnically diverse, and yes, those who identify as LGBTQ+. Being gay, lesbian, or bisexual isn't just about who a person is attracted to; it's a way of seeing the world. We need that perspective in the body of Christ.

Likewise, those who are trans offer us a unique perspective that goes beyond gender. What is the church missing by excluding these voices? Since leaving my former church, I have been privileged to worship alongside people who are openly LGBTQ+. From them, I have learned about what love, strength, and forgiveness look like. I also feel more comfortable being my authentic self in the presence of people who understand what it's like to have to hide parts of themselves and who want better for all of us.

The more I get to know God, the more I am coming to understand how much God loves variety. Scripture says that God's nature is revealed in creation. We could spend a lifetime studying and discovering all of the plants, creatures, and people that populate our world. I am not a debater or a theologian. But I'm convinced that the way to change the tide is not through reason alone. It's through opening our hearts, listening to the stories of others, and telling our own stories of how Jesus changed us. That's why I'm sharing my story with you.

Jackie Inouye is an editor who was a member of a BIC church in the Dillsburg, Pennsylvania, area and is now attending an inclusive church in Harrisburg. She loves the outdoors, reading, baking, playing piano, and watching sci-fi movies with her husband and two kids.

The BIC Church is Failing the Queer Community (and People Are Leaving)

Dinah Knisely

The BIC Church has the best Core Values. If we live by them, there is hope we can reverse course and stem the loss of more and more people from the denomination.

I love the Core Values of the Brethren in Christ (BIC) Church (bicus.org/about/what-we-believe/core-values). They are what drew me and my husband to the BIC, a group we had never heard of before moving to Pennsylvania in 1996. We have been members of The Meeting House (TMH) Dillsburg (formerly Cumberland Valley BIC) since September 1996.

A little background is helpful to our story. It is important to note up front that the plural "our" is very important to an LGBTQIA+ family since church rejection *never* affects only the queer person. (I will use the term "queer" throughout this essay since it is widely accepted and freely used as an all-encompassing term for the LGBTQIA+ community.) While my husband came from a strong, active faith background, I was not raised in a Christian home. I came to faith in Jesus when I was almost thirty years old. We were blessed with two precious children whom we raised in the church from a very young age. You can often hear me say that "our story could be your story." We did all the "right" things and checked all the boxes.

One of the most difficult features of my journey, was the isolation, fear, and loneliness I experienced early on when I was "concerned" our son might be gay. The very place that I had learned should be the safest for me—the church—was, in reality, the very opposite. I quickly learned that the church was *not* a safe place to share and receive much-needed companionship on my journey of being "out" about my son. When a loved one comes "out," there is a process of "coming out" for close family and friends, as well. Tragically, the church has often abandoned, shamed, and traumatized both queer Christians and their loved ones in this process. In my isolation, I was searching for companions, but I was too terrified to tell anyone.

Our son got married in an attempt to fulfill expectations of the way he was raised. This marriage gave us our three precious grandchildren. During that time, I read a book that I highly recommend to new moms on the journey. The book is *How I Sleep at Night* by Sara Cunningham. Sara's story introduced me to a whole world of very loving people (many of them were Christians) whom I believed existed but just hadn't found. To my amazement *and* the preservation of my faith, I was made aware of a private Facebook group of Christian moms who had queer children. I can barely find words to express the lifeline this group of women was and continues to be in my life.

In addition, I have studied Scripture, read many books, and listened to stories told by countless Christian moms with queer kids and by queer people themselves. I also attended two conferences: The Gay Christian Network (now Q Christian Fellowship) and The Reformation Project.

It was at The Gay Christian Network in 2017 that my path was forever changed. I walked into a large conference room where the majority of attendees were queer. The music had begun, and the worship leader was singing. In that space, the presence of God was palpable. These dear followers were experiencing real *freedom* to worship fully and freely. I was completely overwhelmed. I knew deep in my spirit that the Spirit of the living God was in that place. As I worshiped, wept, and prayed, I knew this was a holy moment in my life.

I have spent the last seven years of my journey working to find common ground for queer people, queer Christians, and the Christian church. A fellow mom and I sat before our church board seeking permission to begin a parent support group. Vulnerably, through tears, we shared our stories. Our request was denied.

So, I stepped out on my own to educate believers who were seeking understanding. I have led three groups of local believers through Kathy Baldock's powerful book, *Walking the Bridgeless Canyon: Repairing the Breach Between the Church and the LGBTQ Community*. In addition to this book, a YouTube video of Baldock teaching is available online. Both are excellent resources, and information about them can be found in the "Additional Resources" section at the end of this book. The research that Baldock put into this book is extensive. Her work, and the work of others like Pastor Stan Mitchell, who left his church in Nashville to minister full-time to families working to come together over this topic, is invaluable to the queer community.

Another important part of our journey has been providing a home for our "bonus daughter." Raised in our church, she was rejected by her parents when she came out as gay. She has lived with us for over four years. We proudly affirm and love her and her partner. She recently graduated from college, and we are so proud of her and the young woman she has become.

There has been no attempt at reconciliation by her parents, yet they continue to attend church regularly. This was the breaking point for us. We no longer attend services in that church. These are some of the real-life consequences these precious kids (and their siblings) experience because our churches are silent.

As I am writing this piece, I have just hosted a gathering of Christian moms with queer children. We *need* each other for the support we have not received in our home fellowships. Collectively, we have served in local BIC churches for *decades*. Now, *all* of us have left our BIC churches. Some have found affirming churches to attend, and some are too wounded and disillusioned to start that journey again. We represent elders, worship leaders, pre-school teachers, and youth leaders. Talented and gifted people are leaving the BIC Church because there is no space for us, for allies, or for our kids there.

I am angry and outraged at how the BIC leadership has been unwilling to begin conversation in local churches around this critical topic. There was a group of TMH members who longed to have open dialogue in the church. We even met with our bishop in my home. Still, no change.

The problem is compounded by the way BIC leaders have treated pastors who are affirming. Several pastors whom I know and greatly respect have stepped up to affirm and love the queer community and allies. The result? They were stripped of their BIC ordination and are no longer welcome in the denomination. All their years of faithful leadership and service were stripped away. It is heartbreaking. Many others in the church have also left, feeling their hands are tied, making it impossible for them to teach and lead as they believe.

The gap between the church's position and the LGBTQIA+ community is growing, and we are losing talented and gifted leaders from the BIC. If there was ever a denomination that should be able to bridge this gap, it most absolutely is the BIC. Many of our Core Values speak directly to why we should be affirming. Consider these:

Belonging to the Community of Faith: We value integrity in relationships and mutual accountability in an atmosphere of grace, love, and acceptance.

Serving Compassionately: We value serving others at their point of need, following the example of our Lord Jesus.

Pursuing Peace: We value all human life and promote forgiveness, understanding, reconciliation, and non-violent resolution of conflict.

Relying on God: We confess our dependence on God for everything, and seek to deepen our intimacy with Him by living prayerfully.

Witnessing to the World: We value an active and loving witness for Christ to all people.

It is true that there are *numerous* theological topics we do not all agree on such as women in leadership, participation in the military, and divorce. Still, we can gather together, covered by the grace of Jesus and with our eyes fixed on him, to serve, love, and minister to all the Lord brings our way.

We must choose unity and use the gifting of everyone to express the love of Jesus to a desperate and hurting world.

I long for the BIC to find common ground and not be like other denominations that have chosen to split. Let's be the denomination that does it right: that lives into the Core Values we profess, that honors and values all life above theology, money, and power, that proves we can love and serve together even when we come to different interpretive conclusions, that creates space for all seekers and believers, that cares about experience and stories, and that moves into the margins after the example of Jesus.

Please listen to those of us being cast aside. Learn of the trauma and isolation we are experiencing because of Christian leadership. Understand that many of our queer kids (and their siblings) who have been raised in our churches are traumatized, wounded, and angered by how things have transpired. Many no longer have any interest in spiritual matters focused on Christ. This should cause us to shudder!

Mine has been a painful journey, yet one I would never choose to undo. My eyes have been opened to a much deeper understanding of love and sacrifice than I have ever known, and my faith is stronger and more meaningful in the freedom I have experienced, surrounded by this new community. It is my conviction that the non-affirming church is the one that really loses in the end. And it breaks my heart.

Dinah Knisely *is a native Arizonan who transplanted to Central Pennsylvania twenty-eight years ago. Married with two children (now adults), the family joined The Meeting House, Dillsburg (formerly Cumberland Valley BIC). Over the years they hosted numerous small groups. Dinah led women's Bible study for over twelve years and served as an elder for five years. Currently an LGBTQ ally, she spends time mentoring women, especially moms of LGBTQ children, and she works with adults with special needs. She enjoys photography and gardening on her deck. She and her now-retired husband enjoy traveling.*

The BIC Church Is in Grave Danger

Andrew Larratt-Smith

The BIC Church U.S. is at a crossroads. Failure to reconsider the church's policies and practices with respect to LGBTQ+ people will have disastrous effects for the denomination.

Consider the following statements:

- It would be sinful for me to become romantically involved with someone of the same sex because, based on what I read in Scripture, it is my understanding that same-sex relationships are outside of God's will.

- The only acceptable belief that any member of our denomination may hold is that it is sinful for anyone to become romantically involved with someone of the same sex because the only faithful reading of Scripture is that same-sex relationships are outside of God's will.

There is a world of difference between these two statements.

To be clear, my concern is with the second statement and not the first. While I no longer personally subscribe to the first statement, I can understand why other Christians do, and I respect the commitment to faithfulness, the desire for personal integrity, and the devotion to Scripture that leads them to this position.

But the second statement, which I believe is implied by the current official position of the Brethren in Christ (BIC) Church, causes me deep concern. This position is expressed in both the *Manual of Doctrine and Government* (*MDG*) and the Accents and Issues paper titled "Human Sexuality." It is also expressed through less formal statements, both written and verbal, from BIC leaders and from other church members. As stated in the *MDG*, "Human sexuality is affirmed within the chaste single life or a lifelong marriage between a man and a woman" (Articles of Faith and Doctrine, Article II: God and Creation: Relationships in Creation). Since these are the only acceptable options according to the BIC, the implication is that all members of the BIC should regard same-sex relationships as sinful (as articulated in the second statement above). I believe this view puts our denomination in grave danger, both structurally and spiritually.

In this essay, I argue that this position (1) is not well-defended logically, (2) decenters Jesus and devalues discipleship, and (3) will lead to denominational turmoil and dysfunction that will likely result in decades of declining membership and a loss in ministry effectiveness.

The Position is Not Well-Defended Logically

First, from a purely logical perspective, the second statement is far harder to defend than the first. Unlike the first statement, it is an exclusive claim, asserting not just that its position is a reasonable position, or even the best position, but that all other differing positions are unreasonable, unfaithful, and unacceptable. This is a high bar, indeed.

But the BIC's condemnation of same-sex relationships tends to focus primarily on justifying the rationality of the first statement without seriously considering alternate perspectives and explaining how they are inadequate. For example, I have seen communication from denominational leadership that has framed the alternative to the denominational position as "embrac[ing] all expressions of human sexuality." This is flatly inaccurate and a bad mischaracterization of alternate viewpoints. It fails to consider the possible (and obvious) position of holding heterosexual and same-sex relationships to the same moral standard. Such a position is a far cry from "embracing all expressions of human sexuality." The inaccurate framing of alternative viewpoints serves as a straw man, which functions to make the denominational position appear as the only realistic option.

Furthermore, same-sex sex is often inappropriately associated with sexual infidelity or other sexual transgressions. For example, the *MDG* states that "the practices of premarital sex, extramarital sex, adultery, lesbianism, or homosexuality have no place in the life in Christ" (Statements of Christian Life and Practice, Article 1.3). This conflates and confuses the issues and promotes spurious, slippery slope arguments. Additionally, it besmirches the integrity of LGBTQ+ believers by playing on the trope of insatiable queer carnality.

To be clear, I don't see all this as necessarily malicious or even deliberate on the part of BIC leadership. I understand that it can be easy to unintentionally downplay or mischaracterize other viewpoints, especially around controversial topics.

However, if we as a denomination are going to boldly declare that there is only one acceptable belief on a particular issue, we have an obligation to acknowledge alternative beliefs and rigorously consider them, ideally with an open mind. This obligation is particularly acute on issues that have enormous implications for the lives of BIC members, such as the ability to marry and raise a family while remaining a part of the denomination.

The Position Decenters Jesus and Devalues Discipleship

Second, a commitment to the second statement decenters Jesus and devalues discipleship. It decenters Jesus by making an issue that Jesus is silent about a litmus test for membership. Yes, same-sex behavior is addressed elsewhere in Scripture. And yes, Jesus speaks of the need for sexual holiness and sexual discipleship.

However, faithful Christians can hold a deep commitment to sexual discipleship while maintaining that other Scriptures do not prohibit same-sex relationships when they are properly understood within their historical and cultural context. Jesus did not make same-sex relationships a litmus test for discipleship. When we do so, we are shifting to other criteria, moving away from Jesus and his words as the guidepost for our faith.

Furthermore, gender and sexuality issues are the heart of a deep political debate that is fracturing America. By centering these concerns as a litmus test for denominational membership, at the expense of centering Jesus, we make ourselves vulnerable to those with political agendas who would seek to gain legitimacy and influence through endorsement from religious authorities.

Additionally, I would argue that a commitment to the second statement actively devalues discipleship. Christian faith is, first and foremost, a commitment to following the person of Jesus. When I pray for my children, my hope is that they come to know and follow Jesus through the twists and turns of their lives, not that they subscribe to a particular set of beliefs and behaviors. When we define "acceptable belief" very narrowly on issues that Jesus is silent about, we discourage people from exercising their discipleship muscles.

Over the years, I have known dozens of LGBTQ+ friends. They have taken a variety of approaches to how they view sexuality. Some are in same-sex marriages. Some have remained celibate. Some strongly identify as queer. Some are deeply private about their sexual orientation. Some are in heterosexual marriages. Some have divorced their spouse because they felt they could not continue in a heterosexual marriage. Some started in heterosexual marriages and remained married to their spouse after they transitioned gender.

The one unifying feature I have seen is that my LGBTQ+ friends who are Jesus followers are some of the most earnest Christians I know, following Jesus in all aspects of their lives, particularly when it comes to their sexuality. Uniformly, I have seen them wrestle deeply with Scripture and what it means for them to follow Jesus. The image that comes to mind is Jacob tenaciously wrestling with a mysterious figure, desperate to get a blessing from God (Gen 32:22-32). And while they have walked away with that blessing, they are often limping from the harm they have received from the church.

I am grateful for the way that LGBTQ+ Jesus-followers have modeled discipleship to me, and I am deeply ashamed to admit that some of the harm they have received has come from me. It is high time that we acknowledge and value this community's commitment to discipleship and learn from them rather than treat them as second-class Christians.

Perhaps the most corrosive way the BIC's position erodes sexual discipleship is by creating a double standard. The Accents and Issues paper on human sexuality echoes the *MDG* by describing only two faithful paths: lifelong celibacy or sex within a marriage relationship between a man and a woman. The paper then lists several commonalities between the two paths: "Both paths are difficult and depend on God's grace, both involve the denial of sexual desires, both are blessed by God, both are designed by God to deepen the involvement of individuals in community, and both allow for a full, satisfying human life." This way of framing things suggests that both options are functionally equivalent when, in reality, most believers strongly prefer the path of marriage and family, an option that is foreclosed to same-sex couples. It also papers over a double-standard in which the exact same behavior celebrated in a heterosexual relationship is decried as sin when practiced by a same-sex couple.

As a quick aside, I have heard several BIC members draw parallels between the BIC position on same-sex relationships and its position on non-violence. I disagree. I don't think this analogy works for several reasons. First, the nonviolence position has not become a litmus test for membership or pastoral leadership since it has not been enforced consistently. Second, it does not entail anywhere near the same level of sacrifice. The denominations' position merely forecloses a career in the military or law enforcement as opposed to denying the possibility of a marriage partner and children. Most significantly, the nonviolence position does not present a double standard in which the exact same behavior is celebrated in one demographic and forbidden for another.

My children and their generation are savvy. They see this double standard. When I was their age, most of my queer friends were closeted and ashamed of their sexuality, struggling to understand themselves in a society that marginalized them. In the midst of my own adolescent self-absorption, I was oblivious to their silent struggle. Not so for my children. Their friends are out, often at an early age, and my children are fiercely loyal on their behalf. They immediately recognize the double standard and its implication for their queer friends' ability to marry and raise children.

As a teenager, I made the decision to wait until marriage to have sex. While being nerdy and introverted certainly helped, it took deep internal conviction about the importance of sexual discipleship for me to reach this goal. I see the double standard eroding this conviction in younger

Invitation to Conversation

generations. When they see a sexual discipleship standard being applied inequitably, they lose their conviction about the value of sexual discipleship. Double standards lead to double lives, where people pay lip service to strict religious regulations in church on Sunday morning but behave differently during the rest of the week.

This Position Invites Turmoil and Dysfunction for the Denomination

Taking an inflexible position on gender and sexuality and making it a litmus test for church membership and ministry is likely to result in chaos for the denomination. Let me count the ways. Livelihoods are at stake for pastors who are financially vulnerable. Property disputes are likely when property ownership is asserted by the denomination even though the property has been financed predominantly by local congregations and their congregants. Denominational leaders will be tempted to leverage these vulnerabilities to gain compliance. This will lead to decisions made on the basis of who has power rather than by thorough discourse of the merits of a particular case. It will drive out dissenters or force them to go underground lest they experience disciplinary actions or other forms of retribution. It will produce sloppy reasoning because there is no "iron sharpening iron." This will poison the culture and the climate of the denomination.

These dynamics are further exacerbated by the fact that there are no well-designed off-ramps for congregants and congregations. The *MDG* is vague about the process of disaffiliation. These seeds of discontent are already sprouting. I can point to multiple specific examples where the dynamics I describe above are already playing out.

And there is no end in sight. Even if all the dissenters leave the BIC, the issue will come up repeatedly. Why? Because it is the lives of loved ones that are at stake: our friends, our family members, and our children.

Where To From Here?

We are at a crossroads as a denomination. Are we willing to acknowledge that our position is not well-defended logically, decenters Jesus and devalues discipleship, and will lead to denomination turmoil and dysfunction?

What is important to us? Do we want following Jesus to be the central focus of our faith? Do we want to encourage responsible sexual discipleship born out of internal convictions? If so, then we need to provide enough latitude to church members to faithfully work through these challenging issues related to sexual orientation and gender identity.

But if we continue to make conformity to the current BIC policy on human sexuality the litmus test for church membership, we are stating that what we value most is uniformity of belief on an issue that Jesus was silent about. In so doing, we are putting the church in grave danger and are setting ourselves up for unnecessary turmoil that can, and should, be avoided.

Andrew Larratt-Smith *is an active member of Madison Street Church. He serves in the field of conflict engagement as an ombuds in higher education and previously served in campus ministry with Intervarsity. Andrew holds a Juris Doctor with a specialization in Critical Race Studies and a Master of Dispute Resolution. He lives in Riverside, California, with his spouse, Jen and their two children. Andrew is a proud Canadian and a board game enthusiast.*

The Gift of God is Available to Everyone

Christine Martin

*Since God's love is given to all people without
exception, we should extend that same love to all people,
including those who identify as LGBTQ+.*

Five decades ago, when I was fifteen years old, I heard John 10:10 for the first time and was so moved by these words of Jesus: "I came that they may have life, and have it abundantly" (RSV). The love and generosity expressed by Jesus reached deep into my heart, assuring me that God was good and loving and that he wanted people to experience life with him in a full and beautiful way. Although I had been to church on and off throughout my childhood, this message had never reached me. Once it did, I waded into this new and rich life with God until I was fully immersed.

Throughout high school, I went to a weekly Bible study, a nondenominational youth group, and a Christian summer camp. I had my struggles and doubts, yet the path of following Jesus, which included receiving and sharing God's love and presence, drew me in and was life-giving for me. In college, I continued to meet with the youth group as a youth leader, sharing the good news and the love of God with adolescents.

It was as a youth counselor that I first came to know a person who identified as being queer. Theresa (not her real name) was a delightful teen, full of energy, eager to learn, and fun to be around. And she carried a secret that threatened to tear her apart. Theresa had been coming to Bible study and youth group for about a year when, full of emotion and distress, she shared with me that she was gay. I was surprised and, at first, unsure how to respond. Soon, words of comfort and assurance flowed from my mouth as I told her that her sexual orientation did not change the reality of God's love—or my love—for her. She continued to be involved in the youth group, learning and growing in faith. A couple of years later, Theresa moved away. Sadly, I lost track of her. I deeply hope her faith and love for God continued to flourish as she became an adult and had to face the condemnation, meanness, hatred, and lies that have been poured out upon the LGBTQ+ population by many people, including those within the church.

A few years later, when a group of friends and I were seeking to live life together as a church that would intentionally and faithfully follow the ways of Jesus, we discovered the Brethren in Christ (BIC) Church. The values of the BIC seemed to coincide with who we desired to be: Jesus-centered people who lived simply, communally sharing the mercy, compassion, and generosity of God with others and building the kingdom of God here and now. We were warmly welcomed by Don Shafer, who was then bishop of the Pacific Conference. We felt at home with the denomination and founded the Riverside Brethren in Christ Church (RBIC) in the 1980s.

During those early years, I have no memory of conversations about the LGBTQ+ community in RBIC. I wonder if we were unaware of the need to talk about this, or perhaps we were unwilling to examine our own thoughts and beliefs about sexual orientation and gender identity. I'm sorry to admit that, as a congregation, we've been slow to respond to the injustices and the terrible treatment of the LGBTQ+ population.

In the last few years, questions and concerns raised by a number of people in our congregation have prompted long and deep discussions about how to be faithful and loving when relating to people in the LGBTQ+ community. The people of Madison Street Church (formerly RBIC) have studied Scripture, read books, listened to podcasts, and had long and challenging conversations about these matters, which have allowed the Holy Spirit to guide and move us. While I appreciate all the core values covered in *Focusing Our Faith: Brethren in Christ Core Values*, I think the second one, which relates to the Bible, has special importance for us as we grapple with the issues of human sexuality: "We value the Bible as God's authoritative Word, study it together, and build our lives on its truth." Consider some of these statements found in the chapter on "Believing the Bible" written by John Yeatts, which describes this core value:

- Christians should interpret the Bible together, listening to the insights of others and being held accountable by fellow interpreters (p. 36).
- Christians should diligently interpret Scripture with the tools that biblical scholarship has provided, but be careful in the process to treat the text with respect and integrity (p. 37).
- The Bible's meaning is best interpreted by the gathered community opening it together and reading through the lens of Christ (p. 39).

There is great value in reading and studying Scripture together, listening for the Holy Spirit in the insights of others, interpreting Scripture using the tools that biblical scholarship has provided, and cultivating an understanding of the culture and people being addressed.

As we try to discern God's will regarding issues of sexuality, part of our job will involve reexamining a handful of passages that address same-sex acts in the Bible: Gen 19:4-5; Lev 18:22; 20:13; Rom 1:26-28; 1 Cor 6:9-11; 1 Tim 1:8-11. Rather than simply reading these passages literally, with our minds biased toward non-inclusion, we must come together, under the guidance of the Holy Spirit, to examine them honestly, lovingly, and carefully. As we do, it is helpful to avoid being unduly bound by traditional interpretations as we consider some of the difficulties of translation, their historical and cultural contexts, authorial intent, and other passages in the Bible that shed light on this subject. (For an approach to these passages that challenges the way they have traditionally been interpreted, see *God and the Gay Christian*, by Matthew Vines, and *Unclobber*, by Colby Martin.)

In order to interpret the Bible well, I would encourage the Christian community to read Scripture with certain questions in mind. For example:

Invitation to Conversation

- *How do we read the Bible?*

  Do we read with an "Innocent/Literal" perspective, accepting the Bible without question as authoritative and objective and favoring factual meanings? Or do we read from an "Integral/Literary" perspective, valuing the Bible as a multilayered and complex whole and as a potential source of wisdom and guidance for individuals and groups today? (For these categories and other ways of reading the Bible, see Brian McLaren, *The Great Spiritual Migration*, chapter 6.)

- *Is there inadequate information to make a conclusive decision?*

  If not, we need to broaden our scope to see what the overall message of Scripture tells us.

- *What aspects of this passage are only relevant to its cultural and historical context, and what aspects are essential for all humanity in every time and culture?*

  For example, the story of the destruction of Sodom and Gomorrah in Genesis 19 has often been viewed as an example of God punishing people because of their "homosexual" behavior. As the story goes, two visitors show up at the gates of Sodom, and Lot invites them into his home for food and lodging. All the men of the city come knocking at Lot's door, demanding to have sex with them. Here are some questions that could be used to tease out what is cultural versus what is timeless:

  Could every man in the city be gay?

  No.

  Is this a request to have a loving, mutual relationship with the visitors?

  No.

  What do the men of the city really want?

  To assert their dominance and power over the outsiders by gang raping, humiliating, and dishonoring them.

Therefore, does this passage give us any insight into how God wants us to approach loving, mutual same-sex relationships?

No.

Part of the challenge of using the Bible to address questions about same-sex relationships is the simple fact that the Bible says nothing about sexual orientation. Neither does it make any conclusive statements about gender identity. Although the Bible clearly condemns some same-sex behaviors—acts that are viewed as exploitive, violent, and degrading, such as gang rape and pederasty—it says nothing about faithful, covenantal same-sex relationships. Moreover, if we look at the question of whether sexuality derives from nature or nurture, we need to investigate and discuss current scientific evidence. Such information was not available to the biblical writers. In light of all this, it is possible to read the Scriptures and conclude that the concerns that individuals raise about LGBTQ+ people are disputable. Therefore, it seems our best course of action is to follow Jesus' way of love. We must welcome, accept, and fully include all people regardless of their sexual orientation and gender identity. (See *A Letter to my Congregation: An Evangelical Pastor's Path to Embracing People Who Are Gay, Lesbian, Bisexual, and Transgender into the Company of Jesus* by Ken Wilson.)

Because of what I've learned through study and experience with LGBTQ+ friends, I am deeply concerned about the BIC's rejection of same-sex marriage and its requirement that LGBTQ+ Christians remain abstinent. I see marriage as a beautiful and sacred relationship that God can use in the lives of two faithful people to bring about spiritual growth and transformation. If a same-sex couple wants to make the commitment to love and work for a union that will be used by God, that is a good thing. I'd like to be in a fellowship and denomination that will support that kind of commitment and will celebrate LGBTQ+ marriage.

The restrictive policy maintained by the BIC draws a line that I doubt Jesus would draw. Jesus' love was remarkable in its law-breaking, inclusive nature. Jesus was incredibly loving and inclusive, especially with people who were considered unacceptable and who were marginalized in the culture of his day. It seems that Jesus' boundaries were marked by whether or not a person desired to follow him and attempted to do so. The question Christians should be asking people is, "Do you want to try to follow Jesus with us?" This is, after all, what it means to be a disciple. As Robert Mulholland writes in his book *Invitation to a Journey*:

> Spiritual formation is a process of being formed in the image of Christ, a journey into becoming persons of compassion, persons who forgive, persons who care deeply for others and the world, persons who offer themselves to God to become agents of divine grace in the lives of others and their world—in brief, persons who love and serve as Jesus did (p. 31).

When we surrender ourselves to a God who is consistently "merciful and gracious, slow to anger, and abounding in steadfast love and faithfulness" (Exod 34:6), we give ourselves to living the abundant life with Jesus. This gift of God, abundant life in his presence, is available to everyone, not least of which are those who identify as LGBTQ+.

Christine Martin *is a retired high school teacher who enjoys time with family, friends, and nature. She has a passion for volunteering with teenagers at Habitat for Humanity projects and with Family Promise, a national organization helping unhoused families achieve sustainable independence. She and her husband, Tim, have been active members of Madison Street Church, formerly Riverside Brethren in Christ, since its founding in the 1980s.*

A Pathway to Inclusion in the Anabaptist Vision

Matthew G. O'Brien

The author explores his experience with the Anabaptist vision—what it means to him as a person of privilege and how he sees it as a pathway to inclusion and affirmation of the LGBTQ community.

I can't say for sure who is reading this, but you should know who is writing it. I am a chaplain and chaplain educator. I'm a white, heterosexual, cisgender male and a Christian minister with an advanced degree. I am able-bodied, a member of the military, and I have a supportive network. I'm even right-handed. I am a privileged and sheltered individual.

At first glance, it may seem unlikely that someone like me would be writing an essay for a book like this. I am writing not because I seek to acquire the title of "ally" but to confront my own fragility as a person separated from struggle by privilege. As a straight person in a heteronormative subculture, it is my default to rely on a sense of belonging and assumed right to comfort. However, I am writing because I have witnessed the impact of discrimination and oppression that is rife within spiritual communities, and I choose to join others in their experiences of discomfort and grievance.

My connection to the Brethren in Christ (BIC) goes back many years. I felt found and seen when I started going to a BIC church where I worked as a pastoral associate for five years. Before that, I had sworn off church—another emergent deconstructionist stewing on the sidelines. But this was a restorative experience, one that introduced me to the concept of *ministry as reconciliation* and to moments of ministry as liminality, holding tensions in a fraught world.

As a chaplain educator, I work with aspiring chaplains of all different backgrounds and orientations. Many of these individuals have experienced spiritual trauma in the process of discovering who they are and how they might enfold their true selves into their ministry. There is a generosity and a breadth in the concept of chaplaincy, a professional ministry that welcomes its religious practitioners to serve all people. I witness female chaplains who flourish in the exercise of their pastoral gifts but are not allowed to be pastors in their churches. I witness LGBTQ chaplains offer the kind of unconditional acceptance they never received in their spiritual communities. This is the territory I inhabit, the ground from which I speak and write.

For many years, chaplaincy has echoed the evangelical tradition of conversion, a tradition that often depends on guilt, shame, and fear to manipulate or persuade. I see my ministry as reconciling this historic fact with the path of inclusion, acceptance, and interfaith practice. I am a firm believer that the ministry of reconciliation is about liberation and that Jesus' presence and purpose are to set people free from guilt, shame, and fear. In our present context, I believe that to emulate Christ is to move determinedly towards inclusion.

When I found myself outside the reach of conventional churches, disillusioned with human fragility and failure—both of spiritual leaders and myself—I discovered a way forward in the Anabaptist vision embodied in the BIC Church. In this vision, I found the opportunity to begin to do the work of dismantling my own fragility and privilege in order to see, accept, and empower others.

In my work as an educator, I have consistently heard feedback from LGBTQ students who often feel fear or uncertainty when they first meet me because of my background and the way I carry myself. One day, during my time as a resident chaplain in clinical pastoral education (CPE), I realized that I stood in my own privilege and symbolized, or resembled, in many ways, the oppressor who had afflicted others. The task of overcoming my own fragility in recognizing the experiences of others involved rooting out this resemblance and acknowledging my complicity—the harmful impact I have had and could have on others. Recommitment to liberation meant (and means) acknowledging the need for collective liberation. It is a vital step for spiritual communities to take in order to move towards those who have been marginalized and harmed. For me, to experience divine love and reconciliation is to press into the boundaries of my own fragility and to embrace and empower others. These values consistently support my current work.

I have been inspired and influenced by the principles I learned in the BIC Church about the Anabaptist vision of ministry, principles that can be embodied in the affirming and loving embrace of all people. The seeds of inclusion are there, and the Anabaptist vision points to Christ, the community, and reconciliation as the foundation of spiritual life. If "the arc of the moral universe is long but . . . bends towards justice," to quote Martin Luther King, Jr., the Anabaptist vision proclaims the span. I found these concepts instrumental in my formation as an interfaith chaplain, educator, and minister.

It is Christ who suffers with us, his earthly ministry reflecting compassion for the marginalized and oppressed. Christ, who showed prejudice toward the Canaanite woman, was confronted with his privilege and bias. Christ is our model for the inclusivity and imperfection of our compassion.

It is in community, a karass of love and forgiveness, that we practice the imperfect disillusionment of Bonhoeffer's *Life Together*. The purpose of community is not to be governed by judgment but to root out judgment when it inevitably arises and to reconcile the privileged and the oppressed.

It is reconciliation that I have been trying to write about. *Inclusion, affirmation, belonging, equity, equality, justice,* and the ever-growing list of words that describe the work of welcoming healing in the world are summed up for me in the power of reconciliation. Reconciliation is what I learned from my time in a BIC church, and the arc of reconciliation bends towards inclusion and liberation.

We are not free until we are all free. I am convinced that communities of faith that believe in the God of freedom will move towards affirming all people, including the LGBTQ community. When we include and affirm, we love, and God's light shines on us. In that light, we may truly begin to see and understand the experience of suffering that others have endured and that we may have even caused. And in that light, we may find unity and compassion in the tension and reconciliation of our differences.

Matthew G. O'Brien *holds a B.A. degree from The Master's University in Santa Clarita, California, and an M. Div. degree from Corban University's School of Ministry in Salem, Oregon. Matt has served several Christian faith communities in a variety of pastoral roles and is an ACPE Certified Educator and Chaplain. He is husband to Cristin, father to Olive, and dog-guardian to Rocky. He is especially thankful for his years in community at Madison Street Church, a BIC faith community in Riverside, California.*

"You are My Arm Outstretched"
A Vision for God's People

Mama Sarah

We must open the doors of the church to LGBTQ+ people and embrace them, or we risk losing them forever.

Years ago, I was in prayer, interceding for a gay high school friend named David. I had a vision of the Kingdom of God. There were large black iron gates, and outside the gates were the rejected, including gay people like my friend. I cried out to the Lord, "We can't leave those people behind!" I clearly heard the Lord say to me, "Go get them! You are my arm outstretched!"

From that day on, I knew I had to be a voice and a bridge to make a way for that population of hurting souls to know that they are precious to the Lord.

I am not a debater. I am not filled with vast background and scriptural knowledge about issues related to LGBTQ people. I have not read many books on this topic. I just know that this is a heart issue and that we are dealing with sensitive, wounded souls.

I have three children who have all struggled with identity and who are neurodivergent. I homeschooled them from the beginning until they graduated. During those years, we were part of a very conservative, independent church with mostly homeschooling families. In the insulated "purity culture" of that church and homeschool community, all three of my kids had difficulty fitting in and making friends.

Although my husband and I had started out in a Brethren in Christ (BIC) Church and were active members for several years—from the time I attended Messiah College (now University) until our first two kids were born—we were drawn to this independent church by the homeschooling community, and we stayed there until 2020. That year, facing the COVID crisis, we realized we were diverging from this community in many ways. We finally had to leave, realizing that our issues created debates, hurtful conflict, and rejection from the only social group we had known for fifteen years.

We were drawn back to the BIC Church during COVID because I believed that its policies of outdoor services and mask-wearing exhibited a heart of service and love toward others. I remembered how much the church espoused loving others, accepting others, and serving others, and I wanted to return to that.

At home, we had an open-door policy for all of my kids and for all of my kids' friends. I "adopted" many Messiah University students who were friends of my oldest child and who had faced rejection from family and church. I fed them, loved on them, and let them know they were worthy and loved by God.

After a year or so back in the BIC Church, with two kids in college, it was just my teenager and me attending church. When my teenager expressed to the family that they wanted to change their name and pronouns, we started introducing them in church with the new name. Everyone was so gracious, and it seemed like we would still fit in that congregation. My child, however, started to feel that it wasn't a safe space when a youth leader said to the group, "One of these days, we are going to address the LGBTQ issue." So many questions arose in my kid's mind, and they felt that they wanted to hide. They stopped attending the youth group and the church.

A group of parents of LGBTQ people, along with the pastor, had begun a support group in the church for parents in this situation. We discussed what was happening as my family was processing it. I clearly expressed that my child was teetering on the edge of church. At the time, they were still reading their Bible, still praying, and still wanting to serve the Lord. I did my very best to represent Jesus well and to reach out, just as I had seen in the vision. However, even with my efforts and the pastor's heart to keep them in the BIC fold, they decided to attend a church that is fully "affirming," a church that is careful to respect names and pronouns and that offers outreach and safe haven for LGBTQ youth. It's a church where it's simply not an issue.

I have stopped attending the group for parents of children who identify as LGBTQ because it is too wearisome for me to continue to discuss how to have an open door and how to embrace LGBTQ individuals. Church needs to be a safe space for LGBTQ individuals. Many have been rejected by their own families and/or are suicidal because they have been through so much pain from their own internal conflicts as well as from wounds they received from others.

How can the church continue to reject them? How can we continue to insist that they meet certain standards of holiness before they can fully participate in the life of the church? While we spend precious time debating and deciding how to reach these lost souls, many young people, like my own child, are growing up and leaving the church. Many will never return.

I stayed connected to that dear friend, David, from high school, and I had prayed for him since the 1980s. For years, he lived his life believing that God would never accept him. When his mother passed away two years ago, I had a feeling that I needed to prepare to speak at the funeral, even though I wasn't asked. When the day came, the pastor didn't show up, and I was able to step in to share and pray. David was amazed at how God had seen his situation and cared enough for him in his grief to speak through me as his friend. From that day on, he has given up alcohol and drugs and given his life to the Lord.

Throughout David's adult life, I was the arm of the Lord outstretched. In the life of my children, I am His arm reaching out desperately and hoping they hold on. The arm of the Lord is not reaching out to slap someone with judgment. Instead, we are the arm of the Lord reaching out to save and to embrace the lost, to bring them through the gates, and to offer them a seat at the table.

Mama Sarah *is the mother of three and attends Dillsburg BIC Church. She grew up in a Christian home, studied Social Work at Messiah College, and, in the 1990s, was a member of The Meeting House, formerly Cumberland Valley BIC Church. Sarah has been homeschooling her amazing kids for twenty years. She and her husband have been married for thirty-two years. They have an open door and an open seat at the dinner table.*

The Longing to Belong Is from God (So Why Are We Making Our LGBTQ+ Siblings Sit in the Back of the Bus?)

Elisa Joy Seibert

God has wired the longing to belong into all humans. As representatives of the God of love, Christians should be nurturing our churches into being open-hearted safe havens for all of God's children, including our LGBTQ+ siblings.

In the summer of 2023, Bishop Heather Beaty of the Susquehanna Conference of the Brethren in Christ (BIC) U.S. Church wrote the following in her newsletter to church leaders:

> *Belonging.* For some of us, simply hearing the word *belonging* stirs a deep longing within. Others would describe it as sweetly resonating with our current experience. For some of us, a wall immediately goes up because we have been connected before and have known too many broken relationships to trust again in the idea of belonging.
>
> Yet, this word *belonging* echoes the very heart of the gospel.
>
> We have been created to intimately know and be known by our Creator and Savior. We are called to live out his love in significant relationships of community. . . .

Invitation to Conversation

My prayer for us in the Susquehanna Conference is that we will be a people committed to living out the hopeful blessing of belonging in the context of community. May we each know sweet communion with Christ. May we work to stay connected when distance and difference divide. May we demonstrate the Good News of the gospel through lives that reflect the goodness and graciousness of God at all times. May we bring God glory as we re-commit to Christlike living and loving expressed in our community of belonging.

Yes! This reflects the very heart of God!

Yet here is the irony: these beautiful words appeared in Bishop Heather's newsletter during the same time people in a BIC congregation in the Susquehanna Conference were told—from the pulpit—to have "the right kind of marriage" and to accept the body they were given, messages that feel insensitive, unwelcoming, misattuned, and downright unsafe to LGBTQ+ Christians and those of us who care about them.

It is deeply troubling that devoted followers of Jesus in our congregations, who happen to be in same-sex relationships, are not being allowed to become members or get married in church to the partner they are committed to for life—let alone have that marriage acknowledged and celebrated. As non-members, they must sit on the sidelines during Congregational Council and watch as "real" members vote on the business of the church. Their voices are excluded from these important votes and roles. It's ironic that the church lets these individuals go on a Civil Rights Tour and report back to the congregation about that powerful experience without recognizing that *this is the next civil rights movement right before us*. Yet we in the BIC Church are making our LGBTQ+ siblings sit in the back of the bus!

When those who identify as LGBTQ+ are actively excluded from church membership and various leadership roles, it sends painful messages to each one and to all of us who see and care. It shreds the soul—my soul, too. And it makes the church an extremely unsafe place. We *all* have a longing to belong. It is put there by God. Drs. Sue Johnson and Leanne Campbell, in their *Primer for Emotionally Focused Individual Therapy*, recently put it this way: "Belonging and becoming are two sides of the same coin and, in a truly civilized society, all must belong" (pp. 2-3).

Jesus' invitation is for *everyone* to be part of the kingdom of God, an "upside-down kingdom," as Donald Kraybill aptly called it, one that makes space for the very people society shuns. Jesus stands with the oppressed and the marginalized. The church is also called to stand on the side of the oppressed and never do the oppressing. Yet here we are, Anabaptists, who are called to be radical for Jesus, failing to follow his radical call for unequivocal love when it comes to our LGBTQ+ siblings. That is a huge problem!

This book is inviting the BIC Church to do something really hard: *to change*. This courageous move toward change needs to be motivated by love for those in our midst who are gender diverse and gender expansive and whose sexual orientation is not heteronormative. We need to love each one because they are special to God, created, beloved, worthy, and good. And we love each one because we are all equal at the foot of the cross. No one is better, and no one is less honorable in the Kingdom of God. Status is removed, barriers are brought down, and Christ's love unites us all. That is the goal!

The Journey

It has been a journey to get to the place where I am, and the journey is ongoing. I am thankful for those who stretched me thus far and for those who continue to stretch me. As a cisgender, white, heterosexual woman, I grew up in conservative Christian churches where LGBTQ+ issues were never named, and problematic Scripture passages were read with no commentary. This reinforced the heteronormative and gender-conforming messages I received from the cultural water in which I swam.

The stretching began in my doctoral program at a faith-based institution where I got to know committed followers of Jesus who believed differently than me. This included people who parented well-rounded, emotionally healthy daughters who just happened to be attracted to women. It also included people who put up rainbow flags in their Campus Ministry offices to show that Jesus welcomes everyone and faculty who married their same-sex partner and were so easy to relate to. My stereotypes were challenged. I saw the beautiful humans underneath the labels society had placed on them.

Along the way, I encountered scientific data that showed that sexual orientation and gender identity are biological from birth and not in any way volitional or changeable. I also watched a movie about Matthew Shephard, a kind university student who was beaten, tortured, tied to a fence, and left to die alone in a field just because he was attracted to men. I began to see that Jesus' manner of loving and siding with the marginalized, disenfranchised, and oppressed is how we are called to come alongside our LGBTQ+ siblings today.

I am grateful it was at a place of higher learning, in community, and among other people of faith, that I was gently stretched and invited to think more deeply, engage my biases, and meet people who believed in fresh new ways and who lived in realities I had not experienced. That is the best of what community is called to be, a safe place where we can stumble, struggle, wrestle, question, and grow into open-hearted humans who reflect the image of our open-hearted God. I wish the church and our Christian universities would do more to be safe places that nurture this kind of honest engagement and growth. That would please Jesus immensely!

A crucial turning point in my scriptural understanding came when I read David Switzer's book *Pastoral Care for Gays, Lesbians, and their Families*. He engaged the controversial passages, including those in the Pauline Epistles. He emphasized that when Paul wrote to the churches, there was no societal concept of sexual orientation or same-sex (or other non-heteronormative) attraction. Clearly, Paul was *not* addressing the same set of issues and concerns we are. He was dealing with other matters (such as male prostitution and pagan temple practices) that had *nothing* to do with the LGBTQ+ communities of today.

Some English translations have inaccurately translated a Greek word in 1 Cor 6:9 as "homosexuals" (or something similar) and have done enormous harm to people in the process. But Paul was *never* referencing sexual orientation (a modern concept) in that verse or elsewhere. The church can help us by encouraging intellectually honest interpretive principles and by recognizing the Bible has nothing negative to say about sexual orientation or gender identity because those concepts didn't even exist when the

Bible was written. Instead, the Bible has everything to say about loving our neighbor as we love ourselves, welcoming the marginalized, embracing the oppressed, and being in committed, loving relationships with healthy sexual ethics irrespective of what gender our partner is, how we identify, or how our body is wired.

St. Augustine wisely reminded us that "all truth is God's truth." And John Wesley, the founder of Wesleyanism, a theological tradition that is a key part of our church's heritage, made space for the roles of reason (which includes science) and experience (which includes community), alongside Scripture and tradition, in our understanding of truth. We need to take all of this data into account as we use our God-given intellect to interpret Scripture wisely in light of the best science available. We no longer believe that the Earth is flat or is the center of our solar system, as the Hebrew worldview envisioned. And we no longer shun our BIC congregants for wearing a wedding ring, cutting their hair, or not wearing a head covering, as our BIC ancestors did. The time is *now* for making the next shift in our theological and congregational life as we understand Scripture accurately for what it was and was *not* intending to say.

The Church is Enriched by Inclusion

For the past decade, it has been an honor to get to know people who identify as LGBTQ+, love Jesus, and have grown up in faith-based families, along with getting to know their parents, partners, and friends. I've listened to the stories of my LGBTQ+ siblings in Christ, seen their beautiful hearts and love of Jesus, and witnessed their pure, committed love for their spouse and their generosity in caring for neighbors. The church has much to learn from them.

Many of these individuals have been repeatedly hurt by the church due to its limited welcome and lack of full inclusion. For example, I've seen the pain of LGBTQ+ young adults who have felt abandoned at a crucial time in their lives when they needed support. Yet I'm convinced that if Jesus was here today, these beautiful people are the ones he would be hanging out with!

What is the Church afraid of?

Heterosexual Christians have *nothing* to fear from supporting full inclusion. On the contrary, we have everything to lose by continuing our misinformed, oppressive policies that lead young people to leave the church in droves and cause people who need Jesus to look elsewhere. We all become richer when our communities and congregations include the rich diversity God put in the human race. *That* is a true picture of the kingdom of God! We need each other, *all* of us, to truly be the complete body of Christ.

To be clear, Jesus is not merely calling us to "welcome" LGBTQ+ people. Jesus calls us to *celebrate* each one for the beautiful people they are. We are invited to delight in the diversity God put in humanity, recognizing that *all* people are created in God's image.

A theme I have been hearing again and again in the past year is that when people feel unloved, they don't just want to be "accepted," or tolerated. They actually want (and need) to have people who are safe "rejoice" in them. Think of it this way. Imagine you came home to visit your family at Thanksgiving and saw flat, withdrawn, closed-up non-verbal expressions on your loved ones' faces, along with body postures that clearly said: "It is tolerable that you are here. I 'accept' you, but I clearly am not excited about you, and I certainly don't celebrate who you are. But since Jesus calls me to 'love' you, that's what I'll do. Humph!" Ouch! Wouldn't that feel horrible? To have the people we most depend on merely "tolerate" us is more damaging than being disconnected altogether.

Secure Attachment and Belonging as the Path Forward

Besides having the training of a BIC pastor, I am also an Emotionally Focused (EFT) Couples Therapist who helps people heal their attachment relationships. Science shows us that God has wired into all of us the longing to have at least one other person be there completely for us, to hear us when we call, soothe us when we are in distress, and let us know that we deeply matter. This is called attachment. And, as Dr. Sue Johnson describes in her book, *Created for Connection*, all humans, "from the cradle to the grave," have this attachment system and longing to belong wired in (p. 28).

There are different patterns of attachment we might grow into depending on whether our first families were there for us consistently or not. The most ideal form of attachment is called secure attachment. Secure attachment provides a secure base in which we feel deeply safe and thoroughly loved and lovable. It changes our view of ourselves and our view of others. It helps us be open to the world, share our God-given gifts freely, and love and be loved in ways that make us generous, open-hearted citizens of God's Kingdom and the world.

Parents who want to nurture secure attachment in their children (and give them that amazing gift!) not only need to attune accurately to them but to actually *delight* in them, enter into their space, listen, get to know them, and be curious about them and with them. Rejoicing is a part of that! This, too, is the gift we as the church could offer the world if we would only move beyond our fear of the "other."

Fear makes people uncurious and reactive. For the BIC to move toward full inclusion, denominational leaders will need to discontinue the fear-inducing practice of removing pastors' credentials if they begin this journey and arrive at a different place. Safety and transparency are essential! We can do this! We don't have to be bound by fear any longer. Jesus stands ready to welcome us, and all of God's children, into God's multi-splendored kingdom where all are celebrated and delighted in as beloved of God, equal at the foot of the cross, and able to serve and thrive.

There was a time when the church thought black and brown bodies were "less than," and with God's help and invitation, *we changed*. We are at a similar crossroads now. I pray we choose wisely. What are we waiting for? The time is *now*!

Next Steps

If you are curious about how to begin your journey of becoming more open to being fully inclusive of LGBTQ+ people, take some steps to put yourself in the position for God to gently stretch you. Read a good book like Justin Lee's *Torn* or David Gushee's *Changing Our Mind*. Connect with other Christians who truly want to see anew. Get to know some of the beautiful LGBTQ+ Christians in your church and community. Hear their stories and start a focus group in your church to explore how your congregation can become more welcoming, supportive, and inclusive of these siblings loved by God. And pray and act for our wonderful BIC church to have fears soothed and to open our hearts, minds, and churches to the next Civil Rights Movement and to the change needed in us. God promises to be our secure base and to be with us in this endeavor as we face and process our fears and courageously help our LGBTQ+ siblings truly belong!

Elisa Joy Seibert (Ph.D., M.Div.) *is a Licensed Psychologist, ICEEFT Certified Emotionally Focused (EFT) Therapist and Supervisor, Counselor Educator, former chaplain, and co-founder of the Central PA EFT Community. She is a member of Grantham Church, where she has served on the pastoral staff. She has educated pastors, youth ministers, and lay ministers in the BIC and elsewhere in Pastoral Care and Counseling for over twenty-five years. A graduate of Asbury Theological Seminary and Gannon University, she has a passion for equipping therapists in EFT and specializes in helping couples transform their connections. (www.GrowingConnectionsforCouples.com).*

Are You 100% Sure?

Lin Taylor

For churches to embrace members of the LGBTQ+ community, they need to get training, become more empathic, and reexamine what the Bible actually says.

I grew up in the Brethren in Christ (BIC) Church, and my mother's family has been stalwartly BIC for generations. I honor and value the Bible as the Word of God that reveals the way of salvation and the guide for faith and conduct. I also have two LGBTQ children. For most of my life, I have agreed with the denomination's views about people who identify as LGBTQ.

But I don't anymore.

The change in my views is not because I am ignoring the Bible. Instead, it is because I am taking another look at what it says and what it requires of us.

Thank you for reading this book (hopefully with an open mind and heart). You may have a lot of questions. That is OK. You may think the world is crazy and things are changing all the time, especially when it comes to LGBTQ issues and concerns. That is OK. You may think all these new terms and ways of speaking are awkward and difficult to get used to and remember. That is OK. But for the sake of the gospel, we need to do some hard work. We need to be sure we are not getting this wrong for one simple reason: lives and souls depend on it.

For that reason, I have a few requests.

First, I ask all of our churches to get good training on how to relate to people who identify as LGBTQ. This is especially important for staff and volunteers who work with children and youth. The church should be the safest place possible for these individuals. We all need to know what different terms mean and how to relate to children in various situations—like a child with gay parents, a child who tells you they are gay, or a child who changes their name or pronouns.

Recently, in response to a question about what to do if a child or youth tells you they are gay, a BIC church leader said we should loop in the parents. Wrong! If we don't have appropriate knowledge and fail to handle things correctly in these instances, mistakes will occur. And these mistakes may have serious consequences.

Second, I would like to ask you to put yourself in other people's shoes. Imagine that you are a young person who has become aware that you are exclusively attracted to people of the same gender. If you are straight, you learn in church that your sexuality is a gift from God and that you can find joyous fulfillment of your desires in marriage. If you are gay, however, you hear very different messages. You are told that those desires are not from God and can never be fulfilled. You are told that you cannot marry, and you are informed that the only way you can please God is by a lifetime of celibacy. Every time you fall in love, you will need to deny that love, breaking your heart and possibly the other person's as well.

Imagine you are engaged to someone of the same sex, and you come into a BIC church. Our official policy states that you cannot be married in our church building and that no BIC pastor can officiate your wedding. Instead of being supported, you are instructed to break your engagement and commit yourselves to lives of celibacy.

Or put yourself in the shoes of a married gay couple with children who comes into a BIC church. Hopefully, you would be warmly welcomed. But you would most likely not be allowed to become members and probably could not be baptized. Your marriage would be considered sinful. If you wanted to become members of the church, you would have to divorce, share custody of your children, and commit yourselves to lives of celibacy.

I do not have anything against celibacy. I think it is a gift from God. All of us have had periods of celibacy in our lives, and I think they have a lot to teach us. But I never had to contemplate a *lifetime* of celibacy. As a straight woman, I knew that if I fell in love, I could get married. And I did. Some straight people choose lifelong celibacy for various reasons, but it is *their* choice. They've never had to rule out the possibility of having lifelong companionship, enjoying sexual fulfillment, and starting their own families. We are asking same-sex attracted couples to bear a heavy lifelong burden, a burden that many of us would not accept for ourselves. We have to be 100% sure we are right.

Third, I ask you to study different interpretations of biblical passages used to condemn same-sex expression. Sometimes, the quick and seemingly obvious interpretation is wrong. We have to dig deeper to see what the Bible really means. This is precisely what we have done in other areas, such as the issue of women in leadership.

I won't try to address all the biblical and theological arguments here. This book has a list of resources at the end to help you dig into these things, and I hope you'll do so with an open mind. When I held the traditional view, I was aware that some people believed the Bible could be used to support gay marriage, but I really thought that was wishful thinking, possibly supported by twisting Scripture. Amazingly, a lot of time passed before I took the time to find out for myself.

Once I looked at the Scriptures on my own, I realized there was room for considerable doubt about the traditional view. The verses about "homosexuality" in the Bible are about things such as promiscuous sex and the powerful preying on the weak. There is nothing in the Bible about being in a loving and committed same-sex relationship. Therefore, it seems logical to me that the law of love and grace would compel us to allow gay marriage since the Bible never forbids it. If we have a doctrine that is keeping people out of our church, we have to be 100% sure that we are doing what God wants.

For the sake of the gospel and for the Lamb that was slain, I want us to open our doors as widely as possible. If, on the last day, God tells us that we let too many people into the church, I can accept that. I can't accept it if God tells us that we kept people out.

Lin Taylor *is a computer programmer who grew up in Grantham Church and has attended Harrisburg BIC Church since 1989. She enjoys playing music and hiking with friends. She volunteers for Girls Who Code. Lin lives in Harrisburg with her husband, her youngest child, and their cat, Banjo.*

Extending Grace and Full Inclusion
If Not Now, When?

DANIEL WEATHERFORD

The good fruit Jesus speaks of in Matthew 7:17 is abundantly evident in this beautiful story of a lesbian couple whose fifty-year journey exemplifies faith in Christ, commitment to a fully inclusive faith community, and lives of love and service to marginalized people.

We are immersed in a culture awash in fear. Beset by all manner of crises—political, economic, social, environmental, to name a few—Americans are daily affected by mass-scale disaffection, anger, distrust, and personal isolation. In such an environment, one would hope that the church might be the last bastion of mercy, grace, and love. However, within the church, forces threaten to tear us apart, tempting us to adopt a "divide-and-conquer" mindset that only serves to further embroil us in division and fear. Now, more than ever, we must hold on to the life and teachings of Jesus if others are to know that we are followers of Christ and ministers of reconciliation.

I arrived in Riverside, California, in 1969, at the age of eleven as the result of a third and final adoption. Soon after settling into my new home with my new parents, the Weatherfords, I met Penny, my adoptive mother's twenty-one-year-old niece. Although Penny was living out-of-town by the time I arrived, she had recently lived with my adoptive parents for three years after relocating from her home in Georgia in order to pursue a degree in a nationally ranked nursing program in Riverside.

Invitation to Conversation

This was a formative period in Penny's life. Uprooted from life in a small town in Georgia and thrust into southern California culture and home life with the Weatherfords was a big change for her. It was not an easy transition for any of them, but Penny successfully completed the nursing program and became a Registered Nurse. She met Bobby, a young man in the Navy and a Georgia native like her, and they eventually got married and moved to San Diego, a couple of hours away.

However, over a period of four years, it became clear to both Penny and Bobby that this marriage was a mismatch. They agreed to separate amicably and to end their marriage. Not long after, in 1973, Penny got to know a young woman who had a similar experience with a similar end to her marriage.

Over time, Penny and Janet fell in love and became a "couple." With no legal avenue for a lesbian couple to marry in 1973, they eventually moved in together. Few people could be trusted with the knowledge that they were anything but roommates, so they had to keep up that pretense for all but their very closest friends. They knew that any openness about their true relationship would be met with judgment, prejudice, rejection, and exclusion. Their love held strong, and even without any legal certificate to bind them together, they modeled a relationship of mutual commitment, respect, devotion, and service that many married heterosexual couples would do well to emulate.

When my adoptive mother, Lynette, became aware that Penny and Janet were more than just roommates, her response was instantaneous. She was repulsed by their relationship and completely condemned it. I saw a side to my adoptive mother that personified summary judgment and a willingness to regard Penny as being abnormal and even wicked. In 1973, when I was sixteen years old, homosexuality was just beginning to be seen as a possible (though questionable) "new social convention." It could barely be mentioned or discussed in good company, especially in the company of church people.

Knowing very little about such things at my age, all I could see and understand was that Lynette was both utterly offended by Penny's choice and utterly fearful of the social and religious ramifications should her niece's

244

variant lifestyle become "known." From my vantage point as an adopted son and cousin, I witnessed firsthand what prejudice and outright contempt for non-binary relationships and lifestyles could engender. But here is what made the greatest impression on me at the time. Despite all that my adoptive mother already knew about Penny—that she was sensitive, capable, intelligent, dedicated, and personable, not to mention the Penny was her beloved sister's daughter—it was all readily discarded and replaced with repulsion, animus, and rejection for the *sole reason* that she was a lesbian.

I continued to maintain a healthy, warm, and familial relationship with Penny, who through the years came to be more like a sister to me than a cousin. I also came to view Janet with affection and respect, seeing her as the kind, familial, intelligent, thoughtful, articulate, and politically astute individual that she was. Janet's compassion and concern for people in need had been evident at an early age. When she was only nineteen years old, Janet had joined together with a small group to create a crisis intervention hotline and a halfway house for runaway youth in the Bay Area.

From the outset, it was apparent to me that Penny and Janet belonged together and were devoted to one another—like any other "normal" couple I knew. Having relocated from San Diego to the little Bay Area town of Vallejo, Penny began a long and rewarding career as a nurse as did Janet as a respiratory therapist. They both labored long hours and used their abundant kindness, professional training, and wide experience to serve and care for people in need. Together as respected "aunties," they began to offer generous and tangible aid to multiple nieces and nephews whose family lives were dysfunctional and whose formative years were difficult. Over the years, Penny and Janet have served—and continue to serve—their family and their community in Jesus-like fashion with care, hospitality, and wise counsel, in addition to providing financial support and a stable home environment when needed.

A couple of decades ago, Penny and Janet found safe haven in a Vallejo church that happily and fully included them as fellow followers of Christ. For years, Penny's faith, compassion, and wisdom served the church well in her role as a leadership council member. And Janet's Jesus-like compassion

Invitation to Conversation

and dedication toward people in need found an outlet through her leadership of the church's efforts to serve local unsheltered persons in a weekly food distribution and service effort at a local park. Mirroring Christ's life of service, they have embraced a practice of love, forbearance, inclusion, and grace, providing support for persons whose needs went unmet by their respective communities.

After decades of struggle by activists, the California Supreme Court legalized same-sex unions in 2008. That summer, after thirty-five years of faithful devotion to each other, Penny and Janet celebrated with a big church wedding. Their church's sanctuary was beautifully decorated, and their pastor officiated the ceremony admirably. My wife, our daughter, and I would not have missed it for the world. Along with family members and friends, the whole church showed up for a beautiful celebration of the love that these two women shared.

It is noteworthy that Penny's aunt, Lynette, was also present at the wedding and was celebrating with the others in attendance. Despite my adopted mother's initial contempt for their lesbian "lifestyle," and the 450 mile distance between their home and hers, Penny and Janet had visited her frequently, especially in later years after she became a widow. In fact, it was Penny and Janet who organized and effected Lynette's relocation from Riverside to Vallejo and who took care of her when old age and dementia robbed her of the ability to function independently. Penny readily assumed complete responsibility for her care, settling her into a lovely assisted living home nearby and visiting frequently until her eventual passing. *A greater example of Christ-like love and sacrifice would be hard to imagine.*

In July of 2023, Penny and Janet celebrated fifty (!) years of faithful devotion to each other as a couple. My wife and I wouldn't have missed the party for anything and drove 450 miles to be there. A delicious meal was served, and photo albums at the tables gave evidence of five decades of Penny and Janet's beautiful, shared life. Beloved by the three dozen family members and friends who showed up en masse on a lovely Vallejo afternoon for the backyard celebration, these two beautiful, soulful women mingled amidst the group. A bit uncomfortable with being the center of attention and not without frequent lapses into their usual roles of serving instead of being served, they were surrounded by friends and by many of the family members on whom they had showered love, hospitality, generosity, and care through the years: sisters, nieces, nephews, great-nieces, great-nephews and, of course, Penny's adoring adoptive cousin and his wife.

Now in their mid-seventies, having shared fifty years of devoted commitment to each other, Penny and Janet continue to give evidence that same-sex partners are every bit as able to sustain a monogamous, mutually supportive, faith-filled relationship as any other couple—me and my wife included. Not only this, but they have devoted their lives to using their collective resources to aid, serve, and support friends, family, and people in need. Their lives clearly reflect a Jesus-like love.

It distresses me to know that if Penny and Janet lived near a Brethren in Christ church and wanted to be a part of it in the same way as others who are members, they would be told that would not be possible. They would be told that despite ample evidence of their Christ-like practice and service, they would not have been allowed to have their wedding in a BIC church building and that the BIC pastor of the church would not have been able to officiate at the wedding without revocation of their ministerial credentials. Penny and Janet would learn that despite the longstanding and evident practice of their Christian faith, many leaders in the denomination would consider them to be living in a special category of sin. In many BIC churches, they would experience teaching from the pulpit that would denigrate people like them, if not because of their sexual orientation alone, then certainly because of their same-sex relationship. Penny and Janet's considerable giftedness in leadership within the church would be viewed with skepticism, at best.

Is this the message we want to be sending? Shouldn't we instead be setting our eyes on things of the kingdom? Being like Christ should be our highest aspiration, right? Reserving his harshest judgments for self-righteous, religious people, Jesus demonstrated grace and forgiveness toward the social and cultural outcasts of his day, fully including some of them into his closest circle of disciples. If we call ourselves followers of Christ, shouldn't we follow his example? Shouldn't we do all we can to insist that the BIC Church move toward full inclusion of LGBTQ+ people, people like Penny and Janet, who have so much to offer? I believe we should, and I believe now is the time. Because if not now, when?

Invitation to Conversation

Daniel Weatherford *is a retired high school social studies teacher who is a member of Madison Street Church and serves there as a deacon. He enjoys gardening, exercise, reading, and time spent with friends. He volunteers weekly at the University of California, Riverside, Botanic Gardens. Daniel lives in Riverside, California, with his wife of forty-two years. They share two adult children and one grandson.*

Who's Missing from These Pictures?

Jami West

This short story reveals a lack of welcome for same-sex couples, underscoring how much work remains to be done to promote the acceptance and inclusion of LGBTQ+ people.

Our after-church home groups were designed for adults to gather for spiritual growth, shared understanding, and mutual support. These sessions were intended to offer a safe haven—a place of solace and guidance for all attendees. Unfortunately, one particular meeting left me feeling quite the opposite.

On a sunny afternoon, I entered a home for a Home Group session, keen to bond with others over shared beliefs and teachings. As our discussion ventured deeper into the Scriptures, I found myself distracted by the numerous portraits on the walls. These were images of culturally diverse individuals and heterosexual couples, all seemingly rejoicing in life's milestones. Yet, an obvious omission weighed on my heart: the absence of same-sex couples. When someone remarked that the pictures "really seemed to include everyone," I couldn't hold back.

"Not everyone," I responded.

When probed about who I thought was missing, I pointed out the absence of "same-sex couples." The homeowner's response was swift and dismissive: "Not in my house."

The sting of those words resonated deeply. They served as a vivid reminder that even in spaces dedicated to community and growth, prejudice could still creep in. It wasn't merely about the missing photos; it was the blatant dismissal of the very idea. The message was unambiguous: same-sex relationships were neither welcome nor recognized here.

To say I felt heartbroken, affronted, and isolated would be an understatement. While the Home Group's objective was unity, this encounter accentuated a division.

I wish I could claim this was a one-off experience in my years at Riverside Brethren in Christ Church, but sadly, it wasn't. These experiences, while discouraging, underscored the vital necessity of advocating for inclusivity and understanding in religious settings. I remain hopeful that as we progress, we can turn these moments of pain into catalysts for growth, building a world where every individual feels both welcomed and valued.

Jami West *is the Executive Director and Founder of a non-profit childcare center and a college instructor of Early Childhood Development. She lives in Riverside, California, and celebrates thirty-seven years of marriage. She is a mother of four and a proud grandmother of five. Jami was a member of Riverside Brethren in Christ Church for over twenty-five years.*

Dealing with Reality
Discovering How God Created Our Neighbors

Sam Wilcock

Learning to discover how others were created and being certain to include LGBTQIA+ identities in this discovery better enables us to love as Jesus loves.

As Christians, we believe that all human beings are created by God. They are created according to God's wisdom and plan with a unique combination of talents, abilities, and traits. Some of us enjoy reading and quiet times with family. Others prefer the noisy bustle of a crowded sporting event. Some prefer another combination of things. The diversity of God's creation brings interest to our lives and allows us to have others to rely on in areas where we are not as strong. Scripture is full of stories of God's people learning to appreciate the breadth of creation and being instructed in how to appreciate, not simply tolerate, the "others" they encountered.

As a professor, I find that this diversity of individuals is part of what keeps my job interesting. I teach many of my students for only one semester in an introductory statistics course. Students come from a variety of majors and an even wider variety of backgrounds. Some are in more quantitative majors, while many are from the humanities or social sciences. Many have only had minimal interaction with statistics, while others have taken an entire high school course on the subject. Occasionally, I have a couple of seniors enrolled in the course because they can no longer put it off. Most semesters, there are students who are still in high school and want college credit for the course since they know they will need it later. I've even had several non-traditional students who were in the same face-to-face classroom but were also juggling life at home with a spouse and children. The mix is different from semester to semester, and even within sections in the same semester.

As an instructor, I would be doing my job very poorly if I did not notice this unique mix in each course and make the necessary adjustments to meet students where they are. I need to pay attention to the various forms of feedback that students provide as we move through the required material, and I need to adjust appropriately to those in front of me in order to provide equitable opportunities for success.

I have a better chance of getting to know students I see more often, such as majors who are required to take more than one semester of statistics and especially those who minor in statistics. These students often invite me more deeply into their lives. They come to me for advice about their courses and for their plans after graduation. With these students, I often gain a much fuller picture of what their lives were like before coming to campus. They talk about their families, their high school experiences and teachers, their own expectations, and the pressures they may feel. The more I learn, the more I appreciate how different individual students can be and how these differences should affect my advice. Students with different backgrounds and strengths may require quite different approaches. Some students need to be challenged to step up their work to achieve all that they are capable of (I was one of these), while others—who would wilt if challenged this way—simply need to be encouraged that they really are able to accomplish their goals.

The same rules apply to those of us who are parents. I know my children far better than any student I've ever had, but it can be even more tempting to squeeze my children into a mold of my own creation that does not fit their personality. The reality is that even children who share some of our DNA can be quite different from us. Those of us with foster or adopted children know that sometimes the removal of the biological connection can remind us that our children are their own unique individuals.

Since both my wife and I are college graduates, and since I have a Ph.D. and teach at a university, many people expected we would push our children to go to college without an option to choose otherwise. I have always tried to be clear with my children and with people who have asked that this is not true. Each of my children is unique, with their own special talents, abilities, and interests. Their definitions of "success" may be quite different from ours or from one another's. For some, college may be a logical way for them to develop and enhance their abilities and talents. So far, this is true for my oldest child. As my other children work their way through high school, we wait to see what will work best for them.

By this point, the reader may be wondering how this essay fits within the theme of this collection. To me, the connection is obvious, but I will now make it explicit. Issues of gender and sexuality are deeply ingrained in our definition of who we are. I am a cisgender, heterosexual man. To ignore these parts of my identity will lead to a deep misunderstanding of who I am and how I experience the world. This is equally true for those around us. If I look at my students and don't notice the unique experience of one of the few male nursing majors on campus, I do not fully understand him. If I have LGBTQIA+ students in my classes and am not aware of the potential stresses that they may experience on a campus that has rules limiting their behavioral choices and students who believe that being LGBTQIA+ is inherently sinful, then I may fail to fully understand how to help them when they struggle in my class. The issue may have nothing to do with their ability or effort but with the various other complexities of their lives. Regardless of how an educator thinks theologically about those who identify as LGBTQIA+, to be an effective teacher means addressing their needs and making it possible for them to succeed in the classroom.

To ignore these issues in the classroom or in our home would be an error. This is even more true in the church. The church is the place where we claim that our neighbors can meet the God who loves them unconditionally. Regardless of our theological views, we should always treat people who walk through the doors of our churches or who interact with us in other settings with respect and care. Jesus did not endorse sinful behavior, but we are told in Scripture that "sinners" felt drawn to him. In many cases, lives were changed by his radical acceptance and inclusion.

Invitation to Conversation

The Bible also points toward the inclusion of sexual minorities. In Acts 8, we read about Philip and the Ethiopian eunuch. As a eunuch, this man would have been excluded from full inclusion in Jewish worship (see, for example, Deut 23:1). But nothing prevents him from being baptized by Philip upon hearing "the good news about Jesus" (Acts 8:35-38, NRSVue). And, according to Isaiah 56:1-8, both eunuchs and foreigners, categories of people who had formerly been excluded from full participation in the community of faith, no longer were. Those who would be the equivalent of eunuchs today—such as those who have had vasectomies or hysterectomies—are no longer excluded in any Brethren in Christ (BIC) church of which I am aware.

Other reasons for non-inclusion in Hebraic law existed as well: illegitimate birth (Deut 23:2), being of the "wrong" ethnicity (Deut 23:3), etc. The BIC have agreed that in Christ, exclusions based on gender, ethnicity, or the circumstances of someone's birth no longer apply. What might all this suggest about a move toward full inclusion of sexual minorities in the BIC Church?

For many, the creation story of Adam and Eve precludes discussions of anything more complex than a gender binary and heterosexuality. However, we know that the creation stories in Genesis simplify things immensely. There are only day and night in Genesis 1, but we know about dusk and dawn. There is only dry land and sea, but we know marshes, bogs, and other "in-between" spaces exist. Animals are animals of the land, sea, or air, but we know that there are birds who fly and swim. There are amphibians who live on land and in the sea. These cases do not invalidate the creation stories but should expand our appreciation for the diversity and creativity of the Creator.

In light of all this—the inclusion of people who were formerly excluded and the understanding that reality is more nuanced than Genesis 1 and 2 portrays—why can't we have conversations about full inclusion of our LGBTQIA+ neighbors in our churches? I believe we can and we should. Also, whenever possible, we should not be having conversations *about* our neighbors without *including* our neighbors and being very careful to listen to what they have to say. It would be very strange to have a group of men debating the role of women in ministry without ever listening to the experiences of women and their callings. It would be equally peculiar for a group of white folks to discuss how to increase diversity without ever listening to people of color talk about their experiences in our congregations.

Issues as central to our experience in the world as gender and sexuality must be seriously considered if we are truly to love our neighbors as ourselves. The BIC Church cannot pretend these issues are settled and need no discussion. Our neighbors are more complicated than we have allowed, and when we exclude them in various ways, our witness to God's love for them is severely compromised. We can and must do better! Though we may never fully "arrive," the goal must be to treat the "other" as we want to be treated and to see them as valued members of the family rather than outsiders.

Samuel P. Wilcock *is Professor of Statistics. He and his family currently attend Harrisburg BIC Church after having attended Mechanicsburg BIC Church for over twenty years. He loves Philadelphia sports and watching his five kids do what they love. He and his wife live in Dillsburg with their five children, several cats, and their daughter's dog.*

Appendix

Suggestions for Using This Book

Because we think the message of this book is so important, we hope you will share it with others to extend its reach and influence. There are a number of ways to do this. Here are several ideas to get you started:

1. Give it to a pastor.

    Give a copy of this book to the pastor (or pastors) of your church, and encourage them to read it. Then, invite them to coffee or lunch to discuss the book with them.

2. Lead a Sunday School class.

    Ask your pastor if you can use this book to lead a Sunday school elective in your church. This book would be ideal for a five- or six-week class. Participants could be instructed to read one section each week and then come prepared to discuss what they have read. There are discussion questions at the end of this part of the book that can be used for that purpose.

3. Use it in your small group.

    If you are part of a small group, you could suggest reading and discussing the book during some of your small group meetings. (Again, the discussion questions that follow can help guide the conversation).

4. Promote it on social media.

> Use social media to spread the word about this book. Feel free to post, blog, and podcast about it. Let others know about this book and encourage them to spread the word.

5. Share it with friends and family members.

> Not only would *Invitation to Conversation* make an excellent birthday or Christmas gift, but it would also provide opportunities to talk with family and friends about how the church can do a better job of caring for LGBTQ+ people (and those who love them).

Discussion Questions

These discussion questions are organized according to the five sections of the book. There are also some general, book-level questions at the end.

Part I: LGBTQ+ Individuals Offer Their Perspective

- Which one or two stories from this section were most impactful to you? Why?

- What common themes emerged from the stories in this section?

- Were any of the stories here particularly encouraging? Surprising? Disturbing?

- If you could sit down with one of the authors in this section, who would it be, and what would you want to talk about with them?

Part II: Parents and Grandparents of LGBTQ+ Children Describe Their Experience

- What are some of the unique challenges facing parents and grandparents of LGBTQ+ children?

- What can churches do to be supportive of parents and grandparents of LGBTQ+ children?

- Why would a parent or grandparent of an LGBTQ+ child need support?

- Can you think of examples of BIC (or other) churches that do a good job of supporting parents and grandparents? If so, what does that look like?

Part III: People Explain Their Journey to Inclusion

- What types of experiences and information help people become more fully inclusive?
- What are some of the reasons that lead people to become inclusive of LGBTQ+ people?
- What can the church do to help people become more inclusive?
- Do you think the language of an "inclusive" church is helpful? If not, what other language would be better?

Part IV: Former BIC Pastors Share Their Stories

- What is your reaction to reading these stories? Specifically, how do you feel about the way the church responded to each of these pastors?
- What do you think should happen when a BIC pastor rethinks a theological belief that then puts them at odds with an official position of the denomination?
- What does your pastor believe about people who identify as LGBTQ+ and people who are in same-sex relationships?
- Has your congregation had intentional conversations about the treatment of LGBTQ+ individuals in your midst? If so, how have those gone? If not, why not?

Discussion Questions

Part V: Allies Call for LGBTQ+ Inclusion

- What biblical arguments for same-sex inclusion were most compelling for you? What passages (if any) are still difficult for you to reconcile with greater inclusion?

- What would it look like to include LGBTQ+ folks more fully in church?

- What are the two or three most important ideas you are taking away from this section?

- What are some common characteristics of people who are allies? Do you consider yourself an ally?

General Questions

- If you could identify one essay in the book you felt was exceptionally important, which essay would it be and why?

- What kinds of emotions did you experience reading through this book?

- What stories like the ones included in this book do you know that should be told?

- How did you see God working in the stories included in this book?

- If you had the opportunity to sit down with church leaders what would you say to encourage greater inclusion?

- What do you think is the most important next step for your church to take to become more fully inclusive?

Glossary of LGBTQ+ Terms and Vocabulary

The purpose of this glossary is twofold: 1) to provide definitions for certain words used in this book and 2) to expand an understanding of the considerable diversity that exists in the way sexual orientation and gender identity are experienced and expressed. These terms and definitions are adapted from The Safe Zone Project (https://thesafezoneproject.com/). For a more comprehensive list of terms, see https://thesafezoneproject.com/resources/vocabulary/.

advocate – **1** *noun* : a person who actively works to end intolerance, educate others, and support social equity for a marginalized group. **2** *verb* : to actively support or plea in favor of a particular cause, the action of working to end intolerance or educate others.

ally /"al-lie"/ – *noun* : a (typically straight and/or cisgender) person who supports and respects members of the LGBTQ community. We consider people to be active allies who take action on in support and respect.

asexual – *adj.* : experiencing little or no sexual attraction to others and/or a lack of interest in sexual relationships/behavior. Asexuality exists on a continuum from people who experience no sexual attraction or have any desire for sex, to those who experience low levels, or sexual attraction only under specific conditions. Many of these different places on the continuum have their own identity labels (see demisexual). Sometimes abbreviated to "ace."

biological sex – *noun* : a medical term used to refer to the chromosomal, hormonal and anatomical characteristics that are used to classify an individual as female or male or intersex. Often referred to as simply "sex," "physical sex," "anatomical sex," or specifically as "sex assigned at birth."

bisexual – **1** *noun & adj.* : a person who experiences attraction to some men and women. **2** *adj.* : a person who experiences attraction to some people of their gender and another gender. Bisexual attraction does not have to be equally split, or indicate a level of interest that is the same across the genders an individual may be attracted to. Often used interchangeably with "pansexual".

cisgender /"siss-jendur"/ – *adj.* : a gender description for when someone's sex assigned at birth and gender identity correspond in the expected way (e.g., someone who was assigned male at birth, and identifies as a man). A simple way to think about it is if a person is not transgender, they are cisgender. The word cisgender can also be shortened to "cis."

cisnormativity – *noun* : the assumption, in individuals and in institutions, that everyone is cisgender, and that cisgender identities are superior to trans* identities and people. Leads to invisibility of non-cisgender identities.

closeted – *adj.* : an individual who is not open to themselves or others about their (queer) sexuality or gender identity. This may be by choice and/or for other reasons such as fear for one's safety, peer or family rejection, or disapproval and/or loss of housing, job, etc. Also known as being "in the closet." When someone chooses to break this silence they "come out" of the closet. (See coming out)

coming out – **1** *noun* : the process by which one accepts and/or comes to identify one's own sexuality or gender identity (to "come out" to oneself). **2** *verb* : the process by which one shares one's sexuality or gender identity with others.

fluid(ity) – *adj.* : generally with another term attached, like gender-fluid or fluid-sexuality, fluid(ity) describes an identity that may change or shift over time between or within the mix of the options available (e.g., man and woman, bi and straight).

gay – 1 *adj.* : experiencing attraction solely (or primarily) to some members of the same gender. Can be used to refer to men who are attracted to other men and women who are attracted to women. **2** *adj.* : an umbrella term used to refer to the queer community as a whole, or as an individual identity label for anyone who is not straight.

gender binary – *noun* : the idea that there are only two genders and that every person is one of those two.

gender expression – *noun* : the external display of one's gender, through a combination of clothing, grooming, demeanor, social behavior, and other factors, generally made sense of on scales of masculinity and femininity. Also referred to as "gender presentation."

gender fluid – *adj.* : a gender identity best described as a dynamic mix of boy and girl. A person who is gender fluid may always feel like a mix of the two traditional genders, but may feel more man some days, and more woman other days.

gender identity – *noun* : the internal perception of an one's gender, and how they label themselves, based on how much they align or don't align with what they understand their options for gender to be. Often conflated with biological sex, or sex assigned at birth.

gender non-conforming – 1 *adj.* : a gender expression descriptor that indicates a non-traditional gender presentation (masculine woman or feminine man). **2** *adj.* : a gender identity label that indicates a person who identifies outside of the gender binary. Often abbreviated as "GNC."

genderqueer – 1 *adj.* : a gender identity label often used by people who do not identify with the binary of man/woman. **2** *adj.* : an umbrella term for many gender non-conforming or non-binary identities (e.g., agender, bigender, genderfluid).

heteronormativity – *noun* : the assumption, in individuals and/or in institutions, that everyone is heterosexual and that heterosexuality is superior to all other sexualities. Leads to invisibility and stigmatizing of other sexualities: *when learning a woman is married, asking her what her husband's name is.* Heteronormativity also leads us to assume that only masculine men and feminine women are straight.

heterosexism – *noun* : behavior that grants preferential treatment to heterosexual people, reinforces the idea that heterosexuality is somehow better or more "right" than queerness, and/or makes other sexualities invisible.

heterosexual/straight – *adj.* : experiencing attraction solely (or primarily) to some members of a different gender.

homophobia – *noun* : an umbrella term for a range of negative attitudes (e.g., fear, anger, intolerance, resentment, erasure, or discomfort) that one may have toward LGBTQ people. The term can also connote a fear, disgust, or dislike of being perceived as LGBTQ.

homophobic – *adj.* : a word used to describe actions, behaviors, or individuals who demonstrate elements of this range of negative attitudes toward LGBTQ people.

homosexual – *adj. & noun* : a person primarily emotionally, physically, and/or sexually attracted to members of the same sex/gender. This [medical] term is considered stigmatizing (particularly as a noun) due to its history as a category of mental illness, and is discouraged for common use (use gay or lesbian instead).

intersex – *adj.* : term for a combination of chromosomes, gonads, hormones, internal sex organs, and genitals that differs from the two expected patterns of male or female. Formerly known as hermaphrodite (or hermaphroditic), but these terms are now outdated and derogatory.

lesbian – *noun & adj.* : women who are primarily attracted romantically, erotically, and/or emotionally to other women.

LGBTQ – *abbr.* : shorthand or umbrella terms for all folks who have a non-normative (or queer) gender or sexuality, there are many different initialisms people prefer. LGBTQ is Lesbian Gay Bisexual Transgender and Queer and/or Questioning (sometimes people at a + at the end in an effort to be more inclusive).

outing – *verb* : involuntary or unwanted disclosure of another person's sexual orientation, gender identity, or intersex status.

pansexual – *adj.* : a person who experiences sexual, romantic, physical, and/or spiritual attraction for members of all gender identities/expressions. Often shortened to "pan."

passing – **1** *adj. & verb* : trans* people being accepted as, or able to "pass for," a member of their self-identified gender identity (regardless of sex assigned at birth) without being identified as trans*. **2** *adj.* : an LGB/queer individual who is believed to be or perceived as straight.

queer – **1** *adj.* : an umbrella term to describe individuals who don't identify as straight and/or cisgender. **2** *noun* : a slur used to refer to someone who isn't straight and/or cisgender. Due to its historical use as a derogatory term, and how it is still used as a slur in many communities, it is not embraced or used by all LGBTQ people. The term "queer" can often be used interchangeably with LGBTQ (e.g., "queer people" instead of "LGBTQ people").

questioning – *verb, adj.* : an individual who or time when someone is unsure about or exploring their own sexual orientation or gender identity.

Invitation to Conversation

sex assigned at birth (SAAB) – *abbr.* : a phrase used to intentionally recognize a person's assigned sex (not gender identity). Sometimes called "designated sex at birth" (DSAB) or "sex coercively assigned at birth" (SCAB), or specifically used as "assigned male at birth" (AMAB) or "assigned female at birth" (AFAB): *Jenny was assigned male at birth, but identifies as a woman.*

sexual orientation – *noun* : the type of sexual, romantic, emotional/spiritual attraction one has the capacity to feel for some others, generally labeled based on the gender relationship between the person and the people they are attracted to. Often confused with sexual preference.

sexual preference – *noun* : the types of sexual intercourse, stimulation, and gratification one likes to receive and participate in. Generally, when this term is used, it is being mistakenly interchanged with "sexual orientation," creating an illusion that one has a choice (or "preference") in who they are attracted to.

straight – *adj.* : a person primarily emotionally, physically, and/or sexually attracted to some people who are not their same sex/gender. A more colloquial term for the word heterosexual.

trans* – *adj.* : an umbrella term covering a range of identities that transgress socially-defined gender norms. Trans with an asterisk is often used in written forms (not spoken) to indicate that you are referring to the larger group nature of the term and specifically including non-binary identities, as well as transgender men (transmen) and transgender women (transwomen).

transgender – **1** *adj.* : a gender description for someone who has transitioned (or is transitioning) from living as one gender to another. **2** *adj.* : an umbrella term for anyone whose sex assigned at birth and gender identity do not correspond in the expected way (e.g., someone who was assigned male at birth, but does not identify as a man).

transition / transitioning – *noun, verb* : referring to the process of a transgender person changing aspects of themself (e.g., their appearance, name, pronouns, or making physical changes to their body) to be more congruent with the gender they know themself to be (as opposed to the gender they lived as pre-transitioning).

transphobia – *noun* : the fear of, discrimination against, or hatred of trans* people, the trans* community, or gender ambiguity. Transphobia can be seen within the queer community, as well as in general society. Transphobic – *adj.* : a word used to describe an individual who harbors some elements of this range of negative attitudes, thoughts, and intents towards trans* people.

Resources for Further Exploration

BOOKS

Biblical/Theological

Brownson, James V. *Bible, Gender, Sexuality: Reframing the Church's Debate on Same-Sex Relationships*. Grand Rapids: Eerdmans, 2013.

*Martin, Colby. *Unclobber: Rethinking Our Misuse of the Bible on Homosexuality*. Louisville:

Westminster John Knox, 2016.

*Vines, Matthew. *God and the Gay Christian: The Biblical Case for Same-Sex Relationships*. New York: Convergent, 2014.

Church Focused/Related to Christianity

Baldock, Kathy. *Walking the Bridgeless Canyon: Repairing the Breach between the Church and the LGBT Community*. Reno: Canyonwalker, 2014.

Edman, Elizabeth M. *Queer Virtue: What LGBTQ People Know about Life and Love and How It Can Revitalize Christianity*. Boston: Beacon, 2016.

*Gushee, David P. *Changing Our Mind: Definitive Edition of the Landmark Call for Inclusion of LGBT Christians with Response to Critics*. 3rd ed. Canton, MI: Read the Spirit, 2017.

Oliveto, Karen P. *Our Strangely Warmed Hearts: Coming Out into God's Call*. Nashville: Abingdon, 2018.

Rivera, Bridget Eileen. *Heavy Burdens: Seven Ways LGBTQ Christians Experience Harm in the Church*. Grand Rapids: Brazos, 2021.

Robertson, Brandan J. *The Gospel of Inclusion: A Christian Case for LGBT+ Inclusion in the Church*. Eugene, OR: Cascade, 2019.

Sanders, Cody. *Queer Lessons for Churches on the Straight and Narrow: What All Christians Can Learn from LGBTQ Lives*. Macon, GA: Faithlab, 2013.

*Wilson, Ken. *A Letter to My Congregation: An Evangelical Pastor's Path to Embracing People Who Are Gay, Lesbian, Bisexual, and Transgender into the Company of Jesus*. 2nd ed. Canton, MI: Read the Spirit, 2014.

Wink, Walter, ed. *Homosexuality and Christian Faith: Questions of Conscience for the Churches*. Minneapolis: Fortress, 1999.

Difficult Conversations

Khang, Kathy and Matt Mikalatos. *Loving Disagreement: Fighting for Community through the Fruit of the Spirit*. Colorado Springs, CO: NavPress, 2023.

*Lee, Justin. *Talking Across the Divide: How to Communicate with People You Disagree with and Maybe Even Change the World*. New York: TarcherPerigee, 2018.

Rosenberg, Marshall. *Nonviolent Communication: A Language of Life*. 3rd ed. Encinitas, CA: PuddleDancer, 2015.

Stone, Douglas, Bruce Patton, and Sheila Heen. *Difficult Conversations: How to Discuss What Matters Most*. 3rd ed. New York: Penguin, 2023.

Two Online Resources from Mennonite Central Committee (MCC):

Peaceful Practices: A Guide to Healthy Communication in Conflict, by Jes Stoltzfus Buller. https://mcc.org/resources/peaceful-practices-guide-healthy-communication-conflict.
This Sunday School curriculum is also available in Spanish: *Prácticas pacíficas: Una guía para una comunicación*.

MCC Guide for Having Better Conversations on Divisive Issues, by Myriam Ullah. https://mcc.org/resources/mcc-guide-having-better-conversations-divisive-issues.

Practical Guides

Cantorna, Amber. *Unashamed: A Coming-Out Guide for LGBTQ Christians*. Louisville: Westminster John Knox, 2019.

Cottrell, Susan. *"Mom, I'm Gay": Loving Your LGBTQ Child and Strengthening Your Faith*. Rev. and exp. Louisville: Westminster John Knox, 2016.

*Gainsburg Jeannie. *The Saavy Ally: A Guide to Becoming a Skilled LGBTQ+ Advocate*. Rowman and Littlefield, 2020.

Killermann, Sam. *A Guide to Gender: The Social Justice Advocate's Handbook*. 2nd ed. Austin, TX: Impetus, 2017.

Sanders, Cody J. *A Brief Guide to Ministry with LGBTQIA Youth*. Louisville: Westminster John Knox, 2017.

Stories

Cantorna-Wylde, Amber. *Out of Focus: My Story of Sexuality, Shame, and Toxic Evangelicalism*. Louisville: Westminster John Knox, 2023.

Kreider, Roberta Showalter, ed. *From Wounded Hearts: Faith Stories of Lesbian, Gay, Bisexual, and Transgender People and Those Who Love Them*. 2nd ed. Kulpsville, PA: Strategic, 2003.

*Lee, Justin. *Torn: Rescuing the Gospel from the Gays-vs.-Christians Debate*. New York: Jericho, 2013.

Oord, Thomas Jay and Alexa Oord, eds. *Why the Church of the Nazarene Should be Fully LGBTQ+ Affirming*. Grasmere, ID: SacraSage, 2023.

Robertson, Brandan, ed. *Our Witness: The Unheard Stories of LGBT+ Christians*. London: Dartman, Longman and Todd, 2017.

Trans

Kearns, Shannon T. L. *In the Margins: A Transgender Man's Journey with Scripture*. Grand Rapids: Eerdmans, 2022.

*Hartke, Austen. *Transforming: The Bible and the Lives of Transgender Christians*. Louisville: Westminster John Knox, 2018.

Herzer, Linda Tatro. *The Bible and the Transgender Experience: How Scripture Supports Gender Variance*. Cleveland, OH: Pilgrim, 2016.

Soughers, Tara K. *Beyond a Binary God: A Theology for Trans* Allies*. New York: Church Publishing, 2018.

*Books marked with an asterisk are especially recommended.

Invitation to Conversation

INSPIRATIONAL AND INSTRUCTIONAL ONLINE VIDEOS

"Christianity and Homosexuality"

https://www.youtube.com/watch?v=Ih2vbJDdQ08
Dr. Tony Campolo
Suncrest United Methodist Church
March 1, 2015

"Ending the Teaching of Contempt against the Church's Sexual Minorities"

https://www.youtube.com/watch?app=desktop&v=G2o3ZGwzZvk
Dr. David Gushee
The Reformation Project
November 8, 2014

"Full Inclusion for LGBTQ+ Christians"

https://www.youtube.com/watch?v=V1YLjag_XVU
Dr. David Gushee
The Open Table Collective
June 16, 2023

"The Gay Debate: The Bible and Homosexuality"

https://www.youtube.com/watch?v=ezQjNJUSraY
Matthew Vines
College Hill United Methodist Church
March 10, 2012

"Untangling the Mess"

https://www.youtube.com/watch?v=ziCOOdUW8OA
Kathy Baldock
The Reformation Project
November 26, 2016

"When They Won't Listen: Having Difficult Conversations Workshop"
https://www.youtube.com/watch?v=yJKzvysaXZE
Justin Lee
The Reformation Project
November 19, 2018

ORGANIZATIONS

Canyonwalker Connections

https://canyonwalkerconnections.com/

> Canyonwalker Connection exists to repair the division existing between social and Christian conservatives and the lesbian, gay, bisexual, transgender, and queer (LGBTQ) communities through education, training, encouragement, and dialogue in both secular and religious environments.

PFLAG

https://pflag.org/

> "PFLAG is the nation's largest organization dedicated to supporting, educating, and advocating for LGBTQ+ people and those who love them."

The Reformation Project

https://reformationproject.org/

> "As a Bible-based, Christian organization, The Reformation Project's mission is to advance LGBTQ inclusion in the church."

The Safe Zone Project

https://thesafezoneproject.com/

> "The Safe Zone Project is a free online resource for powerful, effective LGBTQ awareness and ally training workshops."

Invitation to Conversation

Trevor Project

https://www.thetrevorproject.org/

> "The Trevor Project is the leading suicide prevention and crisis intervention nonprofit organization for LGBTQ young people. We provide information & support to LGBTQ young people 24/7, all year round."

Q Christian Fellowship

https://www.qchristian.org/

> "Q Christian Fellowship is cultivating radical belonging for LGBTQ+ Christians and allies."

Just Because He Breathes

LINDA ROBERTSON

This tragic story, poignantly told by Ryan's mother, emphasizes the crucial importance of loving and accepting LGBTQ+ people as they are without trying to change them.

On the night of November 20, 2001, a conversation held over Instant Messenger changed our lives forever. Our twelve-year-old son messaged me in my office from the computer in his bedroom.

> **Ryan says:** can i tell u something
> **Mom says:** Yes I am listening
> **Ryan says:** well i don't know how to say this really but, well……, i can't keep lying to you about myself. I have been hiding this for too long and i sorta have to tell u now. By now u probably have an idea of what i am about to say.
> **Ryan says:** I am gay
> **Ryan says:** i can't believe i just told you
> **Mom says:** Are you joking?
> **Ryan says:** no
> **Ryan says:** i thought you would understand because of uncle don
> **Mom says:** of course I would
> **Mom says:** but what makes you think you are?
> **Ryan says:** i know i am
> **Ryan says:** i don't like hannah

Invitation to Conversation

Ryan says: it's just a cover-up
Mom says: but that doesn't make you gay...
Ryan says: i know
Ryan says: but u don't understand
Ryan says: i am gay
Mom says: tell me more
Ryan says: it's just the way i am and it's something i know
Ryan says: u r not a lesbian and u know that. it is the same thing
Mom says: what do you mean?
Ryan says: i am just gay
Ryan says: i am that
Mom says: I love you no matter what
Ryan says: i am white not black
Ryan says: i know
Ryan says: i am a boy not a girl
Ryan says: i am attracted to boys not girls
Ryan says: u know that about yourself and i know this
Mom says: what about what God thinks about acting on these desires?
Ryan says: i know
Mom says: thank you for telling me
Ryan says: and i am very confused about that right now
Mom says: I love you more for being honest
Ryan says: i know
Ryan says: thanx

We were completely shocked. Not that we didn't know and love gay people—my only brother had come out to us several years before, and we adored him. But Ryan? He was unafraid of anything, tough as nails, and *all* boy. We had not seen this coming, and the emotion that overwhelmed us, kept us awake at night and, sadly, influenced all of our reactions over the next six years, was *fear*.

We said all the things that we thought loving Christian parents who believed the Bible—the Word of God—*should* say:

We love you. We will *always* love you. And this is hard. *Really* hard. *But* we know what God says about this, and so you are going to have to make some really difficult choices.

We love you. We couldn't love you more. *But* there are other men who have faced this same struggle, and God has worked in them to change their desires. We'll get you their books . . . you can listen to their testimonies. And we will trust God with this.

We love you. We are so glad you are our son. *But* you are young, and your sexual orientation is still developing. The feelings you've had for other guys don't make you gay. So please don't tell anyone that you *are* gay. You don't know who you are yet. Your identity is not that you are gay—it is that you are a child of God.

We love you. Nothing will change that. *But* if you are going to follow Jesus, holiness is your only option. You are going to have to choose to follow Jesus, no matter what. And since you know what the Bible says, and since you want to follow God, embracing your sexuality is *not* an option.

We thought we understood the magnitude of the sacrifice that we—and God—were asking for. And this sacrifice, we knew, would lead to the abundant life, perfect peace and eternal rewards, even if it was incredibly difficult.

Ryan had always felt intensely drawn to spiritual things; He desired to please God above all else. So, for the first six years, he tried to choose Jesus. Like so many others before him, he pleaded with God to help him be attracted to girls. He memorized Scripture, met with his youth pastor weekly and went to all the youth group events and Bible Studies. He chose to get baptized and filled journals with his prayers. He read all the Christian books that explained where his gay feelings came from and dove into counseling to further discover the origin of his unwanted attraction to other guys. He worked through difficult conflict resolution with Rob and I, and invested even more deeply in his friendships with other guys (straight guys) just like the reparative therapy experts advised.

But nothing changed. God didn't answer Ryan's prayers—or ours—though we were all believing with faith that the God of the Universe—the God for whom *nothing* is impossible—could easily make Ryan straight. But He did not.

Though our hearts may have been good (we truly thought what we were doing was loving), we did not even give Ryan a chance to wrestle with God, to figure out what *he* believed God was telling him through scripture about his sexuality. We had believed firmly in giving each of our four children the space to question Christianity, to decide for themselves if they wanted to follow Jesus, to truly *own* their own faith. But we were too afraid to give Ryan that room when it came to his sexuality, for fear that he'd make the wrong choice.

Basically, we told our son that he had to choose between God and his sexuality. We forced him to make a choice between his faith and being a sexual person. Choosing God, practically, meant living a lifetime condemned to being alone. As a teenager, he had to accept that he would never have the chance to fall in love, hold hands, have his first kiss or share the intimacy and companionship that we, as his parents, enjoy. We had always told our kids that marriage was God's greatest earthly gift . . . but Ryan had to accept that he alone would not be offered that present.

And so, just before his 18th birthday, Ryan, depressed, suicidal, disillusioned and convinced that he would never be able to be loved by God, made a new choice. He decided to throw out his Bible and his faith at the same time, and to try searching for what he desperately wanted—peace—another way. And the way he chose to try first was drugs.

We had—unintentionally—taught Ryan to hate his sexuality. And since sexuality cannot be separated from the self, we had taught Ryan to hate himself. So as he began to use drugs, he did so with a recklessness and a lack of caution for his own safety that was alarming to everyone who knew him.

Suddenly our fear of Ryan someday having a boyfriend (a possibility that honestly terrified me) seemed trivial in contrast to our fear of Ryan's death, especially in light of his recent rejection of Christianity, and his mounting anger at God.

Ryan started with weed and beer . . . but in six short months was using cocaine and heroin. He was hooked from the beginning, and his self-loathing and rage at God only fueled his addiction. Shortly after, we lost contact with him. For the next year and a half we didn't know where he was, or even if he was dead or alive. And during that horrific time, God had our full attention. We stopped praying for Ryan to become straight. We started praying for him to know that God loved him. We stopped praying for him never to have a boyfriend. We started praying that someday we might actually get to know his boyfriend. We even stopped praying for him to come home to us; we only wanted him to come home to God.

By the time our son called us, after 18 long months of silence, God had completely changed our perspective. Because Ryan had done some pretty terrible things while using drugs, the first thing he asked me was this:

Do you think you can ever forgive me? (I told him of course, he was already forgiven. He had *always* been forgiven.)

Do you think you could ever love me again? (I told him that we had never stopped loving him, not for one second. We loved him then more than we had ever loved him.)

Do you think you could ever love me with a boyfriend? (Crying, I told him that we could love him with fifteen boyfriends. We just wanted him back in our lives. We just wanted to have a relationship with him again . . . and with his boyfriend.)

And a new journey was begun. One of healing, restoration, open communication and grace. *Lots* of grace. And God was present every step of the way, leading and guiding us, gently reminding us simply to love our son, and leave the rest up to Him.

Over the next ten months, we learned to *truly* love our son. Period. No buts. No conditions. Just because he breathes. We learned to love whoever our son loved. And it was easy. What I had been so afraid of became a blessing. The journey wasn't without mistakes, but we had grace for each other, and the language of apology and forgiveness became a natural part of our relationship. As our son pursued recovery from drug and alcohol addiction, we pursued him. God taught us how to love him, to rejoice over him, to be proud of the man he was becoming. We were all healing . . . and most importantly, Ryan began to think that if *we* could forgive him and love him, then maybe God could, too.

And then Ryan made the classic mistake of a recovering addict . . . he got back together with his old friends . . . his using friends. And one evening that was supposed to simply be a night at the movies turned out to be the first time he had shot up in ten months . . . and the last time. We got a phone call from a social worker at Harborview Medical Center in Seattle asking us to come identify our son—that he had arrived there in a coma, in critical condition. We spent 17 days at Harborview, during which time our whole family was able to surround and love on Ryan. We experienced miracle after miracle during that time, things that no doctor had any medical explanation for. God's presence was *tangible* in Ryan's room. But that is a long, sacred story that I'll have to tell another time.

Though Ryan had suffered such severe brain damage that he had almost complete paralysis, the doctors told us that he could very well outlive us. But, unexpectedly, Ryan died on July 16, 2009. And we lost the ability to love our gay son . . . because we no longer had a gay son. What we had wished for . . . prayed for . . . hoped for . . . that we would *not* have a gay son, came true. But not at all in the way we used to envision.

Now, when I think back on the fear that governed all my reactions during those first six years after Ryan told us he was gay, I cringe as I realize how foolish I was. I was afraid of all the wrong things. And I grieve, not only for my oldest son, who I will miss every day for the rest of my life, but for the mistakes I made. I grieve for what could have been, had we been walking by *faith* instead of by *fear*. Now, whenever Rob and I join our gay friends for an evening, I think about how much I would love to be visiting with Ryan and his partner over dinner.

But instead, we visit Ryan's gravestone. We celebrate anniversaries: the would-have-been birthdays and the unforgettable day of his death. We wear orange—his color. We hoard memories: pictures, clothing he wore, handwritten notes, lists of things he loved, tokens of his passions, recollections of the funny songs he invented, his Curious George and baseball blankey, anything, really, that reminds us of our beautiful boy . . . for that is all we have left, and there will be no new memories. We rejoice in our adult children, but ache for the one of our "gang of four" who is missing. We mark life by the days BC (before coma) and AD (after death), because we are different people now; our life was irrevocably changed—in a million ways—by his death. We treasure friendships with others who "get it" . . . because they, too, have lost a child.

We weep. We seek Heaven for grace and mercy and redemption as we try—not to *get* better but to *be* better. And we pray that God can somehow use our story to help other parents learn to truly love their children. Just because they breathe.

This story was originally posted on FaceBook on January 14, 2013, and can be found at justbecausehebreathes.com along with other resources. It is reprinted with permission and has been included here in the Appendix (rather than the main section of the book) because the author comes from outside the Brethren in Christ Church.

Linda Robertson *continues to speak and write about what she has learned from Ryan's life and death, and she finds great meaning in sharing with other parents what she has learned about truly seeing, trusting, accepting, and celebrating all of her children. She leads a year-round virtual drop-in group for Christian parents of LGBTQ kids that is sponsored by Queer Christian Fellowship, where she is a member of the board and leads the Parent Team. She believes passionately in the sacred worth of all people and is happiest when having deep, vulnerable conversations with family and friends while outside running, cycling, or hiking.*

About the Editors

Helena Cicero is an educator with an MA in higher education. She has been a member of three BIC churches throughout her lifetime and has served in various leadership roles in Harrisburg BIC Church. Helena regularly volunteers with a local sexual assault/rape crisis hotline where she comes alongside those who have experienced sexual trauma.

Eric A. Seibert (PhD) is a biblical scholar, author, speaker, and educator. He has published numerous books and articles, most recently *Redeeming Violent Verses*. Eric is a lifelong member of the BIC Church and was a licensed BIC minister for over a decade. He currently attends Grantham Church and serves on the Peace and Social Justice Commission.

Julie Weatherford is a spiritual director and a founding member of Madison Street (BIC) Church. She holds an MPH from Loma Linda University and an MA in theology from Fuller Seminary. Julie is retired from a career in public health and has served on BIC (and BIC-related) boards at regional, national, and binational levels.

For more information about this project, check out our website:
www.invitation2conversation.com

ALSO FROM
SacraSage Press...

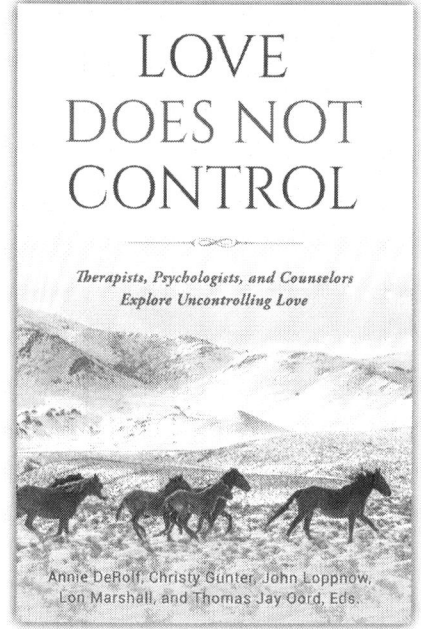

WHY THE CHURCH OF THE NAZARENE SHOULD BE FULLY LGBTQ+ AFFIRMING

THOMAS JAY OORD and ALEXA OORD, editors

LOVE DOES NOT CONTROL

Therapists, Psychologists, and Counselors Explore Uncontrolling Love

Annie DeRolf, Christy Gunter, John Loppnow, Lon Marshall, and Thomas Jay Oord, Eds.

SACRASAGEPRESS.COM

Made in the USA
Middletown, DE
30 June 2024